For
Harold Steinberg
Agonist

Preface

A book might seem an anomaly that offers itself as a unity in design and theme, but includes chapters on the ancient religion of Gnosticism, on Freud, on Emerson and Whitman and Hart Crane, on American Jewish cultural prospects, and on the author's own theories of fantasy, of the Sublime and of poetry and its interpretation. What, beyond the aggressive personalism of the author, can hold together so eclectic a range? I deny the eclecticism, though I would not attempt to refute a charge that this book attempts to transcend what is generally considered to be literary theory and its working through in practical criticism. Revisionism is this book's subject, and revisionism, in personal life, in society and its institutions, in religion, and in the arts and sciences and all the academic disciplines, is a fierce process, however that process conceals itself in the codes of civilization. It is revisionism, and not repression or supposed sublimation, that is the discontent in civilization Freud most truly explored. But what is revisionism? To that question, this book attempts some partial answer, as these chapters direct themselves towards the theory of revisionism its author hopes to live to write.

Whatever revisionism is, as a process or even as a dialectic, why should someone coming out of (or working at the outer limits of) literary criticism attempt to theorize about its nature? Revisionism pragmatically has become only a trope for Romanticism, just as Romanticism earlier became a trope for the European Enlightenment, the Enlightenment for the Renaissance, and the Renaissance for the Ancients. But there is a telling (and a killing) difference. Revisionism, as Nietzsche said of every spirit, unfolds itself *only in fighting*. The spirit portrays itself as agonistic, as contesting for supremacy, with other spirits, with anteriority, and finally with every earlier version of itself. Burckhardt, Nietzsche, Huizinga are the cultural theorists of the agonistic spirit, from the Greeks and the Hebrews onwards, but Freud is the prophet of agon and of its ambivalences. The first theologians of agon were the Gnostics of Alexandria, and the final pragmatists of agon have been and will be the Americans of Emerson's tradition. As my first chapter attempts to adumbrate, that is the center of this book: the American religion of competitiveness, which is at once our glory and (doubtless) our inevitable sorrow.

But again, why should someone crossing out of literary criticism address the problematics of revisionism? What else has Western poetry been, since the Greeks, must be the answer, at least in part. The origins and aims of poetry together constitute its powers, and the powers of poetry, however they relate to or affect the world, rise out of a loving conflict with previous poetry, rather than out of conflict with the world. There is, despite much contemporary criticism, a referential aspect to a poem, which keeps it from coming into being only as a text, or rather keeps a text from being merely a text. But this referential aspect is both masked and mediated, and the agent of concealment and of relationship always is another poem. There is no unmediated vision, whether in poetry or in any other mode, but only mediated revision, for which another name is anxiety, in the Freudian sense of "anxious expectations."

Freud, in his final phase, showed that anxiety was pre-emptive, that it established itself prior to any stimulus, and so in some sense created the catastrophe of such a negative stimulus. This peculiarly creative aspect of a kind of primal anxiety is the tendency or process I have called "poetic misprision" and attempted to portray in a number of earlier books. My concern in this book is to extend the study of misprision to Freud himself, to the Gnostic model that first made revisionism into negative theology, to Emerson and Whitman and their American tradition, and to literary arenas including the genre of fantasy and the instance of the Sublime. Finally, this book reaches out to the American Jewish cultural dilemma, in which it necessarily shares. The religion of Akiba is not dead, whether in America or elsewhere, but the burdens of revising so rugged a tradition are as strong today as they were for the Jewish Gnostics, for Philo and the Jewish Platonists, and for their mixed descendants, the Kabbalists. From its first chapter, on the concept of "agon," to its penultimate, on the dark cultural prospects of American Jewry, this book searches for the revisionary gift that Emerson called "self-reliance" and made into the American religion, a purified Gnosis. Against its only apparent eclecticism, this book proclaims a religious intention, but with the Emersonian or American difference—a literary one, as the book's Coda cries out.

New Haven   H.B.
June 1981

Contents

The divine bards are the friends of my virtue, of my intellect, of my strength. They admonish me that the gleams which flash across my mind are not mine, but God's; that they had the like, and were not disobedient to the heavenly vision. So I love them. Noble provocations go out from them, inviting me to resist evil; to subdue the world; and to Be. And thus, by his holy thoughts, Jesus serves us and thus only.

EMERSON, "The Divinity School Address"

Having studied the mocking-bird's tones and the flight of the moun-
    tain-hawk,
And heard at dawn the unrivall'd one, the hermit-thrush from the
    swamp-cedars,
Solitary, singing in the West, I strike up for a New World.

WHITMAN, "Starting from Paumanok"

AGON

A Prelude to Gnosis

Gnosticism began as a religion of the intellectuals in Hellenistic Alexandria, perhaps initially in the purely pagan Hermetic writings. But Alexandria also became the center of Christian Gnosticism, and very likely of a Jewish Gnosticism as well. Both these phrases—"Christian" and "Jewish" Gnosticism—are in a sense oxymorons, figurative paradoxes, when regarded from the orthodox perspectives of Church and Synagogue. Yet the Valentinian Gnostics, like most of the major sects, considered themselves the true Christians, and their gospel as the *Gospel of Truth*. And the entire tradition of what Gershom Scholem calls "Jewish mysticism" can be described as Jewish Gnosticism, a description that Scholem himself frequently has adopted.

There is a massive and augmenting historical scholarship devoted to Gnosticism. I am not a historian of religion, and can make no contribution whatsoever to such scholarship. This book is not history or scholarship, but only a personal blend of my individual religious experience with my own literary theory and criticism. In this blending, it differs from my earlier book *Kabbalah and Criticism*, whose sole concern was to use Kabbalah, or Jewish Gnosticism, and Scholem's analyses as paradigms for a theory of reading poetry. Though I still am concerned with Gnosticism as a mode of interpretation, even as a way of telling a story, or reading a poem, I care more now for Gnosticism as such, by which I do not mean primarily the historical phenomenon of a Hellenistic religion of the first two centuries of the Common Era. I mean a timeless knowing, as available now as it was then, and available alike to those Christians, to those Jews and to those secular intellectuals who are not persuaded by orthodox or normative accounts or versions of religion, and who rightly scorn the many mindless, soft pseudo-transcendentalisms now swarming, but who know themselves as questers for God.

Though Hans Jonas, the most distinguished philosophical historian of Gnosticism, calls one of his books *The Gnostic Religion*, I am uncertain as to whether Gnosticism, ancient or modern, ought to be considered a "religion" in the sense that Christianity, Judaism and Islam are religions. Gnosticism polemically is decidedly not a faith, whether in the Christian sense, *pistis*, a believing that something was, is, and will be so; or in the Hebraic sense, *emunah*, a trusting in the Covenant. If religion is a binding, then Gnosticism is an unbinding, but not for the sake of things or persons merely as they are. Gnostic freedom is a freedom for knowledge, knowledge of what in the self, *not* in the psyche or soul, is Godlike, and knowledge of God beyond the cosmos. But also it is a freedom to be known, to be known by God, by what is alien to everything created, by what is alien to and beyond the stars and the cosmic systems and our earth.

There is no Gnosticism without Gnosis, yet there is a Gnosis without Gnosticism, as Emerson, Blake and others have shown in their lives and writings. I write this book as a Jewish Gnostic, trying to explore and develop a personal Gnosis and a possible Gnosticism, perhaps even one available to others. But I begin by attempting an exposition of Gnosis apart from Gnosticism, which means that I need to investigate three kinds of material—historical, literary and psychological—which hardly can be kept apart, since in a sense all are necessarily textual.

Gnosis is not rational knowledge, but like poetic knowledge (I suspect "like" to be my evasion) Gnosis is more-than-rational knowledge. Writing upon the nature of Gnostic "knowledge," Hans Jonas distinguishes it from Greek *theoria*:

> There, the object of knowledge is the universal, and the cognitive relation is "optical," i.e., an analogue of the visual relation to objective form that remains unaffected by the relation. Gnostic "knowledge" is about the particular (for the Transcendent deity is still a particular) and the relation of knowing is mutual, i.e., a being known at the same time, and involving active self-divulgence on the part of the "known."

Gnosis alters both knower and known, without blending them into a unity. But we have, in the West, no ways of knowing, rational or irrational, that we can describe without Greek models of description, and whatever the origins of Gnosticism, it found its tongue through Greek, not through Hebrew or Persian or any other language. Though Gnosticism was a late, Hellenistic phenomenon, its speculative principles stemmed ultimately from earlier Greek religious crises of the fifth century before the Common Era, and from Plato's reactions to those crises. Like Neoplatonism, like Stoicism, possibly even like Pharasaic Judaism and like virtually all varieties of Christianity, Gnosticism is inconceivable without Plato. But this is, for Gnosticism, a troubled ancestry, almost as troubled as the notorious relation, perhaps even one of descent, of Gnosticism to the Jewish Bible.

E. R. Dodds is the classical scholar whose writings most illuminate the Hellenic descent and nature of Gnosticism, particularly *The Greeks and the Irrational* and its near-sequel, *Pagan and Christian in an Age of Anxiety*. In his chapter on Plato and the Irrational Soul, in the first of those books, Dodds traces Plato's spiritual evolution from the pure rationalist of the *Protagoras* to the transcendental psychologist, influenced by the Pythagoreans and Orphics, of the later works, culminating in the *Laws*. The Pythagoreans and the Orphics were the source of a dualistic distinction that the Gnostics inherited from Plato, and then strongly misread into their genuinely unprecedented doctrine.

Pythagoras traditionally received his wisdom from the Orphics, but we know nothing certain about Orpheus or the Orphics, except that they introduced among the Greeks the shamanistic notion of what Dodds calls an "occult self." Fifth-century B.C.E. Greek writers used *psyche* to mean the emotional, anxious self, but not the rational soul. Dodds remarks, as does Bruno Snell in *The Discovery of the Mind*, that the *psyche* as anxious self is descended from the Homeric *thumos*, an intranslatable word, but akin to the Freudian concept of the drive. A different notion of the self, Dodds's "occult" one, came down from the north, from Scythia and Thrace, where the religious culture was shamanistic. The perhaps mythical Orpheus and the quite historical Pythagoras are Greek versions of shamans, and the legend of Pythagoras actually identifies him with the Hyperborean Apollo, god of Scythia and Thrace. Empedocles, coming after Pythagoras, presents himself both as shaman and as god, with "a detachable soul or self, which by suitable techniques can be withdrawn from the body even during life, a self which is older than the body and will outlast it" (Dodds).

This daemonic self, transmigrated from body to body, represented a source of power to Empedocles, but this power was paid for by an ascetic revulsion from the body, the first such *askesis* in Greek tradition. This *askesis* made unattractive the fifth-century identity between the *psyche* and an empirical self or personality. An ontological self, the *daemon*, is said by Empedocles to persist from life to life as "the carrier of man's potential divinity and actual guilt" (Dodds). Both divinity and guilt belonged to what Plato in the *Laws* was to call "the old Titan nature," referring to the sin of the Titans in rending and devouring Dionysus (akin to the Dionysiac Maenads' *sparagmos* of Orpheus).

Dodds defines Plato's mature doctrine of the soul, his "transcendental psychology," as "the identification of the detachable 'occult' self which is the carrier of guilt-feelings, and is potentially divine, with the more rational Socratic *psyche* whose virtue is a kind of knowledge." This grand misprision, as I would call it, is a strong misreading of shamanistic doctrine, and made possible the belated notion of Gnosis, another creative misreading, in that case a mis-reading of Plato himself. As in Pythagoras and Empedocles, the shamanistic metempsychosis is intact in Plato. But shamanistic trance became Platonic rational concentration; shamanistic Gno-sis, or knowledge acquired in the trance state, became Platonic metaphysics; recollection of past bodily lives became recollection of the Ideal Forms as a foundation for epistemology; shamanistic journeyings through sleep and Hades became the Platonic myth of Er in *The Republic*.

These Platonic persuasive revisions, handed down throughout Hellenistic culture, gave the Neoplatonists an account of the soul they could accept, but repelled the Gnostics, who needed a more radical dualism, and probably found it in ancient Persian religion. But St. Paul also needed (or wanted) a more radical dualism than Platonism afforded, and though he denounced the Gnostics, he relied upon a Gnostic, rather than a Platonic distinction, between "pneumatic man" and "psychic man" (or "natural man," as the King James Bible translates *psychikos*). The *pneuma* is the trans-cendental self in Paul as in the Gnostics. Jonas observes: "It is re-markable that Paul, writing in Greek and certainly not ignorant of Greek terminological traditions, never uses in this connection the term *psyche*, which since the Orphics and Plato had denoted the divine principle in us."

Psyche and *daemon* (in its fresh guise of *pneuma*) thus became a new kind of dualism, cosmic soul against acosmic self. In a poem like Yeats's A *Dialogue of Self and Soul* this dualism attains a modern apotheosis. Why St. Paul should be both so close and so opposed to the Gnostic dualism is a puzzle I reserve for some later surmises. But the Gnostic dualism of soul or *psyche* against self or *pneuma* or "spark" is crucial for seeing just what Gnostic knowing, or Gnosis, takes as its quest.

Like the ontological self or daemon of Empedocles, the *pneuma* of Gnosis is a figurative expression for which we ought not to seek an empirical referent, because that would belong to human rather than divine knowledge. In this respect, it is Heraclitus who is the ultimate philosophical forebear of both Gnosticism and Christianity, with his insistence, as Bruno Snell puts it, "that his comprehension of the role of the deity in the world transcends the opinions held by the mass of the people." As a mythological comparison, rather than a scientific analogy, the Gnostic contrast between *psyche* and *pneuma* lends itself to Jonas's Heideggerian distinction between an orthodox or Platonic concept of being, the *psyche*, and a Gnostic concept of happening, the *pneuma*. Being is static; happening, or movement, leads to a difference: "The knowledge is of a history, in which it is itself a critical event" (Jonas).

How much can you know of your own history, when your knowing is itself a crucial movement in that history? The illuminating analogues to this dilemma seem to me to reside in reading poetry, rather than in undergoing psychoanalysis. The peculiar rigors of transference and counter-transference and the waywardness of the unconscious combine to prevent psychoanalysis from becoming a Gnosis, that is, from getting beyond an uneasy knowledge of the multi-layered text of the *psyche*. But in the deep reading of a poem what you come to know is a concept of happening, a realization of events in the history of your own spark or *pneuma*, and your knowing is the most important movement in that history. A reader who has known Browning's *Childe Roland*, or Stevens's *The Idea of Order at Key West*, or some comparable poem, will discover that the knowledge is a Gnosis, or can become one. Since I intend a precise analogue here, involving two stringent nihilisms—true poem and reader's *pneuma*—considerable elaboration is necessary.

The Gnostic's spark or spirit or inmost self is absolutely alien to the cosmos, to everything natural. Even so the reader's *pneuma* transcends what is known and knowable by nature, or more simply, something unknown but supremely valuable in the reader quests for a knowledge that the poem can give. I will expound Emerson's own Gnosis (certainly *not* a Gnosticism) later in this book, but I rely upon him here because of his extraordinary sense of *the reader's Sublime*. Here is a passage from the Journals that Stephen

Whicher, in a fine insight, chose to print as a kind of *summa* to a selection of Emerson's prose:

> It is the largest part of a man that is not inventoried. He has many enumerable parts: he is social, professional, political, sectarian, literary, and is this or that set and corporation. But after the most exhausting census has been made, there remains as much more which no tongue can tell. And this remainder is that which interests. This is that which the preacher and the poet and the musician speak to. This is that which the strong genius works upon; the region of destiny, of aspiration, of the unknown. Ah, they have a secret persuasion that as little as they pass for in the world, they are immensely rich in expectancy and power. Nobody has ever yet dispossessed this adhesive self to arrive at any glimpse or guess of the awful Life that lurks under it.

What is here called a "remainder" is the *pneuma* or spark, the "awful Life" that lurks beneath the "adhesive self" or *psyche*. If this is what the poet speaks to, then this is what must answer that call by a knowing, a knowing that precisely is not that which is known, or has any relation to "firm recorded knowledge," as Emerson goes on to say, in a passage of Sublime aspiration:

> Far the best part, I repeat, of every mind is not that which he knows, but that which hovers in gleams, suggestions, tantalizing, unpossessed, before him. His firm recorded knowledge soon loses all interest for him. But this dancing chorus of thoughts and hopes in the quarry of his future, is his possibility, and teaches him that his man's life is of a ridiculous brevity and meanness, but that it is his first age and trial only of his young wings, and that vast revolutions, migrations, and gyres on gyres in the celestial societies invite him.

With so fervent a vision of transcendence, there must be an implication of a radical dualism, despite Emerson's professed monistic desires, his declarations that he is a seer of unity. For this too is the Emersonian accent on the nature of resurrection: "It is the revelation of what is, and the transformation of things, and a transition into newness." I quote that sentence however from the Valentinian *Treatise on Resurrection*, late second century c.e. I remember quoting, in an earlier book (*Poetry and Repression*, 1976) the Gnostic Monoimos as an even uncannier prophecy of Emerson:

> Cease to seek after God and creation and things like these and seek after yourself of yourself, and learn who it is who appropriates all things within you without exception and says, "My God, *my* mind, *my* thought, *my* soul, *my* body," and learn whence comes grief, and rejoicing and love and hatred, and waking without intention, and sleeping without intention, and anger without intention, and love without intention. And if you carefully consider these things, you will find yourself within yourself, being both one and many like that stroke, and will find the outcome of yourself.

This Gnosis too, like Emerson's, is a reader's Sublime. Such a Sublime answers Emerson's rhetorical question: "Is not the sublime felt in an analysis as well as in a creation?" The hereseologist Hippolytus condemned Monoimus for misprision of the most Sublime of poems, *The Iliad*, a "misreading" that substituted for *Iliad* XIV, 201—"Ocean, the origin of gods, and the origin of men"—the interpretation that Man was the Ocean, the Abyss, the Alien God, and so Man was "the origin of gods, and the origin of men." In the conclusion of the passage from Monoimus quoted above, "that stroke" refers to the single stroke of the iota, which being numeral as well as letter, stands for the number ten, and so serves as a synecdoche for all other numbers. Monoimus, as witty as Emerson, makes "that stroke" also the stroke of interpretation, of a Gnostic analytical allegory:

> This Man is a single unity, incomposite and indivisible, composite and divisible; wholly friendly, wholly peaceable, wholly hostile, wholly at enmity with itself, dissimilar and similar, like some musical harmony, which contains within itself everything which one might name or leave unnoticed, producing all things, generating all things. . . .

Gnosis has uncovered in Homer's Ocean its own concept of happening, Primal Man, but this uncovering indeed is an event in the history of the *pneuma* of Monoimus (and now of ourselves as readers). Two strict negatives, poem and reader's spark, have combined in a movement that leads to a difference, and that difference is an example of Gnosis. But since readers do not tend to read Gnostic sages such as Monoimus the Arabian, I will illustrate my analogy between Gnosis and the deep reading of poetry by proceeding to give an interpretation of a poem by Wallace Stevens, himself scarcely more Gnostic than Homer was. But I wish to be Monoimus or Emerson to Stevens's Homer, as it were, and to illustrate how poetic knowledge is a Gnosis; or rather, how much closer poetic knowledge is to Gnosis than to philosophical knowledge of any kind. My text is Stevens's *The Sail of Ulysses*, written in 1954, when the seventy-five-year-old poet was less than a year from his death. I can think of no finer instance of an American Gnosis than this poem's opening section. Ulysses, "symbol of the seeker," reading his own mind, states the Emersonian manifesto: "As I know, I am and have / The right to be." And then guiding his boat beneath the night sky, he orates his Gnosis:

> If knowledge and the thing known are one
> So that to know a man is to be
> That man, to know a place is to be
> That place, and it seems to come to that;
> And if to know one man is to know all
> And if one's sense of a single spot
> Is what one knows of the universe,
> Then knowledge is the only life,
> The only sun of the only day,
> The only access of true ease,
> The deep comfort of the world and fate.

What can knowledge be here except a Gnosis? How far would it extend Stevens to name the known man as Primal Man, and the known place as what the Gnostics called the place of the Pleroma, the All, the Original Fullness, the Abyss? And what is "fate" here if not the Gnostic Heimarmene, the cosmic *Fatum* that the knower fights to evade?

What Stevens calls "knowledge" and praises as "the only life, The only sun of the only day," must be transcendent and negative, in relation to nature. This transmundane knowing severely mitigates the apparent pathos of the section following, where the "luminous companion" cannot be another self, but must be the answering voice of one's own spark or *pneuma:*

> There is a human loneliness,
> A part of space and solitude,
> In which knowledge cannot be denied,
> In which nothing of knowledge fails,
> The luminous companion, the hand,
> The fortifying arm, the profound
> Response, the completely answering voice,
> That which is more than anything else
> The right within us and about us,
> Joined, the triumphant vigor, felt,
> The inner direction on which we depend,
> That which keeps us the little that we are,
> The aid of greatness to be and the force.

Since Gnosis, as opposed to philosophy, is interested only in *religious* knowledge, and since Stevens is decisively *not* a religious poet, what does it mean to call his "knowledge" here a Gnosis? There can of course be a kind of religious knowledge on a rational basis, but Gnosis is more than or other than rational, and so is Stevens's "knowledge." Gnosis never yields to a process of rigorous working-through; when the call is heard, the hearer *knows*, and if the call truly is *to him*, then even a single moment suffices. And yet this need not be considered either a mystical or a visionary experience, since in Gnosis the knowledge is neither of eternity nor of this world seen with more spiritual intensity. *The knowledge is of oneself.*

But this is not the Greek adage "Know yourself," since Gnosis is uncanny, very much in the Freudian sense of *unheimlich;* for what is called to and answers the call, however new it seems, is precisely *what is oldest in oneself.* Stevens is friendly both to body and to world, and so is no Gnostic, but towards time and history Stevens does share in an Emersonian Gnosis. Gnosis, whether in Gnosticism or in Emerson, emphasizes that *transition* is more real than being. The psyche belongs to experience, to time and history, to what is moment-to-moment; but the knowing of Gnosis is momentary and beyond experience. As performative knowledge, Gnosis is pragmatic and particular, and it is performative, not cognitive knowledge, that informs Stevens's *The Sail of Ulysses*.

The transition from a knowing that is being to a Gnosis is the kernel of section V of Stevens' meditation:

> Yet always there is another life,
> A life beyond this present knowing,
> A life brighter than this present splendor,
> Brighter, perfected and distant away,
> Not to be reached but to be known,
> Not an attainment of the will
> But something illogically received,
> A divination, a letting down
> From loftiness, misgivings dazzlingly
> Resolved in dazzling discovery.

This life, beyond this present knowing, to be known, is precisely a revelatory and performative knowledge, a *praxis*. Known, it will bring about a "vigilance" that Nietzsche prophesied for his Overmen:

> In which the litter of truths becomes
> A whole, the day on which the last star
> Has been counted, the genealogy
> Of gods and men destroyed, the right
> To know established as the right to be.

With so strenuous a prophecy of genealogical undoing, congenial to Gnosticism, it is hardly surprising that Stevens should go on to a vision of the true oracular and ontological self, *pneuma* or spark, diamond paralleling the Gnostic pearl:

> It is the sibyl of the self,
> The self as sibyl, whose diamond,
> Whose chiefest embracing of all wealth

> Is poverty, whose jewel found
> At the exactest central of the earth
> Is need. . . .

The Emersonian trope of "poverty" as imaginative need is more Gnostic than it is Platonic, more a calling and an answering than it is an Eros. From *The Sail of Ulysses* until his death, Stevens's final poems explore a calling, "a scrawny cry," that is "like / A new knowledge of reality." Feeding "on a new known," the poet breathes in an air that "is clear of everything. / It has no knowledge except of nothingness. . . ." The final version, *Of Mere Being*, makes the flickering of that being into a performative knowing:

> You know then that it is not the reason
> That makes us happy or unhappy.
> The bird sings. Its feathers shine.

The bird may or may not be a phoenix, and the palm in which it sings rises not in the Pleroma but in the literary cosmos of Paul Valéry. Even so, the knowledge is like bird and palm in being transmundane, "beyond the last thought." Poetic knowledge is revealed as a Gnosis, reliant upon evasion and not substitution as its idea of order. What is oldest in Stevens is called to by the bird, answers the call, and in that response achieves a final knowledge; "irrational" only in being more-than-rational. Is it possible to clarify this Stevensian Gnosis without being reductive? Can we hope to be formulaic enough to catch what is distinctively *poetic* about this poetic knowledge, and yet also preserve what is a *knowing* in it that transcends the epistemology of tropes, the cognitive aspects of rhetoric?

Gnosis, as an instance of what Emerson called Power, is a persuasive rhetoric, a language of desire and possession, or in Freudian terms a repressive discourse, unconsciously but purposefully in flight from the obsessive universe of human repetitions, and from the necessities of sublimation. Gnosis is therefore, considered merely as literary language, both an early and a belated chapter in the history of the Sublime. Early, because ancient

Gnosticism reached its highest development in the second century c.e., when the Western literary Sublime was first formulated, and belated both because the Sublime was always belated (being Hellenistic rather than Hellenic) and because that belatedness has intensified necessarily in every fresh Sublime down to Yeats and Lawrence in Britain and Stevens and Hart Crane in our country.

A juxtaposition of Gnosis or poetic knowledge and the Sublime inevitably centers upon the ideas of the Negative and negation, for what belated poetry and Gnosticism always shared and share is that they were and are two extreme manifestations of what historically has been termed negative theology. I reserve an account of negative theology for a future book, on historical Gnosticism, and turn here to Stevens's mode of negation, whose strategy is always one of evasion.

Of Mere Being is a purified Gnosis, because in it Stevens is most himself, that is to say, his *pneuma* speaks, and what it says is not philosophic but evasive, evasive of all philosophy and of every other circumscribed mode of cognition. Stevens indeed was a man to whom things spoke—Ruskin's way of defining a poet; and like Ruskin Stevens quested after a Gnosis, after a dialectic that might evade that speaking, in favor of listening to a call from what was oldest in himself. The critic Denis Donoghue wisely remarked, partly in reference to Stevens, "Evasion plays no part in knowledge, and is a scandal to epistemologists, but it is crucial if you want to escape or refute your fate." I would add to Donoghue that evasion is Stevens's greatest poetic strength, and that strong poetry shares with Gnosticism, rather than with Judaism or Christianity, a linguistic and psychic cunning that truly can be equated with what Romanticism called the Imagination. That cunning, when it is realized as poetic knowledge, is very nearly identical with the knowledge exalted by the Gnostics. In writing this book, I seek an alliance between the traditions of poetic knowledge and of Gnosis, and such an alliance, as I will argue throughout, may help to make possible a new or purified Gnosticism, a kind of American Gnosis prophesied by Emerson, and still to be realized among us.

1
Agon: Revisionism and Critical Personality

A critical theory and *praxis* that teaches the defensive necessity of "misprision" or strong "misreading" cheerfully accepts even the weakest misreadings of its doctrines and techniques. If they persist in their folly, all these outraged reviewers will become wise. Defense is therefore not the purpose of this chapter. All of us, despite our overt desires, are doomed to become the subjects of our own need for demystification, and I overtly desire to go on demystifying my own ideas about interpretation. Three of these seem to me likeliest to yield to self-clarification. I behold no differences, in kind or in degree, between the language of poetry and the language of criticism, and yet I continue to bring forward critical vocabularies for which poetry seems to yield no precedents. I go on wondering why the long history of rhetoric always analyzes tropes as though they were synchronic, and yet my rhetorics of rhetoric always themselves fall far short of being truly diachronic. Finally, I return obsessively to what seem radically incompatible paradigms for poems and interpretations: Gnostic catastrophe creations and Freudian conflicts of heightened emotional ambivalence. Meditating upon these splits or gaps in my own theorizings and practical criticism is not an activity designed to make my work more acceptable or even useful, whether to others or to myself. But I have a design, and it may transcend even a drive for self-demystification. I became cathected upon poems very early, when

I was about ten years old, and I have spent forty years trying to understand that initial cathexis. Every love, including a love for poetry, requires reductive examination, even if, as with Stevens's Mrs. Alfred Uruquay, reduction can lead to our wiping away moonlight like mud. There is no redemptive virtue in loving poetry any more than there necessarily is in loving persons or in loving moonlight. There is not even, alas, any redemptive virtue in loving interpretation for its own sake. A man or woman who tells me that he or she loves God makes me feel very awkward, partly because "God" then seems to become a trope for some very imaginative perversions indeed. Reviewers, whether journalistic or academic, who chant malice while they proclaim their love for poems, interpretations, and the persons of poets, dead or quick, generally trope also, and for defensive purposes all their own. What do we mean when we think we love poems, and what does that love defend, or defend against?

I have come to a conviction that the love of poetry is another variant of the love of power, a conviction in which I am happy to note I have been preceded by Hazlitt. But more precisely even than Hazlitt, I would locate this love's object as a particular power, the power of usurpation. We read to usurp, just as the poet writes to usurp. Usurp what? A place, a stance, a fullness, an illusion of identification or possession; something we can call our own or even ourselves. Reading seems to me now not so much Nietzsche's Will to Power over texts, as Schopenhauer's power to will texts, or rather texts of the Sublime, which is to say, of the Abyss. Emerson, in his final phase, defined that Abyss: "There may be two or three or four steps, according to the genius of each, but for every seeing soul there are finally just two facts—I and the abyss." I interpret Emerson here as meaning the Abyss in its Gnostic sense: the forefather or foremother, before Creation, who was usurped by the Demiurge, that Demiurge being what Platonists, Jews and Christians call God the father. Loving poetry is a Gnostic passion not because the Abyss itself is loved, but because the lover longs to be yet another Demiurge.

I proceed therefore to make approaches near the abyss. The language of criticism shatters the vessels always prematurely, since the critic too becomes a Demiurge, perhaps despite himself. But the critic should be a de-idealizing Demiurge, unlike the belated poet, who can choose to deceive himself, if it helps him to do his work.

Most of what the Academy considers acceptable critical style is of course merely a worn-out Neoclassical diction, garlanded with ibids, and civilly purged of all enthusiasm. I will not labor this happily obvious truth, particularly since it has been elaborated, with his customary learning and eloquence, in a recent book, *Criticism in the Wilderness*, by my worthy constituent, Geoffrey Hartman. But the partial or cognitive return of the repressed, through what Freud called "negation," always keeps taking place in criticism, and truly constitutes its history, since that is all that is ever memorable in criticism. Dr. Johnson condemning *Lycidas* as being easy, vulgar and therefore disgusting; Blake and Hazlitt cheerfully assuring us that the grandest poetry is immoral; Empson asserting that Milton's God deliberately provoked all the trouble anyway; these are the authentic instances of the voice of the critic. The great theorist of that voice *as voice* remains Oscar Wilde, when he reminds us, following Walter Pater, how important it is that the critical imagination never fall into careless habits of accuracy. We must see the object, the poem, as in itself it really is not, because we must see not only what is missing in it, but why the poem had to exclude what is missing. Carlyle and Ruskin, Pater and Wilde are strong critics, but Matthew Arnold is not a critic at all, only a passing bell, or the School Inspector upon his rounds. "They do not know enough," he keeps telling us, and his ephebe, T. S. Eliot, continued that telling. Wordsworth and Blake, Shelley and Keats, Browning and Tennyson, Whitman and Emerson, they do not *know* enough. Enough, or too much, and so I pass on to how and what the language of criticism knows, and how this relates to what the language of poetry knows.

That *language* itself *knows* anything is a considerable trope, re-

flecting a currently fashionable shibboleth, Franco-Heideggerian
and monolithic, that is another usurpation, language-as-Demiurge
replacing the self-as-Abyss or even the self-as-Jehovah. But here I
will not dispute the trope, reserving that polemic for later. Of
course I won't accept it either, because I think it is at best gorgeous nonsense, and at worst only another residuum of the now
wearisome perpetual crusade of intellectual Paris against its own
upper middle class, and this just has no relevance to, or in, our
perpetually Emersonian America. We *do* have a national criticism,
as we have had a national poetry since Whitman and Dickinson.
There is an American or non-Hegelian Negative, and it is indebted
to Emerson for having pioneered a diachronic rhetoric. For now,
I give a passage from Emerson as an instance of the language of
criticism and its way of knowing, and then I will proceed to some
passages from Whitman for a counter-example of how the language of poetry knows what it appears to know. "Every form is a
history of the thing," Emerson wrote in *The Uses of Natural History*, by which he strangely meant what Stevens intended by:
"The first idea is an imagined thing." Emerson's first idea was the
root meaning of "first idea," which is to *see earliest*, and this I
take it is the Emersonian or American difference from Carlyle and
Ruskin. As seers, they followed Coleridge in urging their public to
see, just to see, but Emerson's prophecy to his countrymen was
that we had to see as though no one, British or Germans, or even
Greeks or Hebrews, ever had seen *before* us. The language of
American criticism ought to be pragmatic and outrageous, or perhaps I verge on saying that American pragmatism is a truly outrageous philosophy, or as Richard Rorty says, post-philosophy.
American pragmatism, as Rorty advises, always asks of a text: what
is it good for, what can I do with it, what can it do for me, what
can I make it mean? I confess that I like these questions, and
they are what I think strong reading is all about, because strong
reading doesn't ever ask: Am I getting this poem right? Strong
reading *knows* that what it does to the poem is right, because it
knows what Emerson, its American inventor, taught it, which is

that the true ship is the shipbuilder. If you don't believe in your reading, then don't bother anyone else with it, but if you do, then don't care also whether anyone else agrees with it or not. If it is strong enough, then they will come round to it anyway, and you should just shrug when they tell you finally that it is a right reading. Of course it isn't, because right reading is not reading well, and can be left, as Yeats grandly would have said, to our servants, except that we haven't got any servants.

The language of strong criticism has to be at least as pragmatic as the language of poetry, because you cannot achieve a stance, in our belatedness, without pragmatism, and our strong poets-as-poets necessarily know this. But perhaps I ought to evade my own obsessive rhetoric of belatedness, since Vico tells us that the first strong poets or Magic Primitives were highly pragmatic, and Emerson, who can be called the American Vico (amidst much else), liked to remind us that the originals were not original anyway. The relation of Emerson to both Nietzsche and William James suggests that Emersonian Transcendentalism was already much closer to pragmatism than to Kant's metaphysical idealism. Emerson wants his tropes to be independent, fresh, but above all *useful*, and he offers tropes rather than a Coleridgean metaphysical method because he knows that methods are just changes in diction, and that new methods always yield to newer ones. Rorty is splendidly useful when he sees that pragmatism and currently advanced literary criticism come to much the same cultural enterprise, and I add only that Emerson, more than Carlyle or Nietzsche, is the largest precursor of this merger. Freud thought that his personal "science" could assert an ascendancy over not only philosophy and religion but over literature also. Emerson, a shrewder prophet, could have told Freud that psychoanalysis was another form of the triumph of literary culture over science, as well as over religion and philosophy. Usurpation is a high art in Freud, but Emerson formulated the dialectics of that art, and Nietzsche and William James took some crucial early lessons from Emerson.

Emerson's language of criticism and its relation to Whitman's poetic language is my declared subject, and I will proceed to some texts, but I want first to suggest that on a pragmatic view there is no language *of criticism* but only of an individual critic, because again I agree with Rorty that a theory of strong misreading denies that there is or should be any common vocabulary in terms of which critics can argue with one another. Gnostic and elitist, a strong reading, like Emerson's, champions the literary culture of the isolate individual, the solitary construer, a Dickinson or Thoreau or Whitman. When Nietzsche wrote that every word was a prejudgment, he spoke for every strong misreader after him. Every word in a critic's vocabulary should swerve from inherited words, and when Emerson speaks of a "poem" he does not mean what Coleridge meant, but something well under way toward what Whitman wanted to mean in saying that the United States were themselves the greatest poem. This mode of swerving still goes on when Stevens calls my own favorite among all his poems *The Poems of Our Climate,* meaning the inner weathers we contrive as well as the texts we write.

The strongest of all texts urging strong misreading is Emerson's *Self-Reliance,* and I break into it just before my favorite moment in Emerson, the daemonizing chant of the paragraph that begins: "And now at last the highest truth on this subject remains unsaid . . . ," the truth being that of the American Sublime proper. I have published several commentaries on this paragraph, but have evaded until now the two superb paragraphs that precede it:

> Man is timid and apologetic; he is no longer upright; he dares not say "I think," "I am," but quotes some saint or sage. He is ashamed before the blade of grass or the blowing rose. These roses under my window make no reference to former roses or to better ones; they are for what they are; they exist with God today. There is no time to them. There is simply the rose; it is perfect in every moment of its existence. Before a leaf-bud has burst, its whole life acts; in the full-blown flower there is no more; in the leafless root there is no less. Its nature is satisfied and it satisfies nature in all moments alike. But man postpones or remembers; he does not live in the present, but

with reverted eye laments the past, or, heedless of the riches that surround him, stands on tiptoe to foresee the future. He cannot be happy and strong until he too lives with nature in the present, above time.

   This should be plain enough. Yet see what strong intellects dare not yet hear God himself unless he speak the phraseology of I know not what David, or Jeremiah, or Paul. We shall not always set so great a price on a few texts, on a few lives. We are like children who repeat by rote the sentences of grandames and tutors, and as they grow older, of the men of talents and character they chance to see,—painfully recollecting the exact words they spoke; afterwards, when they come into the point of view which those had who uttered these sayings, they understand them and are willing to let the words go; for at any time they can use words as good when occasion comes. If we live truly, we shall see truly. It is as easy for the strong man to be strong, as it is for the weak to be weak. When we have new perception, we shall gladly disburden the memory of its hoarded treasures as old rubbish. When a man lives with God, his voice shall be as sweet as the murmur of the brook and the rustle of the corn.

I call this theoretical literary criticism, or the theory of strong misreading, but I have no objections to someone else calling it heretical religion, or American moral philosophy, or psychology or whatever, and it is a kind of prose poetry also. Its language delighted Nietzsche, rather lukewarmly stirred Carlyle, and is already very close to the language of Pater and Wilde a generation later. By the word "language" here I am troping also, as even the driest and deadest among us necessarily trope when they tell us that literature is only another form of language. But my trope is stolen from Shelley and from Emerson, and it tells us that language is only dead literature, fossil poetry, the wreck of an abandoned cyclic poem. So Emerson commences here by telling us that we have fallen from the true Adamic stance or upright posture, and he warns me also to say "I think" or like Jehovah "I am" but not to be timid or apologetic, and not just to quote Emerson, that admirable saint and sage. The soon-to-be-Whitmanian blade of grass and the soon-to-be-Wildean blowing rose do not postpone and do not remember, being unconcerned with anteriority or futurity. But of course Emerson is hyperbolical; he knows well enough that all roses *do* make reference to former roses, just as Paul de Man, prince of deconstructors, knows well enough that all poems *do* make reference to former poems. Deniers of genealogy (and Nietzsche is the link here between the otherwise totally disparate Emerson and de Man) are lying against time, and to such lying I grant all honor. So far, in this first paragraph, Emerson's language of criticism might be called the wistful-hyperbolic, or as the sage himself taught us to say, in the Optative Mood.

"This should be plain enough," he charmingly begins the next paragraph, but since it never can be made plain enough, he leaps into elaboration with a touch of eloquent exasperation. If David or Jeremiah or Paul were perfect, then why is Emerson or Bloom or you alive? At what price to ourselves do we so highly value the Bible or the text of Shakespeare or the life of Jesus or the life of Sigmund Freud? The question is either painful or meaningless, and I join Emerson in trying to render it painful. For this is all that the strong misreading of the strong misreading that is our literary culture can hope to teach us. What does the love of great poems or of great lives cost us? What *is* the price of the reading experience? I think the question is truly painful because in a literary culture we necessarily lose all capacity to answer it, and by "a literary culture" I do mean Western society now, since it has no authentic religion and no authentic philosophy, and will never acquire them again, and because psychoanalysis, its pragmatic religion and philosophy, is just a fragment of literary culture, so that in time we will speak alternatively of Freudianism *or* Proustianism. The necessary dualism of a literary culture has usurped the spirit, pragmatically and materially, so that to question the moral efficacy of reading now inherits the shock once attached to putting into question the moral value of prayer, or of metaphysical speculation. Again, it is clear that the only apparent contemporary rival of literature is merely its disguised double, as it is quite some time since I have heard one of my friends chiding another for entering upon, rather than abandoning, a psychoanalysis. "He or she won't go to an analyst" is our mournful variant upon "He or she doesn't read much anymore."

Emerson urges new perception, whether of the text of nature or of books, but primarily of the strong self, by which he means the Gnostic *pneuma* or spark and not the mere *psyche*, so that he would have been hardly bothered by our current Gallic deconstructions of the *psyche*. That is why, after the Sublime paragraph I skip over here, he goes on to a passage upon which I found my critical idea of poetic crossings, those meaningful disjunctions that are the black holes of rhetoric:

> Life only avails, not the having lived. Power ceases in the instant of repose; it resides in the moment of transition from a past to a new state, in the shooting of the gulf, in the darting to an aim.

Power-as-meaning hides in the crossing, yet Emerson hardly would deny power to the achieved aim. But that is bound power and not freedom. For a prophet of power so to trope as to exalt transition over object, threshold over desire, is to have appropriated a language for criticism as rugged and tricky as any language of poetry and of Eros. The usurpation of freer voice is apparent in the outburst following directly after:

> This one fact the world hates; that the soul *becomes*; for that forever degrades the past, turns all riches to poverty, all reputation to a shame, confounds the saint with the rogue, shoves Jesus and Judas equally aside. Why then do we prate of self-reliance? Inasmuch as the soul is present there will be power not confident but agent. To talk of reliance is a poor external way of speaking. Speak rather of that which relies because it works and is. . . .

Now, to "rely" is to bind or covenant, as in "religion," and to prate of "self-reliance" is to make a covenant with one's own *pneuma* or spark-of-the-primal-Abyss. But if the true soul is in fullness of presence it is not the *psyche* but that spark, and the rich internal way of speaking is of what works and is. If that verb "works" is translated as "reads" then what "is" had better be the strong misreader, or the Emerson who wrote the astonishing paragraph in between that I now cease to evade:

> And now at last the highest truth on this subject remains unsaid; probably cannot be said; for all that we say is the far-off remembering of the intuition. That thought by what I can now nearest approach to say it, is this. When good is near you, when you have life in yourself, it is not by any known or accustomed way; you shall not discern the footprints of any other; you shall not see the face of man; you shall not hear any name;—the way, the thought, the good, shall be wholly strange and new. It shall exclude example and experience. You take the way from man, not to man. All persons that ever existed are its forgotten ministers. Fear and hope are alike beneath it. There is somewhat low even in hope. In the hour of vision there is nothing that can be called gratitude, nor properly joy. The soul raised over passion beholds identity and eternal causation, perceives the self-existence of Truth and Right, and calms itself with knowing that all things go well. Vast spaces of nature, the Atlantic Ocean, the South Sea; long intervals of time, years, centuries, are of no account. This which I think and feel underlay every former state of life and circumstances, as it does underlie my present, and what is called life and what is called death.

Again, I hear the voice of the critic, and I call this theory of poetry, because its concern is the powers of poetry, their origin and their aim. Its language is a language of criticism for which Longinus (and Plato before him) serve as precedent, but which is surprisingly absent from poetry, despite our impulse to seek it there. Such images of desire, possession and power, such gorgeous tropes of restitution, super-mimetic in their drive, come either directly or more frequently by Gnostic misprision out of broad Platonic tradition. If I encountered this Emersonian rhapsody in the Valentinian *Gospel of Truth*, or in a fragment of Basilides, I would know where I was: in the Pleroma, in the Fullness of our Forefather the Abyss, where however if you do dwell, you cannot know that you dwell. "It was a Great Marvel that they were in the Father without knowing Him."

Rather than comment as yet upon the Emersonian Pleroma, I want to contrast Emerson's language of criticism with the language of poetry it most deeply influenced, Whitman's. Whitman first published the originally untitled work that was to be called *Song of Myself* not as a poem in fifty-two sections but as one in thirteen hundred and thirty-six lines. That 1855 text both is and is not what we think of as *Song of Myself*. It opens:

> I celebrate myself,
> And what I assume you shall assume,
> For every atom belonging to me as good belongs to you.

When Whitman revised the first line into the now-familiar "I celebrate myself, and sing myself," he made more explicit his antithetical relationship to epic tradition. But his more vital revision was of himself, since he had come to understand that his truest contest was with his own earlier text. What is now the received version indeed is *Song of Myself*, rather than *Song of My Soul* or *Song of the Real Me or Me Myself*. There are at least three Whitmans in the poem, and it is problematic which of the three is the proper reference of the belated title. We can call these Whitmans (following their author) my self, my soul and the real Me or Me myself. I would translate these respectively as: my masculine *persona*, Walt Whitman, one of the roughs, an American; the American soul (largely as expounded by Emerson); my more ambiguous *persona*, somewhat feminine, somewhat boyish. Freudian translations will not work: the rough Walt is not wholly an id; the quasi-Emersonian soul does not operate like a superego; the real Me is hardly an ego, not even the narcissistic, partly unconscious ego of Freud's later thought. All three of these Whitmanian visions or fictions participate in all three of the Freudian notions, and it is one of Whitman's uncanny powers that he cuts across all available maps of the mind.

There are psychosexual implications in Whitman's chart of

being, and Justin Kaplan's biography has confirmed some of my purely random guesses. Thus, as I read Whitman's work and life, he is far more autoerotic than homoerotic. *Song of Myself* celebrates the poetic power of masturbation, not of sexual intercourse. I doubt that Whitman had much if any homosexual experience in any complete sense, though the winter of 1859–60 seems to have held some kind of sexual crisis, on the basis of the *Sea-Drift* elegies. *Song of Myself* celebrates two kinds of union, a curious opening embrace between self and soul, and a mid-poem crisis in which the self—Whitman as one of the roughs—makes love to the real Me or Me myself, who laments but then is won over. What the poem excludes is the third union, between soul and the real Me, which Whitman acknowledges at the start of section 5:

I believe in you my soul, the other I am must not abase
    itself to you,
And you must not be abased to the other.

    I is: "Walt Whitman, a kosmos, of Manhattan the son, / Turbulent, fleshy, sensual, eating, drinking and breeding." "My soul" appears to be Whitman's image of voice, what later he will call "the tally of my soul," and here in section 5 its embrace transcends any human mode of sexuality:

Loafe with me on the grass, loose the stop from your throat,
Not words, not music or rhyme I want, not custom or lecture, not
    even the best,
Only the lull I like, the hum of your valvèd voice.

I mind how once we lay such a transparent summer morning,
How you settled your head athwart my hips and gently turn'd over
    upon me,
And parted the shirt from my bosom-bone, and plunged your tongue
    to my bare-stript heart,
And reach'd till you felt my beard, and reach'd till you held my feet.

    That delicious gymnosophistry is a trope for Whitman's annunciation, or the revisionary replacement of the transparent eyeball by a transparent summer morning's loafing on the grass. But the truest, which is to say most agonistic revision, is the nature of "the other I am," the charmer whose first appearance precedes the soul's advent. In section 4, Whitman catalogs aspects of Walt Whitman, a kosmos, but then adds ruefully: "But they are not the Me myself." My own favorite passage in the poem then suggests the realities of the Me myself, with whom it is difficult for the reader not to fall in love:

Apart from the pulling and hauling stands what I am,
Stands amused, complacent, compassionating, idle, unitary,
Looks down, is erect, or bends an arm on an impalpable certain rest,
Looking with side-curved head curious what will come next,
Both in and out of the game and watching and wondering at it.

The erotic detachment of this figure is remarkable, and inevitably attractive. But nothing is got for nothing, according to Emerson's dark law of Compensation, and it is the Me myself who suffers the curious masturbation-rape of section 28 (for which see chapter 7, pp. 188-89, below). The revenge of the Me myself in Whitman is reserved for *As I Ebb'd with the Ocean of Life*, where as "the real Me" this inmost self all but destroys the outward *persona* of the poet:

O baffled, balk'd, bent to the very earth,
Oppress'd with myself that I have dared to open my mouth,
Aware now that amid all that blab whose echoes recoil upon me I have
　　not once had the least idea who or what I am,
But that before all my arrogant poems the real Me stands yet
　　untouch'd, untold, altogether unreach'd,
Withdrawn far, mocking me with mock-congratulatory signs and bows,
With peals of distant ironical laughter at every word I have written,
Pointing in silence to these songs, and then to the sand beneath.

To see the continuity of these two passages, of the Me myself both in and out of the game and watching and wondering at it, and of the real Me mocking Whitman with mock-congratulatory signs and bows, is to see what Whitman's language knows by virtue of his poetic stance. In *As I Ebb'd* the real Me preserves her/his original personality of estrangement, here called "untouch'd, untold, altogether unreach'd, / Withdrawn far." Yet there has been an advance in aggressivity. The "amused, complacent, compassionating, idle, unitary" Me myself would have looked with side-curved head curious at the anguished Walt on the beach, watching and wondering what had become of him. This later real Me *mocks* in the cruelest way, contrasting *Leaves of Grass* with the nihilistic "sand beneath." What she/he *knows* is that Whitman's language has failed him, or rather that Whitman has failed his language. One answer then to my earlier question is that the language of American poetry, at its strongest, knows that the poet's subjectivity has failed it. And here I locate the difference, if any, between precursor-critic and ephebe-poet, between Emerson's language and Whitman's. Emerson never believes or acknowledges that he has failed his language; what he insists upon knowing is that his language, language itself, always fails his soul, or rather the Oversoul, which indeed transcends the dance or interplay of tropes.

What the language of Emerson and of Whitman knows then is something about adequacy or inadequacy, something about agon, about the struggle between adverting subject or subjectivity and the mediation that consciousness hopelessly wills language to constitute. In this agon, this struggle between authentic forces, neither the fiction of the subject nor the trope of language is strong enough to win a final victory. There is only a mutual Great Defeat, but that Defeat itself is the true problematic, the art of poetry and the art of criticism. In that defeat, there are no losers, only intrepid agonists who never yield up their own recalcitrance. Call this recalcitrance a trope of death *or* of birth—which is another thrust upon my part at the critical theorist who (after Nietzsche) troubles and wounds me most, Paul de Man. For de Man, every authentic poetic or critical act rehearses the random, meaningless act of death, for which another term is the problematic of language, which again I reject.

For the problematic-of-problematics, in Freud as in the poets, and in us as their descendants, cannot be language, cannot even be the struggle of language against language. Language is not the Demiurge, breaking the vessels to a fresh creation of catastrophe. Catastrophe is indeed already the condition of language, the condition of the ruins of time, and of the defense against time, the deep lie at every reimagined origin. Freud posited a fundamental fusion/defusion of the two drives, love and death, as his reimagined origin of primal human ambivalence. Drive is a mythological image, and the aim of drive is always revisionary. Image, even when it is the image of voice, sees again even as it aims again, and if it sees language, it sees phantasmagoria also, and phantasmagoria need not be language. Finite men and women struggle in and against time, and with one another. Even in loving they cannot breathe without ambivalence, and where there is ambivalence there can be war to the death. Language does not become poetry for us until we know that language is telling us lies, because the truth is ambivalence and so also already death. Poetry has to be loved before we can know it as poetry, and must inspire ambivalence in us at the center of that love. Language does not require love from us, and if it provokes ambivalence, that ambivalence need not be as primal, as mythological, as the domain of the drives.

What is the motive, the drive, for all those problematics of deconstruction, via language, from Heidegger on to Gallic Post-Structuralism? Are these not the death-throes of German Romantic philosophy, and can they go beyond Nietzsche, who died that death for all of us? An Anglo-American poem is after all a richly confused relational event, from the standpoint of any Continental dialectical philosophy. Assimilations of Wallace Stevens to Heidegger or to Derrida rather than to William James or even to Dewey are on their face considerably less persuasive even than it would be to assimilate Stevens or Hart Crane to Hegel rather than to Emerson. Poems, however strong, lie against time and protest place only by being embedded in time and place, and American poems tenaciously remain texts resembling Walt Whitman and not Stéphane Mallarmé. A Derridean reading of Stevens is as charming a notion as a William Jamesian reading of Mallarmé; I long to see the advanced journals crowded with articles on the pragmatic principle at work in *Un coup de dés*, but my longing is likely to go unanswered, and not because it is less sublime than the contrary longings now being so manifestly indulged.

Reading, as an art, depends upon fundamental previsions of what is being read, so that in order to read a poem you necessarily start with an idea of what a poem is, or can be. Is it sweetness and light, as modern humanistic criticism from Matthew Arnold to M. H. Abrams tells us it is going to be? Is it the working through of the epistemology of its tropes, as modern deconstructive criticism from Heidegger to Paul de Man insists upon telling us? Increasingly I suspect that Abrams and Hillis Miller, when they debate interpretive modes, truly dispute only degrees of irony, of the human gap between expectation and fulfillment. Deconstructive *praxis*, in reading a poem, looks more and more like a refinement upon, but not a break with, the well-wrought Cleanth Brooks. I am moving towards the assertion that my kind of antithetical criticism makes an authentic break with rhetorical criticism, of whatever philosophical antecedents; but here I need to clear some ground first, since what I think is least understood by others in my own work is the rather extended concept of trope that I employ, a concept that follows the language of poetry and even of theosophies of several varieties, but that goes beyond trope as expounded by any rhetorician, ancient or modern, though here as elsewhere I happily acknowledge the example of Kenneth Burke.

Rather than ask again: what *is* a trope? I prefer to ask the pragmatic question: what is it that we want our tropes to do for us? The guide in that dark region of the will is the modern Orpheus, Nietzsche, in *The Gay Science*, where our ultimate gratitude to art as "the cult of the untrue" falls short of the magnificence of Oscar Wilde in *The Decay of Lying*, but has its own strength:

> . . . we do not always restrain our eyes from rounding off and perfecting in imagination: and then it is no longer the eternal imperfection that we carry over the river of Becoming—for we think we carry a *goddess*, and are proud and artless in

rendering this service. As an aesthetic phenomenon existence
is still *endurable* to us. . . .

Despite his partly ironic gratitude, Nietzsche pays poetry a
dubious compliment; the truth would kill us, so art as a beneficent
illusion helps sustain us. This is not far from Freud's condescen-
sion, at certain moments, to poetry. A trope is thus a way of carrying a perpetual imperfection across the river of Becoming, while
thinking we carry a goddess. But what trope is troping the concept
of trope here? Transumption or metaleptic reversal, I would say,
which is Nietzsche's favorite figure, the entire basis of his Zarathustra's rhetoric. The erotic image of carrying the goddess, lest
Becoming inundate her, is the prior trope *for* trope, while the
Nietzschean transumption says that Being is no goddess but an
eternal imperfection, or Poverty as Emerson liked to call her.
Being *is* belatedness, troping seeks to reverse such belatedness,
and Nietzsche transumes all troping, all art, by genially shrugging
at the self-deception involved. What we want our tropes to do for
us Hart Crane splendidly conveyed in a Nietzschean outburst in
the "Dance" section of *The Bridge*: "Lie to us! Dance us back our
tribal morn!" How does Crane's trope differ from Nietzsche's own
admonition: "Try to live as though it were morning," or if there
is no difference, is Crane merely repeating Nietzsche?

I think not, and I cite again the Emersonian difference, which
is to say, the American difference: a diachronic rhetoric, set not
only against past tropes, as in Nietzsche, but against the pastness
of trope itself, and so against the limitations of traditional rhetoric.
Here is Emerson at his subtlest, in that devious essay *The Poet*:

> If the imagination intoxicates the poet, it is not inactive in
> other men. The metamorphosis excites in the beholder an
> emotion of joy. The use of symbols has a certain power of
> emancipation and exhilaration for all men. We seem to be
> touched by a wand which makes us dance and run about hap-
> pily, like children. We are like persons who come out of a cave
> or cellar into the open air. This is the effect on us of tropes,
> fables, oracles and all poetic forms. Poets are thus liberating

gods. Men have really got a new sense, and found within their world another world, or nest of worlds; for, the metamorphosis once seen, we divine that it does not stop. I will not now consider how much this makes the charm of algebra and the mathematics, which also have their tropes, but it is felt in every definition; as when Aristotle defines *space* to be an immovable vessel in which things are contained;—or when Plato defines a *line* to be a flowing point; or *figure* to be a bound of solid; and many the like. What a joyful sense of freedom we have when Vitruvius announces the old opinion of artists that no architect can build any house well who does not know something of anatomy. When Socrates, in Charmides, tells us that the soul is cured of its maladies by certain incantations, and that these incantations are beautiful reasons, from which temperance is generated in souls; when Plato calls the world an animal, and Timaeus affirms that the plants also are animals; or affirms a man to be a heavenly tree, growing with his root, which is his head, upward; and, as George Chapman, following him, writes,

"So in our tree of man, whose nervie root
Springs in his top;"—

when Orpheus speaks of hoariness as "that white flower which marks extreme old age"; when Proclus calls the universe the statue of the intellect; when Chaucer, in his praise of "Gentilesse," compares good blood in mean condition to fire, which, though carried to the darkest house betwixt this and the mount of Caucasus, will yet hold its natural office and burn as bright as if twenty thousand men did it behold; when John saw, in the Apocalypse, the ruin of the world through evil, and the stars fall from heaven as the fig tree casteth her untimely fruit; when Aesop reports the whole catalogue of common daily relations through the masquerade of birds and beasts;—we take the cheerful hint of the immortality of our essence and its versatile habit and escapes, as when the gypsies say of themselves "it is in vain to hang them, they cannot die."

Definition here is a mode of divination, and the point of troping, in Emerson's diachronic sense, is that as he says: "it does not stop." A turning is a flowing, a becoming, an Orphic metamorphosis, and its *aporia* aspect yields "a joyful sense of freedom." Our essence is immortal only because of its evasiveness: "its versatile habit and escapes." This is precisely Stevens's "intricate evasions of as," and is by no means a Nietzschean "as if." If Nietzschean transumption is the parodistic version of repetition, or the Eternal Recurrence, then Emersonian transumption indeed is more whimsical. Nietzsche remains a rhetorician, albeit a profound one, and has more in common with Carlyle, whom he loathed, than with Emerson, whom he adored. Carlyle cannot do without the old descriptions of the world, and neither can Nietzsche's Zarathustra, for all his protests. Both prophets remain Protestants, however displaced, but Emerson has entered upon the American religion, Orphic and Gnostic, rather than Protestant.

Diachronic troping, in the Emersonian mode, depends upon a technique that Emerson may have derived from Milton, and for this variant of transumption I refer now to the chapter "Milton and His Precursors" in my *A Map of Misreading*. Like Milton, Emerson establishes as the basis of his figuration three temporal zones: the true origins, everything false ever since, and the truth of the eternal now, the Miltonic poetic presence or the Emersonian oratorical presence. The Miltonic or American text is true; what happened at the start is true; all of literature and history and religion, all text in between, is false. But again there is the Emersonian or American difference; the origins are not in the Creation, whether of world or man. The world, though glorious, is a catastrophe, and man was never created, but is himself the origin. But that formula is Sophistic, and not philosophic, which returns us to the agon between the Sophists and Plato.

In pursuit of a truly diachronic rhetoric, where should we flee ultimately except to those great figures, the inventors of rhetoric, our ancestors the Sophists? Protagoras and Gorgias are the authentic origins of an antithetical criticism, particularly when expounded by their definitive scholar, Mario Untersteiner, in his grand book *The Sophists* (translated from the Italian by Kathleen Freeman; Oxford, 1954). Let us, as critics, abandon Aristotle to the Formalists, and Plato to the Platonists (which these days may mean the Deconstruction Road Company). Untersteiner splendidly translates the famous apothegm of Protagoras not as: "Man is the measure of all things" but as: "Man is the master of all experiences," necessarily including (as I would adumbrate) the experience of reading or interpreting texts of any and every kind. The doctrine of Protagoras begins with the central idea developed in early Greek lyric poetry, and which has dominated Western lyric ever since: "two logoi in opposition to each other," which pragmatically means an overt recognition of the relativity of all values, and metaphysically means a kind of phenomenalism. Rhetorically, in Protagoras, the two logoi become multiform, suggesting to me the tropological perspectivism with which Western lyric poetry always confronts us. Deeper than this perspectivism is what might be called the modified logocentrism of Protagoras; he teaches, as Gorgias will, the relativity of meaning, but meanings for him *are* presences, not absences, though these are flickering presences, perpetually in flux.

The crucial term in Protagoras is *metron*, "mastery over something," which for the purposes of literary criticism I would translate as "poetic misprision" or "strong misreading." Untersteiner says of *metron* that by it Protagoras portrayed Man as "master of experiences" precisely in order to overcome "the logoi in opposition to each other," which is to say that *metron* comes into play in order to master the tragic difficulties that both produce and are lyric poetry. But we know Protagoras largely through the ironic if respectful misprision of Plato, and Protagoras refused to propound an art of rhetoric all his own. Gorgias may have been the lesser consciousness, but we actually have his great orations, the *Helen* and the *Palamedes*, and in him we have a deliberate and aggressive art of rhetoric as immediate and available as the work of our contemporary Gorgias, Kenneth Burke.

I invoke Burke as prelude to Gorgias partly because the Burke of *The Rhetoric of Religion* waits all coiled up at the end of the labyrinth of this my discourse, but also because I rely as much upon Burke as upon Untersteiner when I try to translate Gorgias

to my own purposes. For Burke as for Gorgias and for the School
of Deconstruction, the trope is a figure of knowledge. For me, it
is always a figure of willing and of not-knowing; and in fact I have
a suspicion that an uncertainty in Gorgias also fixes the will as
decisive, there at the origins of rhetoric.

The *Helen* certainly does turn upon the dramatic process of
knowing, since the *Helen* is a defense, and you cannot defend
without appearing to *know* the nature both of your client and of
the indictment. Still, of the four causes that Gorgias finds to account for Helen's apparent desertion of her domestic duties, the
will, albeit divine, takes priority over force, eloquence and necessity. Even the divine will must transform itself into the laws of
reality, or into what Gorgias distinguishes as the two major aspects
of rhetoric, the "persuasion" of logos and the "deception" of logos.
This ambivalence of logos, so pervasive in Gorgias, is something
more lost than found in most of our uses and understandings of
rhetoric. Even persuasion, to the Greeks, meant such irreconcilable
qualities as the force of reason and the powerful violence of the
daemonic. Deception was even more ambivalent because of its
reliance upon the difficult concept of *kairos*, now so peculiar for
us to apprehend because of the Christian modifications of the
notion. Pythagoras and Pindar, as Untersteiner demonstrates, are
our inevitable guides to the meaning of *kairos*, a term so ambivalent as to sum up everything that Freud came to call primal
ambivalence, or the fusion/defusion of the fundamental drives,
love and death.

Kairos, in Pindar, is what Untersteiner calls "the knowledge of
the right moment, that is, of the instant in which the intimate
connection between things is realized." Yet this instant can be
called a negative moment also, the antithesis in which what we
could call the intimate disconnection between things is surprisingly
known. Gorgias, following the poets, essentially founds the aesthetic upon the pragmatic, because his idea of rhetorical deception
is what we would call more a critical than a metaphysical idea.
Poetry *is* in effect criticism, because *kairos* is the heart of poetry,

and *kairos* testifies to the non-rationality of the cosmos. True feeling is the capacity to be deceived, prompting the famous joke that when Gorgias was asked: "Why are the Thessalians the only people you do not deceive?" he replied: "Because they are too lacking in sound feeling to be deceived by me." Or, as Gorgias said another time, poetry provokes "a lamentation which loves sorrow."

Neither a Formalist nor a Deconstructor nor an Idealizer of any kind would define a logos as a lamentation in love with sorrow (strangely Rilkean language!), but such would be my point against those critical modes, that they know less than Gorgias did about what he called "the inspired incantation of the opportune" or poetry. What Gorgias knew was that knowledge itself was tragic or poetic, because *kairos* itself is an altogether agonistic concept. Logos, confronted by the figure of the human, breaks into antithetical forces that work to destroy rationality. And here I want to quote Untersteiner directly, because his paraphrase of Gorgias sums up my own stance against all those, culminating in Paul de Man, who would make criticism into the science of the epistemology of tropes:

> Epistemology, when it is transferred from its own proper theoretical plane to the realm of the practical, becomes will, decision, which was realised in a *kairos* endowed with the property of breaking up the cycle of the antithesis and creating something new, irrational: that epistemological process defined as "deception," "persuasion," the power of which lies in the imposition of one of the two alternatives.
>
> The ethic, aesthetic and rhetoric of Gorgias are all based on *kairos*.

Untersteiner demonstrates that Gorgias represented a swerve away from his precursor, Protagoras:

> The dissolution of experiences into antitheses represents the inverse process to the speculation of Protagoras, which had reconstituted the antilogies as a unity either by the agency of the individual or by that of universal man. Gorgias' epistemological treatise takes its stand as an antithesis to the rationalistic phenomenalism of Protagoras.

Untersteiner sees an inverse relationship between the visions of Protagoras and of Gorgias; man as the master of all things, including texts, is irreconcilable with the tragic incanter of *kairos*. But an antithetical criticism also can absorb this antithesis between the two great Sophists. Gorgias' poet or orator is a *psychagogos*, a leader of souls to only relative truth, or to the relativity of truth, by an antithetical incantation, which tropes upon every definition, and contrasts every conception with its alternative. A poem or any verbal invention must exemplify *kairos*, not in the later Christian sense of the acceptable time but in the imaginative sense of "the opportune," of the *possible* image. *Kairos* is the weather of the mind, or the poem as fiction of duration; within a poem it is tone or stance, or the location of crisis-points in argument and in cognitive emotion. The *metron* of Protagoras and the *kairos* of Gorgias have in common not only the Sophistic "relativism" that Plato despised, but what I would call a knowing tropological perspectivism. As I have translated *metron* as "poetic misprision" or "strong misreading" so I would render *kairos* as "image of voice" or "crossing" or more broadly as poetic stance, in the most agonistic sense, which is stance against all competition, or in Freud's terms, primal ambivalence, due to the fundamental fusion/defusion of the two drives, Eros and Thanatos. *Kairos* is ambivalence-in-motion, or a figuration for poetry itself. Or even, as I would now add, a metaphor for criticism itself, both in theory and in practice.

I hope to have made clear, by now, that in expounding my own critical theory and practice, I neither want nor urge any "method" of criticism. It is no concern of mine whether anybody else ever comes to share, or doesn't, my own vocabularies of revisionary ratios, of crossings, of whatever. What Richard Rorty cheerfully dismisses as "the comfort of consensus" I too am very glad to live without, because I don't wish to privilege any vocabularies, my own included. Autonomy and novelty are the goals of strong reading as they are of strong writing, so that I am charmed when I observe Frank Lentricchia ending his recent book *After the New Criticism* by saying that my desire to be an original theorist is what is most retrograde and anti-intellectual in contemporary criticism. "Intellectual" seems to mean "consensus" in that view, a view held in common by traditionalist academics and by post-Heideggerians. They want agreement, as though an MLA election or a Deconstructive banquet would suffice either to arrive at a common meaning or at a decision that meaning cannot be decided. Agreement suffices for those who want it, and I don't find much pragmatic difference between the academic moldy figs who cry out slogans of ideas and meanings, and the augmenting textualists parroting the new dogmas that there are only texts, that there is nothing outside the text, and that the texts, to become texts, had to suspend their referential aspects. Nor can I discover a pragmatic difference between traditionalist insistences that all literary influence is benign, and Deconstructionist assertions that every text is cut off from literary influence, a text being as random and discontinuous an event as is any human death. That my own views are regarded as traditionalist by Deconstructors, and as deconstructive by traditionalists, adds to the charm of the situation in criticism. What is a poem *for* anyway? is to me the central question, and by the question I mean pragmatically what *is* the use of poetry or the use of criticism? My answer is wholly pragmatic, and therefore unacceptable either to those who call themselves humanists or to those of the supposedly new modes. Poetry and criticism are useful not for what they really are, but for whatever poetic and critical use you can usurp them to, which means that interpretive poems and poetic interpretations are concepts you make happen, rather than concepts of being. I love scores of poems by Stevens, but that love pragmatically does not differ in kind from my love for the house I live in, or for a particular caved-in huge old armchair in my study. My caved-in armchair doesn't have a meaning or meanings, and the sonorous declaration that there is nothing outside of the text only says, to me, that there is nothing like my caved-in old armchair except for some other caved-in old armchair, or as Richard Rorty again observes, that all descriptive vocabularies are mortal. Rorty's source is William James, mine is the aspect of

Emerson that triumphs in the essay *Experience* and subtly prophesies the pragmatism of James, Peirce, Dewey. I will go further;
those elements in Stevens and in some later poets that some critics
now want to call deconstructive are actually American pragmatic,
and are caught in a fine prolepsis by James at his most central:

> Metaphysics has usually followed a very primitive kind of
> quest. You know how men have always hankered after unlawful
> magic, and you know what a great part in magic *words* have
> always played. If you have his name, or the formula of incanta-
> tion that binds him, you can control the spirit, genie, afrite, or
> whatever the power may be. Solomon knew the names of all
> the spirits, and having their names, he held them subject to his
> will. So the universe has always appeared to the natural mind
> as a kind of enigma, of which the key must be sought in the
> shape of some illuminating or power-bringing word or name.
> That word names the universe's *principle*, and to possess it is
> after a fashion to possess the universe itself. "God," "Matter,"
> "Reason," "the Absolute," "Energy," are so many solving
> names. You can rest when you have them. You are at the end
> of your metaphysical quest.
>
> But if you follow the pragmatic method, you cannot look on
> any such word as closing your quest. You must bring out of
> each word its practical cash value, set it at work within the
> stream of your experience. It appears less as a solution, then,
> than as a program for more work, and more particularly as
> an indication of the ways in which existing realities may be
> *changed*.
>
> *Theories thus become instruments, not answers to enigmas,
> in which we can rest.* We don't lie back upon them, we move
> forward, and, on occasion, make nature over again by their aid.
> Pragmatism unstiffens all our theories, limbers them up and
> sets each one at work. Being nothing essentially new, it har-
> monizes with many ancient philosophic tendencies. It agrees
> with nominalism for instance, in always appealing to particulars;
> with utilitarianism in emphasizing practical aspects; with posi-
> tivism in its disdain for verbal solutions, useless questions and
> metaphysical abstractions.

The heart of this, for me, is that: *"Theories thus become instruments, not answers to enigmas, in which we can rest. We don't lie*

back upon them, we move forward, and, on occasion, make nature over again by their aid." Substitute "poetry" and/or "criticism" for "nature" in that formulation, and you have my view of the proper function of critical theory at this time. It cannot answer the enigma of what poetry truly is, or whether the meaning of a poem can be decided. But it can change our notion of a poem, of a poet, of poetry, though that change will be a mortal change, finite and limited, and good only for particular purposes for a particular time. Lentricchia severely says that my view of theory "invites an interpretive anarchy: a programmatic subjectivism that can only lead to the purist of relativisms." His fear is that this could debase all talk about poetry to trivia. I could reply, with the late Mayor Daley of Chicago: "They have vilified me, they have crucified me; yes, they have even criticized me." A little dialectical awareness is a better reply: beware the rhetorical or ironic impersonalist, whether traditionalist or deconstructionist, whose cool tone is a reaction-formation defense of a private quest for power. The self-dramatizing pragmatist, whatever his defenses, is more authentically representative of the perpetual otherness of poetry. "Interpretive anarchy" is an anxious name to give the necessity for misreading, which Emerson called self-reliance. Need I say here that by "misreading" I do not mean dyslexia? Great criticism has achieved its curious universalism only by the same merely apparent interpretive anarchy that strong poetry has manifested. Criticism and poetry are not primarily political, social, economic or philosophical processes; they are barely epistemological events, which is why Foucault, whatever use he may have for the history of ideas, is so massively irrelevant a theorist for the history of poetry and criticism, by which I mean a poetic and critical view of history. For poetry and criticism (by which I do continue to mean a single entity) have always been pragmatic events. They are not measurements of duration, but fictions of duration, and they are closer to lies and self-deceptions than to any other fictions. If we ever get a vigorous philosophy of the lie, then we may be close to a useful philosophy of poetry. Until then our criticism must be what it was in Samuel Johnson, William Hazlitt, John Ruskin, and in Carlyle and Emerson and Nietzsche, a dialectical war of the will against itself while simultaneously warring against anteriority, even in the name of rescuing and preserving anteriority. Bertrand Russell warned that pragmatism could lead only to warfare. So be it. Every great critic has asked himself pragmatically: what has reading this poem by another person *cost me*, what is the loss that accompanies my gain? What Lentricchia calls interpretive anarchy, James calls instrumentalism, and Rorty, as James's true heir, calls devising new ways of speaking that could help us get what we want. Criticism is not going to discover the truth any more than philosophy is going to uncover any truth; if there were poetic truth then there might be *the* Stevens, *the* Shelley, *the* Wordsworth. Emerson and Nietzsche and James and Pater and Wilde all teach us that *the* Emerson and *the* Nietzsche and so on just do not exist, except as critical fictions. Lentricchia's "Bloom" does not exist; he is Lentricchia's critical fiction, very useful for finishing a book. As a fellow-pragmatist, I can't begrudge Lentricchia his instrument, but as a precursor I urge him to remember that he is out of James and not Foucault, out of Frost and Stevens and not Derrida; he is an American critical pragmatist trying to deceive himself into an illusory rigor, on which I again cite the pragmatic Rorty:

> The *weakest* way to defend the plausible claim that literature has now displaced religion, science and philosophy as the presiding discipline of our culture is by looking for a philosophical foundation for the practises of contemporary criticism. That would be like defending Galilean science by claiming that it can be found in the Scriptures, or defending transcendental idealism as the latest result of physiological research. It would be acknowledging the authority of a deposed monarch in order to buttress the claims of a usurper. The claims of a usurping discipline to preside over the rest of culture can only be defended by an exhibition of its ability to put the other disciplines in their places. This is what the literary culture has been doing recently, with great success. It is what science did when it displaced religion and what idealist philosophy did when it briefly displaced science. Science did not *demonstrate* that religion was false, nor philosophy that science was merely phenomenal, nor can modernist literature or textualist criticism

demonstrate that the "metaphysics of presence" is an out-dated genre. But each in turn has managed, without argument, to make its point.

So far I have given only a prelude to a discourse upon interpretive paradigms, and hope to have made two points: models for criticism should be pragmatic, and *not* traditionally philosophical; and they cannot be hedges against "interpretive anarchy." Paradigms for criticism are instruments; I use them to replace other instruments, because every criticism depends upon a paradigm, even without awareness. Deconstructive and other post-Heideggerian paradigms tend to the so-called linguistic model, which reduces to the very odd trope of a demiurgical entity named "Language" acting like a Univac, and endlessly doing our writing for us. I don't find this trope any more persuasive than the traditionalist trope of the Imagination as a kind of mortal god endlessly doing our writing for us. Richard Wollheim likes to ask the new followers of the Language Demiurge how, in their view, meaning ever gets started anyway, which is quite unanswerable upon deconstructive terms, but has never been answered by the devotees of the Imagination Demigod either. I have three answers, two of which at least are incompatible, and all of which turn upon usurpation, upon violence, because *contra* Foucault the human mind cannot conceive of interpretive power without the king. Interpretation is implicitly hierarchical, and cannot proceed without a usurpation of authority. Meaning gets started by a catastrophe that is also a ruining and breaking creation—originally a Gnostic formulation. Or else meaning gets started by a transference of a purely fictive earlier authority to a later representative—originally a Hebraic formulation. Or else meaning gets started by an act of violence, textual or physical, in a family grouping—originally what Vico called a Gentile formulation, both Asiatic and Greek. Freud is not the only major speculator of the last century to merge these three formulations; Schopenhauer and Nietzsche and even Hegel could provide roughly similar blendings, as could Carlyle, Emerson and Pater in our language. But Freud is inescapable, since more even than Proust his was the mythopoeic mind of our age, as much our theologian and our moral philosopher as he was our psychologist and our prime maker of fictions. Meaning gets started, for him, by catastrophes at our origins; by family passion and strife in our development; by transferring repressed earlier ambivalences onto later authority figures in our maturer educations, loves and therapies. I prefer Gnostic and Kabbalistic catastrophe creations to the more muted versions in Freud, Ferenczi and Rank, and I have begun to question severely my own use for criticism of the Freudian "family romance." In the course of writing a full-scale commentary upon all of Freud's major books and essays, concentrating upon issues of transference and authority, my labors have convinced me that Freud's most important book, not for its intellectual contribution, but for the pattern of his work, is *Totem and Taboo*. Freud dissimulated, productively and shrewdly, by using his own mythopoeic versions of taboo and totemism as the covert models for the analytical transference. At the close, Freud said that the theory of the drives was his mythology. What he could not admit was that his therapy also was his mythology, since there is no warrant for analytical authority over the emotions except for the role that the totem-analyst plays in regard to the taboo-transference.

There are vivid insights into the role of interpretive models in Thomas Kuhn's *The Structure of Scientific Revolutions* and in Max Black's *Models and Metaphors*, but here as elsewhere I take my starting point from Kenneth Burke, particularly from the later Burke of *The Rhetoric of Religion*. Rather like Emerson in the essay *Experience*, Burke does not secularize the Augustinian enabling fiction of the Fall, but instead he shows that such a "god-term" is a necessity of the Negative in language, where the Negative performs the work of God or, as I would say, of the Demiurge. Meaning gets started all right, but by denial, the self-contradictory denial of any anteriority. If you want a trope of a language machine, then I would say: "Excellent, provided you recognize that such a trope is as much a perspectivism, is as turning a stance, as is denial." Heidegger asks us to believe that he finds a way through the woods so as to take up language's very own stance towards itself. But that, even if it *were* some part of some truth, immediately privileges language itself as a mode of explanation. Burke, as an American pragmatist, shrewdly evades such a privileging. The Negative in language, like God in theology, simply is a trope *that works*, and that helps Burke to set going various machines for criticism.

Can we read strongly, that is to say, critically, without machines to aid us? A not wholly unfriendly critic, Neil Hertz, characterized my own work as a blend of Rube Goldberg and Piranesi, or a *mélange* of homemade contraptions and imaginary spaces. I accept this but universalize it: all criticism, from the rival formulations of Aristarchus of Alexandria and Crates of Mallos down to our moment, is a volatile mixture of Rube Goldberg and Piranesi. The triumphant point of a Rube Goldberg is not that it is a twittering machine, or that it goes through amazing, far-fetched convolutions in order to perform a simple operation in a howlingly complicated way, *but that it works*—not by getting a job done, but by an audacious inventiveness that exposes, however parodistically, the truth that the job's aim cannot be distinguished from its origins. Or, to leap out from these tropes, that the idea of poetry always is more founded upon the idea of criticism than criticism ever is founded upon poetry. To mend a formulation I ventured too long ago, criticism is not so much prose poetry as poetry is verse criticism. My statement that all criticism was prose poetry gave much offense; the other and more useful notion should have given and go on giving offense, for even a Shelleyan love lyric is as much verse criticism as are Horace and Pope. We need paradigms for deciding meaning in poems because poems themselves rely upon paradigms, indeed *are* commentaries upon paradigms. With my customary arbitrariness, or as one critic said, brutal over-simplifications, I assert that there are three major paradigms that poems tend to rely upon: catastophe creation, agonistic strife, transference of ambivalence. I shall take these up in that order.

I translate an apothegm of the Yiddish poet Leivick as saying:

"A song means filling a jug, and even more, breaking the jug; breaking it to pieces; in the language of the Kabbalah we perhaps might call it: 'Broken Vessels.' " Certainly the major Gnostic poet in the language was Yeats, and either his natural Gnosticism or his traditions gave him the powerful trope that he calls "breaks," as in: "Marbles of the dancing floor / Break bitter furies of complexity" after the smithies of Byzantium "break the flood." I would say now that the spirits who are that flood are primarily the precursors: Blake, Shelley, Keats, Pater and Nietzsche, the antithetical fivefold who from their ephebe's perspective most truly represent "bitter furies of complexity." They are "furies" because they are avenging daemons, whom Yeats must placate, and whose "complexity" he feels he must "simplify" into his own "intensity." But why are they "bitter"? Stevens, in *The Poems of Our Climate*, notes that in "this bitterness," in the imperfect that is our paradise, delight lies in flawed words and stubborn sounds. To be imperfect is to be unfinished, and in both poets to be "bitter" means to be broken, or to be in brokenness. Bitterness is to lie among the broken vessels, to tell the lie of the perpetual breaking of the vessels, a lie because here "breaks" also means "makes" or the creation by and in catastrophe.

Stevens prefers placing his jugs and jars, his cold porcelains, to breaking them, but such placement, as he knew, is a breaking anyway. That breaking is named fashionably "intertextuality," but what is called "intertextuality" these days is an ancient critical and poetic phenomenon, more traditionally subsumed under the broad categories of echo, allusion and influence. I myself prefer "intratextuality," since "inside" and "outside" are wholly figurative notions in relation to poems. What matters is the sense or senses in which poems are internal to one another, say as the *Ode on a Grecian Urn* of Keats internalizes itself as "porcelain" in Stevens's poems:

> The eye believes and its communion takes.
> The spirit laughs to see the eye believe
> And its communion take. And now of that.
> Let the Secretary for Porcelain observe
> That evil made magic, as in catastrophe,

If neatly glazed, becomes the same as the fruit
Of an emperor, the egg-plant of a prince.
The good is evil's last invention. . . .

                    *   *   *
               . . . The day itself
Is simplified: a bowl of white,
Cold, a cold porcelain, low and round,
With nothing more than the carnations there.

                    *   *   *
      . . . It is desire, set deep in the eye,
Behind all actual seeing, in the actual scene,
In the street, in a room, on a carpet or a wall,

Always in emptiness that would be filled,
In denial that cannot contain its blood,
A porcelain, as yet in the bats thereof.

Keats is the Secretary for Porcelain in Stevens's Academy of
Fine Ideas, and he is urged to observe what he already knew too
well in his own meditation upon the Grecian Urn: evil which, in
Stevens as in Keats, means the necessary pain and suffering of
being part of nature, is made magic through the catastrophe creation that is poetry. The complete simplicity of the Stevensian day,
with Keats's cold Pastoral reduced to "cold, a cold porcelain," is
another creative catastrophe, and so will be the desire or poverty
that would be filled by the poem or porcelain as yet in its bats or
chunks of unbaked clay. Poems or porcelains differ from one another as Stevens differs from his precursors Keats and Whitman,
because no catastrophe is quite like another, as Yeats might have
remarked, thinking both of love affairs and of poems. His actual
statement, in *Per Amica Silentia Lunae*, was that no disaster, erotic
or poetic, is like another and so there must be always "new bitterness, new disappointment." I add to Yeats here only that the critic
as reader must join the poet as reader in the finding of a "true
mask" of personality, in the Wildean sense, though the finding of
such a mask, and the work of meditating upon it, will not make
fresh suffering less necessary.

For Criticism is a communicable art, dependent upon instruction, and then upon revisionary invention. It is no more a social science or human science than poetry is. Its earliest master was Aristophanes (an insight I owe to Bruno Snell). That criticism should have found its origins in satire and farce surely ought not to be forgotten when we brood upon the nature of this literary art. Oscar Wilde, a strong critic who was at his best in dialogue, gave us the added insight that criticism was the only civilized form of autobiography. The true critic, whether Aristophanes or Wilde or Kenneth Burke, knows that criticism, like poetry, cannot be an escape from personality. The various waves of Modernism from Eliot to the belated Modernism of Barthes and Foucault have played at emptying out the authorial subject, but this is an ancient play, and recurs in every Modernism from second-century B.C.E. Alexandria down to our moment.

Personality in any case cannot be voided except by personality, it being an oddity (perhaps) that Eliot and Barthes matter as critics because they are indeed critical personalities, if less intense and vivid say than Hazlitt and Wilde. Critical personality does not seem to me to differ in degree or in kind from poetic personality, and personality in this sense seems to me as much a cognitive as an affective term. A critical or poetic personality can be reduced rhetorically to stance or tone, perhaps even to diction, but the limits of rhetorical reduction are reached quickly enough. We read criticism as we read poetry (or ought to), so that we can acquire a further sense of what Milton's Satan calls "quickening power." Such a sense depends upon what Blake and Pater called "spiritual form" as opposed to "corporeal form," or more simply upon what even the wary Stevens had to call "the spirit":

> For she was the maker of the song she sang.
> The ever-hooded, tragic-gestured sea
> Was merely a place by which she walked to sing.
> Whose spirit is this? we said, because we knew
> It was the spirit that we sought and knew
> That we should ask this often as she sang.

That Stevens seeks the spirit as Muse to revive his poetry is beautifully clear. Less clear, but as crucial, is the erotic ideology of

The Idea of Order at Key West, since the power of the poet's mind over the tragic-gestured sea or universe of death is also an erotic power, or a restitution of a wounded Narcissism. Most of us are neither artists nor ideologues, though as readers and viewers we are all critics. The pragmatic mode akin to art and ideology for most of us is no longer religion but Eros, or even the religion of Eros, or for many of us, psychoanalysis. This means that most of my own readers will have confronted revisionism primarily in their erotic lives, which are quite simply now our spiritual lives. Revisionism in Eros is always a mode of narcissistic mobility, whether we are in the rejecting or the rejected posture. This means that erotic choice and change are always instances of self-revisionism, whatever idealizations we cultivate about the erotic partner. But what are erotic choice and change? How do we reject, or how are we rejected?

In a love affair, as in a poem or a film, there are always crises, significant disjunctions in which meaning appears to be collected. I remember, some years back, distributing photocopies of one of my early maps of misprision or misreading to a startled and properly skeptical Yale graduate seminar, to whom I observed that even if the Kabbalistic chart proved useless for interpreting poems, it would still be highly serviceable for plotting the vicissitudes of their love affairs. My observation was founded upon the ethos of Freud, which argues that influence or transference is a process that trades in three prime concepts: power, authority, tradition. Power in this context can be defined as the capacity to wound; authority may be identified as what we all sense has been lost from our world; tradition appears now to be the trope of usurpation and imposition. If power always includes violence, however psychic or internalized, then authority cannot be a concept involving violence, any more than it comprehends persuasion, whether rational or imaginative. As for tradition, since it has to do as much with group repressions as with individual vicissitudes, it becomes the largest and loosest of the three terms, and does not exclude internalized violence nor any mode of persuasiveness. Erotic choices and rejections, whether of poems or persons, are transactions in power, authority and tradition, and not just interplays of language. Falling out of love, whether with poem or person, may be more of a revisionary act than falling in love, be it textual or sexual. What ought to be seen more clearly is that revisionism is an energizer even when it works through loss. But loss of idealization, whether in regard to poems or to persons, is very difficult for almost anyone to accept.

When I was a young man, deeply in love with the whole range of Romantic poetry, British and American, I would have been distressed to believe that there was an essential continuity, rather than a violent discontinuity, between the European Enlightenment and Romanticism. Blake then seemed to me a *nabi*, a Hebrew prophet somehow born belatedly in the London of 1757. Had a critic presented a Blake not so much a visionary as a shrewd revisionist, obsessed with his own defensive gestures, which is to say a Blake closer to Alexander Pope than to Ezekiel, I would have been offended. Presenting just such a Blake in the lectures that became *Poetry and Repression*, I gave precisely such offense, to auditors as to readers. But the idealizations of poets and poetry do not serve the spirit. Instead, they weaken the spirit by investing value in a context that cannot sustain value, in itself. Perhaps no context can, and yet it seems no surprise that poetry should entice so many of its readers into illusions. Matthew Arnold's abiding legacy was his curious hope that poetry would take the place of empty heaven and its hymns (in Stevens's phrasing). The hope was wrongheaded, because it got the truth of the relation between poetry and belief just exactly backwards. That relation has never differed, in kind or in degree, from the agonistic interplay of any two poems, or of any two beliefs.

Agon, as a cultural concept, returns us, via Freud, Nietzsche and Burckhardt, to the Greeks, and ultimately to Plato's contest with Homer. Later contests by the Gnostics with Plato were less violent than the Gnostic struggle to the death with the Hebrew Bible, or with the Church's own readings of the Christian Bible. My prelude to Gnosis in this book explains my choice of the Gnostics as a paradigm for the revisionary agonist in America, whether she or he be critic or poet. That agonist belongs to Stevens's Academy of Fine Ideas and shares, as best he can, in its belated version of the Emersonian program:

> He wanted that,
> To face the weather and be unable to tell
> How much of it was light and how much thought,
> In these Elysia, these origins,
> This single place in which we are and stay,
> Except for the images we make of it,
> And for it, and by which we think the way,
> And, being unhappy, talk of happiness
> And, talking of happiness, know that it means
> That the mind is the end and must be satisfied.

2
Lying Against Time:
Gnosis, Poetry, Criticism

Valentinus, whose fragments show a mythopoeic power beyond that evidenced in any complete Gnostic text we possess, wrote this in a letter, as reported by Clement of Alexandria:

> Even as fear fell upon the angels in the presence of Adam when he uttered greater sounds than his status in the creation justified, sounds caused by the one who invisibly had deposited in Adam seed of celestial substance so that Adam expressed himself freely, so also among the generations of men of our world, the works of men become objects of fear to their own makers, as in the instances of statues, images and everything which hands fashion in the name of a "god." For Adam, being fashioned in the name of "man," inspired angelic fear of the pre-existent man because pre-existent man was in Adam. They, the angels, were terrified and quickly concealed or ruined their work.

An exegesis of the literary strength of this magnificent fragment is the starting point for my attempt to expound part of the "meaning" of Gnosis. My way into Gnosis is not psychological, philosophical or historical, and may or may not be "religious." Within the necessary limitation of my own misreading of Gnosis, I would want to call it a Gnostic way, because I have found that my mode of interpreting literary texts can be described more accurately as a Valentinian and Lurianic approach than as being Freudian, Nietzschean or Viconian. A Valentinian and Lurianic stance makes possible, at least for me, an "antithetical" and revisionist way of reading Wordsworth and Shelley, Emerson and Whitman, Yeats and Stevens. And perhaps a kind of literary criticism opened up by Gnostic and Kabbalistic dialectic can be turned back upon Gnostic texts, so as to see how the Valentinians and Lurianics read when they are read as Emerson or Yeats can be read.

What is the fear that falls upon sculptor and poet, according to Valentinus, when they behold the statues and images that they have fashioned in the name of a "god"? We might think of the dramatic speaker of Blake's *Tyger*, who fears what turns out to be an image he himself has framed, except that Blake himself is hardly one with that frightened speaker. What is it in an artist that can look upon his own handiwork and find it frightening? For "a god" here we can read "the daemonic" or, in our Age of Freud, "the uncanny" (*unheimlich*). Valentinus gives us two clues for interpretation, both analogical. Adam frightened the angels because his voice reverberated with the power of a pre-existent Man, a Primal or Divine Anthropos or Adam Kadmon, in whose name Adam had been fashioned. The angels were terrified because they realized that a greater power or freedom of expression than they enjoyed thus belonged to Adam, who by sharing in the name of pre-existent Anthropos stood over them in hierarchical rank and stood before them in priority of genesis. In their terror, the angels rapidly hid or botched their work, which can only have been the cosmos, the world into which Adam has been thrown, but which would have been inferior to Adam (and to us) even if the demiurgical angels had not lost their nerve.

Our exegesis hardly has begun to open up the splendors of this Valentinian fragment. The two analogical clues—the angels' fear of Adam, and their ruining of their work—are at once oddly alike and different, in that the angels' fear of Adam is their fear *of a name*, just as the human artist's fear is of a daemonic name; while the angels' botching of Creation comes rather from their lacking a name greater than their own in which their creation can share, unlike the frightened human artist who does not conceal or ruin his work, despite his terror. To understand these diverse analogical hints, I suggest that we read Valentinus's brief text antithetically, which is precisely how that text itself interprets the texts having priority over it, Genesis and Plato's *Timaeus*, and perhaps, more subtly, the Gospel of John. Valentinus is troping upon and indeed against these precursor authorities, and the purpose and effect of his troping is to reverse his relationship to the Bible and to Plato, by joining himself to an asserted earlier truth that they supposedly have distorted. The greater sounds uttered in his letter testify to the belatedness of the Bible and of Plato, who like the terrified angels have concealed or ruined their creation.

Valentinus, as we would expect of him, does not distinguish between Creation and Fall in regard to the cosmos, the work of the angels. His attitude to art is rather Paterian, in that the statue or poem exceeds in power what it represents, exceeds and surprises the artists' expectations, because sculptor and poet do not know that they work in the name of a "god." The cosmic Creation falls below angelic design, but the human creation rises above artistic design, because it sounds in the name of pre-existence. What seems the kernel of Valentinus's mythmaking here is this formula: *to fashion in the name of* a being more Sublime, that is a being higher in an agonistic hierarchy of measurement. The angels are ignorant, artists are ignorant, and Adam is evidently ignorant also. The pre-existent Man is not ignorant, because presumably to be a God-Man *is* to be the Gnosis, is to be free.

Does Valentinus's fragment imply that artistic fear is the *consequence* of angelic fear, or that it is only the analogy of the earlier terror? I come forward eighteen centuries from the Valentinian myth to its parodistic and ironic equivalent in Thomas Mann's "Descent into Hell" that is the "Prelude" to his Joseph tetralogy. Mann calls Gnosticism "man's truest knowledge of himself," and celebrates what he calls

> the figure of the first or first completely human man, the Hebraic *Adam qadmon*; conceived as a youthful being made

out of pure light, formed before the beginning of the world as prototype and abstract of humanity.

Mann describes the Gnostic and Manichean vision, which he compounds, as a "narcissistic picture, so full of tragic charm," and he names the Gnostic quest pattern as "the romance of the soul." Erich Heller, commenting on the Joseph saga, makes the Mannian judgment that the "Gnostic tradition is the exact theological version of Schopenhauer's metaphysics." I think that this should be modified from "exact" to "approximate," except in regard to that part of Schopenhauer's metaphysics which constitutes his aesthetic of the Sublime, as Schopenhauer's Sublime does seem to me exactly Gnostic.

Heller speaks of Mann's theology as being "the theology of irony," and I will suggest later that irony is, in the rhetoric of Gnosis, only a preparatory trope. Mann therefore, in his playfulness, does not seem to me a Gnostic writer, as compared to Kafka, Rilke, and Yeats in our century, or in the nineteenth century, Emerson and Melville, Balzac and Victor Hugo, Novalis and Nerval, among others. Mann indeed seems hardly Gnostic compared to such genuinely mixed cases as Carlyle, Gnostic in his view of man but not in his vision of nature, or Blake, wholly Gnostic in his stance towards nature, but opposing the Gnosis in his vision of man.

Mann plays at Gnosticism precisely because it gives him a model for his own perhaps equivocal Modernism, and that is why Mann can be useful in answering our interpretative question about Valentinus's fragment. The Modernist or mock-Gnostic would attribute artistic anxiety and fear of the created work to an angelic or daemonic fear or loss of nerve, but the truly Gnostic interpreter would find artistic anxieties-of-representation to be only analogous to the angelic failure of courage. The analogy touches its limit where Valentinian Gnosis properly begins, which is in a liberating knowledge that excludes all aesthetic irony, precisely because the inaugurating realization in such knowledge makes of all Creation and all Fall one unified event, and sees that event as belonging altogether to the inner life of God, and not to the life of man, except insofar as man is Anthropos or pre-existent Adam, that is, not part of the Creation.

A Gnostic aesthetic would say that works of artists become objects of fear, even to those artists, because the statues or poems are works of true knowledge. Yeats remarked, at the end of his life, that man could embody the truth, but could not know it, which is an inverted Gnostic formulation. Friedrich Schlegel said that the true aesthetic was the Kabbalah, an insight partly worked out in our time very seriously by Walter Benjamin, a true Gnostic, and parodistically by Borges, like Mann a Modernist pretending to a Gnosticism. I would revise Schlegel by asserting that the truest aesthetic is the Valentinian Gnosis, and its surprisingly close descendant in the Lurianic or regressive Kabbalah, and I return now to Valentinus's fragment to begin a sketch of this truest aesthetic.

The Adamic "greater sounds" that frighten the angels are necessarily poems. To ask how poems can be the Gnosis is to ask what is it that poems know, which in turn is to ask what is it that we can come to know when we read poems? But to make the question itself Gnostic we need to cast away nearly the entire philosophical tradition of knowledge. I say "nearly" because of my respect for and debt to Hans Jonas, whose work has demonstrated the authentic resemblances between Gnosticism and the Heideggerian revision of ontology and epistemology. But the Heideggerian revision, in its aesthetic implications, has fostered the capable critical school of Deconstruction, which has touched its limit precisely in the tracing of any poem's genuinely epistemological or negative moments. To get beyond that critical dilemma or *aporia* or limit of interpretability, I suggest that we abandon Heidegger for Valentinus and Luria. "Poetic knowledge" may be an oxymoron, but it has more in common with Gnosis than it does with philosophy. Both are modes of *antithetical* knowledge, which means of knowledge both negative and evasive, or knowledge not acceptable as such to epistemologists of any school.

"Know," as an English word, goes back to the root *gno*, and one of its most frequent current usages is not far from Gnosis: "To perceive directly whether with mind or with the sense; to apprehend clearly and certainly." We need amend this only by asking: *what* does the Gnostic perceive directly with his mind, *what* does he apprehend clearly and certainly? Jonas answers: "The 'what' of the knowledge contains the explanation of its own origin, communication, and promised effect." Jonas's language here is the language of the poetic Sublime, rather than of philosophy, and Jonas is centered even more firmly in literary tradition when he wisely goes on to describe the typology of Gnosis in terms of its imagination and mood as well as its thought. A knowledge that is at once "secret, revealed and saving" is indeed the language of a "transcendental genesis." Like Milton's Satan in his fall from the Godhead, a fall that opens up a new, Sublime, negative Creation in the Abyss, so the Valentinian Creation/Fall brings about a Sublime and Negative cosmos, with the difference that the Gnostic Fall is *within* the Godhead, and not just *from* it. Jonas sees the Valentinian cosmos as being a "stratification along a vertical axis, on the antithesis of the heights and the depths."

In this cosmos, a negative movement of knowledge ensues, from divine loss of knowledge to demiurgical lack of knowledge to human want of knowledge until at last the dialectic of negation brings about a human restoration of knowledge as the vehicle of salvation. Jonas's commentary again is far closer to a poetic than a philosophical vision of time.

> This progressive movement constitutes the *time* axis of the gnostic world, as the vertical order of aeons and spheres constitutes its space axis. Time, in other words, is actuated by the onward thrust of a mental life. . . . It is a metaphysic of pure movement and event.

Jonas packs in so much here that it wrongs him to analyze only the time-element in his remarks. But time is the puzzle that Gnosis and modern poetry meet in sharing. By "modern poetry" here I now mean the Renaissance and later, down to our various contemporary Modernisms. Puech and other scholars have emphasized the Gnostic hatred for time, but only Jonas has caught the precise accent of belatedness that characterizes what is unique to Gnosis. Comparing Valentinus and the early Heidegger, Jonas brings them together in their abolishment of the present moment, in their destruction of the temporal aspect of metaphorical presence. Valentinianism, Jonas observes,

> makes no provision for a *present* on whose content knowledge may dwell and, in beholding, stay the forward thrust. There is past and future, where we come from and where we speed to, and the present is only the moment of *gnosis* itself, the peripety from the one to the other in the supreme crisis of the eschatological *now*.

Jonas is unsurpassed in his rapid characterization of what he calls Heidegger's "breathless dynamism," with its precise analogues to the Valentinian *Augenblick:*

> . . . "facticity," necessity, having become, having been thrown, guilt, are existential modes of the past; "existence," being ahead of one's present, anticipation of death, care, and resolve, are existential modes of the future. No present remains for genuine existence to repose in. . . .

I follow Jonas then in reading the Gnostic temporal dilemma as being caught at the crisis-point between past and future, a dilemma perhaps more Kafkan even than it is Heideggerian. But here I come to the darkest puzzle that Gnosis and belated poetry share: what is it that can be known when there is no present moment in which a knowing can take place? I take it that this is why a Gnostic never *learns* anything, because learning is a process *in time.* I think that the poet in a poet, the strong poetic self, also cannot learn anything. The thought-form of the Hebrew Bible depends upon a movement in the fullness of time, a movement in which moral learning can take place, which is another reason why both Gnosis and belated poetry are so remote both from Hebrew ideas of reality, and from the Hebraic mode of listening to the voicing of the Word. Belatedness sees a writing in space; it cannot hear a voicing in time. What is known through seeing a writing is more problematic than the urgency of an oral revelation, the urgency of a time always open to redemption.

What a Gnostic or a strong poet knows is what only a strong reading of a belated poem or lie-against-time teaches: a freedom compounded of three elements, and these are: negation, evasion, extravagance. It is the mutual audacity of belated religion or Gnosis, and of belated poetry or Petrarch and after, to create a freedom out of and by catastrophe. I will examine first the dialectic of negation, evasion, and extravagance in Valentinianism, and then suggest a version of the same dialectic in the history of poetry.

Negation in Gnosis needs to be distinguished from negation in Hegelian philosophy and from what Freud calls negation, though the distance from psychoanalysis is not nearly so great as it is from philosophy. If philosophy is, as Novalis said, the desire to be at home everywhere, then Gnosis is closer to what Nietzsche thought the motive of art: the desire to be elsewhere, the desire to be different. Jonas illuminatingly contrasts Gnosis to its own contemporary philosophic rival:

> . . . Gnostic emanationism, unlike the harmonistic one of the Neoplatonists, has a catastrophic character. The form of its progress is *crisis*. . . .
> . . . For tragedy and drama, crisis and fall, require concrete and personal agents, individual divinities. . . . The Plotinean descensus of Being, in some respects an analogy to the gnostic one, proceeds through the autonomous movement of impersonal concept, by an inner necessity that is its own justification. The gnostic descensus cannot do without the contingency of subjective affect and will. . . .

Following Jonas, I turn to Gnostic negation as the first movement of that affect and will. Whereas Hegelian negation also insists that true knowledge begins when philosophy destroys the experience of daily life, such destruction is a phase on the way to a universal, and so Hegelian truth finally negates both the *per se* existence of the object and the individual ego. But Gnosticism would not accept this shifting of the truth to a universal. The warrant for the truth remains personal, indeed *is* the true personal, the *pneuma* of the Gnostic, his self as opposed to his mere *psyche* or soul. Shall we say, against the philosophers, that Gnosis is the rapid, impatient labor of the Negative?

Freudian negation, perhaps because of its hidden root in Schopenhauer's concept of the Sublime, has one revelatory resemblance to Gnostic negation. In the Freudian *Verneinung*, a previously repressed thought, feeling or desire enters consciousness only by being disowned. A kind of truth is thus acknowledged intellectually, even as it is given no emotional acceptance. This psychical duplicity or metapsychological dualism empties out the presence of the present moment just as the Hegelian Negative does, but it carries also the implicit "thesis that there is sense in everything, which in turn implies that everything is past and there is nothing new," to quote J. H. Van den Berg's critique of Freud. What Freud calls the bodily ego's negation by a mingled act of projection and introjection is very close to the Gnostic negation of time and of the Creation. But here I enter again upon the Gnostic vision of time, which is the ultimate form of Gnostic negation, and I will discuss this darkest of visions in some detail.

The Hermetic *Asclepius* sets all time into the context of the lie by its declaration that "where things are discerned at intervals of time, there are falsehoods; and where things have an origin in time, there errors arise." Much fiercer is the vision given to us of Ialdabaoth the Demiurge in the Gnostic *Apocryphon of John*, where that deluded creator is said to have "bound the gods of the heavens, the angels, the demons, and men in measure, duration, and time, in order to subject them to the chain of destiny." *Heimarmene*, cosmic fate, is our sleep, our exile, our anxiety, and above all our ignorance. Time is thus the supreme negation, because it parodies the truth of Gnosis.

Time in Gnosis is what Shelley called "an envious shadow,"

and aesthetically is an acute withdrawal or contraction *of meaning*. In strictly poetic terms, the time of the Gnostics is any poem's fiction of duration, that is, its way of figurating the illusion of a temporal sequence. Mallarmé may seem more a Hegelian than a Gnostic in his negative moments, but his tropes of duration and visions of the void are thoroughly Gnostic. When the serene irony of the eternal blue stuns the poet in what he called a sterile desert of sorrows, and what the Gnostics called the Kenoma, then he inhabits the cosmos of Valentinus and not of Hegel. It is a cosmos of mirrors that mirror only nothing or the void, in a fall in which we never stop falling, hence the terrible Mandaean formula: "How long I have endured already and how long I have been dwelling in this world."

This demonic temporality becomes necessarily the most extreme mode of negative theology ever known, far surpassing the Christian negative theology that was to stem from the Neoplatonic temporal vision of pseudo-Dionysius the Areopagite. A God who transcends the principles both of deity and goodness of course transcends all temporality also; there is nothing left of the Hebraic hearing of the dynamic motion of God in time, in the vision of the pseudo-Dionysius, which is really a belated exercise in Platonic theology, and yet became a permanent element in Christianity. But Gnostic negative theology is yet more drastic because Gnostic transcendence really needs a word beyond transcendence to designate so hyperbolic a sense of being above the world, "that world." our mere universe of death. Gnostic metaphor depends therefore upon the most outrageous dualism that our traditions ever have known. In a Gnostic metaphor, the "inside" term or *pneuma* and the "outside" cosmic term are so separated that every such figuration becomes a catachresis, an extension or abuse of metaphor. Metaphors of time become particularly abused, as in the Valentinian parody of Plato's *Timaeus*, where I again follow Jonas's path-breaking work.

Freud says that "negation, the derivative of expulsion, belongs to the instinct of destruction." Developing Freud's remark in his

book *Allegory*, Angus Fletcher points to the near-identity between
a kind of satire and Gnosticism:

> In a way Freud's term "negation" names the process by which,
> unconsciously, the mind selects terms to express its ambiva-
> lence. Extreme dualism must cause symbolic antiphrases. One
> gets the impression sometimes that the most powerful satirists
> are dualists, users of "negation," to the point that they become
> naive gnostics. They, like Gnostics, hover on an edge of extreme
> asceticism which can drop off absolutely into an extreme
> libertinism. . . .

Something of the destructive, ambivalent satire that Fletcher
describes can be seen in the sophisticated Gnosticism of the
Valentinians when they directly parody Plato. Something indeed
of the violence of the Gnostic satire of Plato can be surmised by
the counter-violence of the ordinarily gentle Plotinus, when he
writes "Against the Gnostics; or Against Those that Affirm the
Creator of the Cosmos and the Cosmos Itself to be Evil":

> Misunderstanding their text [Plato's *Timaeus*] . . . in every
> way they misrepresent Plato's theory as to the method of crea-
> tion as in many other respects they dishonor his teaching. . . .

What exercised Plotinus (as Jonas and others have shown) was
the Gnostic misprision of that beautiful passage in the *Timaeus*
(37c ff.) where Plato makes the best case he can for time. For
Plato, time's positive and formal aspect is that it reflects and imi-
tates its original, eternity, but its negative and qualitative aspect
is that the mimesis is necessarily imperfect:

> When the father and creator saw the creature which he had
> made moving and living, the created image of the eternal gods,
> he rejoiced, and in his joy determined to make the copy still
> more like the original, and as this was an eternal living being,
> he sought to make the universe eternal, so far as might be. Now
> the nature of the ideal being was everlasting, but to bestow this
> attitude in its fullness upon a creature was impossible. Where-
> fore he resolved to have a moving image of eternity, and when
> he set in order the heaven, he made this image eternal but

moving according to number, while eternity itself rests in unity, and this image we call time.

What Plato gives here has been a kind of analogical model for literary criticism from second-century B.C.E. Alexandria down to the orthodox academic present. Indeed, this appears to be the ultimate model for the benign notion of literary influence as a positive transmission from source to later text, and from writer to reader, throughout Western history. Though there is some loss acknowledged and regretted by Plato in this passage, the loss is a necessity of demiurgical creativity, and the clear implication is that every subsequent and even more belated poet *must* imitate the Demiurge. Alexandrian or analogical literary criticism, from Aristarchus to modern American Formalism or New Criticism, assumes the image of a verbally represented temporality as a fit mimesis for a fullness somehow present beyond time. The analogists of Alexandria followed Plato and Aristotle in being able to assume that literary texts were analogous to their interpretations, and since the Greek "analogy" means "equality of ratios," such an assumption allowed a literary text the status of a unity that might have a fixed meaning. Opposed to the Library of Alexandria in the second century B.C.E. was the Library of Pergamon, as headed by Crates of Mallos. Crates set the Stoic concept "anomaly" or "disproportion of ratios" against the Platonic-Aristotelian "analogy." To apply a Stoic anomalistic or allegorical reading to a literary text is indeed to see it not as a unity but as an interplay of disproportionate ratios or differences. A meaning rising out of such ratios will not be fixed but wavering, or as we say these days, "intertextual." Valentinus, beginning again in Alexandria four centuries after Aristarchus, accepts the Stoic system of interpretation by anomaly and applies it to Plato, much to the dismay both of Neoplatonists and of the Great Church. For here is the Valentinian reading of the Platonic "moving image of eternity":

> When the Demiurge further wanted to imitate also the boundless, eternal, infinite and timeless nature of [the original eight

Aeons in the Pleroma], but could not express their immutable eternity, being as he was a fruit of defect, he embodied their eternity in times, epochs, and great numbers of years, under the delusion that by the quantity of times he could represent their infinity. Thus truth escaped him and he followed the lie. Therefore he shall pass away when the times are fulfilled.

The Stoic mode of allegory or irony as produced through the operation of anomaly, or disproportion of revisionary ratios, makes this Valentinian parody also an allegory of reading, and again an allegory of misprision. By misprision I mean literary influence viewed not as benign transmission but as deliberately perverse misreading, whose purpose is to clear away the precursor so as to open a space for oneself. For Plato, the Demiurge is a valiant though finally inadequate yet faithful copyist. For Valentinus, the Demiurge is a liar, whose lie is *about* Eternity and also *against* Eternity. Valentinus, in opposition, also lies, but his lie is not *about* time, but rather *against* time. This is a remarkably Nietzschean lie or parody or antithetical fiction, for as a lie it expresses the will's resentment against time, and even more against time's cruel statement: "It *was*." Valentinian negation is thus the opening movement in a poetic dialectic, and so is remarkably akin to its collateral descendant in the Lurianic *Zimzum*, or creative contraction of the Divine, upon which Gershom Scholem has been the definitive and invaluable commentator. Both mythopoeic motions fall away from time by a catastrophic account of origins.

Lying against time, despite Plotinus's attack on the Gnostics, is as much a Neoplatonic as it is a Gnostic starting point. Jonas, in one of his later essays, *The Soul in Gnosticism and Plotinus*, notes that at the "critical point—when the question is: why there should be this lower world at all outside the Intelligible—Plotinus cannot make do without the same language of apostasy and fall for which he takes the Gnostics so severely to task." Jonas's acuity can be evidenced by contrasting Plotinus's mockery of the Gnostic myth of the soul's fall with Plotinus's own gnosticizing account of the origin of time. Here is Plotinus against the Gnostics:

To those who assert that creation is the work of the Soul "after the failing of its wings," we answer that no such disgrace could overtake the Soul of the All. If they tell us of its falling, they must tell us also what caused the fall. And when did it take place? If from eternity, then the Soul must be essentially a fallen thing: if at some one moment, why not before that?

Yet here is Plotinus himself, on "Time and Eternity":

> Time was not yet there, or was not for those intelligible beings. . . . But there was there a nature which was forward and wished to own and rule itself and had chosen to strive for more than it had present to it. Thus it started to move, and along with it also moved time. . . . the Soul first of all temporalized herself, generating time as a substitute for eternity.

Jonas comments that this Neoplatonic myth "tells of forwardness and unrest, of an unquiet force, of unwillingness or inability to remain in concentrated wholeness, of a power that is thus at the same time an impotence, of a desire to be selfsubsistent and separate." I would add to Jonas's commentary only the observation that such a myth of negation, at the origins, is a necessity for any poetic of belatedness, and Neoplatonism, despite itself, is in the same cultural stance of belatedness as is Gnosticism, Kabbalah or post-Miltonic poetry. I think that this shared problematic of belatedness accounts for why Kabbalah was able to merge two such incompatible visions as those of Neoplatonism and Gnosticism, and also for why poetic mythology from the Renaissance to the present day has been able to blend together so easily all three of these different esotericisms, as well as other *arcana*.

The stance of belatedness, as a cultural manifestation, has been studied hardly at all, partly because belatedness is invariably adept at disguising itself either as one Modernism or another. The English word "late" goes back to an Indo-European root meaning "to let go" or "to slacken," and thus there is a sense of weariness and entropy held back even in the prehistory of the word. Valentinian Gnosis, like literary Modernism, is an Alexandrian invention, and I think we can speculate that belatedness, as a cultural stance, is uniquely the product of Alexandria in its six great centuries, from the mid third century B.C.E. through the mid third century C.E. Belatedness is a highly dialectical notion, and so by no means wholly a negative one, even if its cutting edge or initial trope is negation. F. E. Peters, in his massive history *The Harvest of Hellenism*, credits the later Hellenes of Alexandria with taking the creative insights of the Greeks from Homer to Aristotle and distilling them "into principles and norms which could be *taught* rather than merely transmitted." The monuments of Hellenistic Alexandria, as Peters summarizes them, are "gnosticism, the university, the catachetical school, pastoral poetry, monasticism, the romance, grammar, lexicography, city planning, theology, canon law, heresy and scholasticism." Peters seems to me to be definitive in this catalog of belatedness, and I like his putting Gnosticism first on his list, because we can call Gnosticism the essence of belatedness, and Valentinianism the purest version of that essence.

Belatedness is perhaps best defined by the traditionalists who cannot bear it, in every major sense of the verb "bear." Here is Charles Williams, one of the neo-Christian Inklings of the C. S. Lewis–Tolkien-Eliot-Auden school, rather unhappily characterizing Gnosticism in his celebrated book *The Descent of the Dove*, subtitled *The History of the Holy Spirit in the Church*. Williams calls Gnosticism a Christian "grand intellectual Romantic movement . . . almost a literary movement," and he adds that in an age of printing, Gnosticism would have been a literary movement, though a deadly one. In fairness, I quote Williams again, though I have not encountered a more misleading description of Gnosticism than this:

> The lost or pseudo-Romantic, in all times and places, has the same marks, and he had them in the early centuries of the Faith. He was then called a Gnostic. . . . The Gnostic view left little room for the *illuminati* to practise love on this earth. . . . The Church anathematized the pseudo-Romantic heresies; there could be no superiority except in morals, in labor, in love. *See, understand, enjoy*, said the Gnostic; *repent, believe, love*, said the Church. . . .

Williams is not very interesting when he identifies true Romanticism with the Church and false Romanticism with Gnosticism. Such identification makes Eliot and Auden truly Romantic, while Yeats somehow is not. But Williams is interesting and valuable for the understanding of Gnosticism if we read him with an eye to his anxieties and to the defenses his anxieties spur. The peculiar mark of his neo-Christianity is his obsessive concern with the idea of *substitution*, an idea which in the Gnostic dialectic is usurped by the idea of *evasion*. Substitution, Williams implies in his Postscript, is the truly Christian idea of order, giving a properly rhetorical meaning to the doctrine of co-inherence, the "taking of the Manhood into God." Now substitution, whether in erotic, religious or literary contexts, is always the doctrine of the Second Chance. Gnosticism evades, rather than substitutes, because like every mode that battles its own belatedness Gnosticism insists upon the First Chance alone. Hating time, Gnosticism insists upon evading time rather than fulfilling time in an apocalyptic climax, or living in time through substitution. It is a familiar formula to say that failed prophecy becomes apocalyptic, and that failed apocalyptic becomes Gnosticism. If we were to ask: "What does failed Gnosticism become?" we would have to answer that Gnosticism never fails, which is both its strength (through intensity) and its weakness (through incompleteness). A vision whose fulfillment, by definition, must be always *beyond* the cosmos, cannot in its own terms be said to fail *within* our cosmos.

How can evasion be an idea of order? Only by identifying itself with an elitism, is probably the only answer, whether one thinks of evasion in erotic, religious or literary terms. Evasion is in flight from or represses fate, and again, whether erotic, religious or literary, the principle of evasion denies that existence is historical.

Without evasion or the lying against time that brings back the First Chance, no mythology is possible, and Gnosticism brought mythology back to monotheism. Evasion, on the rhetorical level, is always misinterpretation or misreading, and in such revisionary hermeneutic, Gnosticism was a great innovator. Irenaeus, furious at the capture of the Pauline term Pleroma, or "fullness," by Valentinus, says that Valentinianism "strives . . . to adapt the good terms of revelation to [its] own wicked inventions." Certainly, it is one of the achievements of Valentinus that Paul's term is now forever the mythological possession of Gnosticism. Evasion, in poetry, can be manifested only as the faculty of invention, and invention in turn depends always upon strong interpretation of prior texts. Jonas summarizes "the speculative principle of Valentinianism" as being a knowledge that "affects not only the knower but the known itself; that by every 'private' act of knowledge the objective ground of being is moved and modified." To which I would add that such motion and modification textually must be misprision or creative misreading. Hence Jonas's observation that "the speculative principle of Valentinianism actually invited independent development of the basic ideas by its adherents," and hence the complaint of Irenaeus that Jonas cites: "Every day every one of them invents something new, and none of them is considered perfect unless he is productive in this way." Nothing like that freedom of invention was to be seen again in the psychopoetics of theology until the disciples of Isaac Luria began to elaborate upon him, some fourteen hundred years later.

So far in this account of Valentinian dialectic I have shown negation taking the place of fate, and evasion substituting itself for the logos or freedom of meaning. The third term of the triad is extravagance, the restitution of power by a mode of figuration that moves from the symbolic or synecdochic through the Sublime or hyperbolic and ends in an acosmic, anti-temporal trope that reverses the Alexandrian predicament of belatedness. This final extravagance is the earliest instance I know of the rhetoric of transumption, which is the ultimate modal resource of post-Miltonic poetry, and which projects lateness and introjects earliness, but always at the expense of presence, by the emptying out of the living moment.

Near the close of *The Gospel of Truth*, Valentinus (or his disciple) bids farewell to us, with a graciousness that only the conviction of an achieved earliness is likely to permit in a heresiarch:

Such is the place of the blessed; this is their place. As for the others, then, may they know, in their place, that it does not suit me, after having been in the place of rest, to say anything more.

Such majestic certitude reflects earlier celebratory statements in this text, that "each one will speak concerning the place from which he has come forth" and that for each "his own place of rest is his pleroma." I shall conclude by bringing together these Valentinian assurances with the fundamental concerns of our own belatedness when we study poetry and its criticism. Walter Benjamin beautifully remarked of his favorite writer that "Kafka listened to tradition, and he who listens hard does not see." When I reflect upon Benjamin's aphorism, I recall that from Akiba until now, the rabbinical tradition insists that the authority of Torah as Yahweh's Word is absorbed *by listening*. Hence the rabbinical tradition *did not see*, which made room for the oxymoron of a Jewish Gnosis in the Lurianic Kabbalah. Poetry and criticism after Milton in our language are attempts to see, in frequent contradistinction to the main Protestant tradition of listening to the Word. But they are attempts to *see earliest*, as though no one had seen before us. Is this not the mark of Gnosis, that seeing is the peculiar attribute of certain spiritualized intellectuals, Faustian or favored ones, whose particular knowledge *is* itself the highest power? When you have the Gnosis, when you see truly, then you are in the place of rest, you are in your own internalized pleroma.

The modern study of Gnosticism begins with Mosheim in 1739, in the Age of Sensibility during which the Enlightenment waned rapidly. This was no more accidental than was the onrush of studies in Gnosticism in the High Romantic period, with Horn in 1805, Lewald in 1818 and Matter in 1828. In poetry, a "place" is *where* something is *known*, but a figure or trope is *when* something is willed or desired. A Classical or Enlightenment "commonplace" is where something is already known, but a Romantic or Post-Enlightenment "place" is a more inventive and indeed a Gnostic "knowing," a knowing in which one *sees* what Walter Benjamin called the *aura*. In the *aura* what is known knows the knower, what is seen sees the seer, but the *aura* is principally visible in its disintegration, its Gnostic disappearance at the moment of acosmic, atemporal shock.

A Gnostic "place," like the classical topos or "commonplace," is always a name, but the anomaly or difference of the Gnostic name is best conveyed by the notion of name as an "image of voice" as *The Gospel of Truth* once calls it. Such a Gnostic or Romantic name comes by negation; an un-naming yields a name. A written space has been voided of its writing, so that the Gnostic place displaces a prior place. This is why the best model for Post-Romantic poetic place or image of voice is the Valentinian Pleroma or its curiously similar analogue in the Lurianic *tehiru*. The Pleroma or *tehiru*, like the Romantic and Modern poetic place, is both a fullness and an emptiness.

Any new poetic place, or image of voice, empties out a previous place *in the same spot*. Into this emptiness, a new fullness is placed, but a revisionary fullness, one that postpones or defers the future. Walter Benjamin says of Kafka's stories that in them "narrative art regains the significance it had in the mouth of Scheherazade: to postpone the future." Gnosticism would go further and banish the future altogether, until that acosmic, atemporal restoration to the Pleroma takes place, of all pneumatics simultaneously. Perhaps this is the ultimate difference between orthodoxy and the Gnosis. The rabbis said of God that "he is the place of the world, but the world is not his place." With the second half of this topological aphorism, the Gnostics were in agreement, but they dissented altogether from the first half. This dissent implicitly commits Gnosticism to an aesthetic that is neither mimetic, like Greek aesthetic from Plato to Plotinus, nor anti-mimetic, like Hebraism from the Bible to Jacques Derrida. Gnostic writing, when strong, is strong because it is super-mimetic, because it confronts and seeks to overthrow the very strongest of all texts, the Jewish Bible. That super-mimesis is an intolerable burden, whether for literature or for the fallen poetry of theology. But out of the titanic efforts to bear that burden have come the equivocal triumphs of the Romantic tradition, in poetry, in criticism and in theology as well. Valentinus, who taught us what Hans Jonas eloquently calls "the self-motivation of divine degradation," is the truest precursor of our own divinely degraded visions of belatedness.

3

Catastrophe Creation:
Gnosis, Kabbalah and Blake

Call it "Creation: The Arena of the Demiurge's Drama." It is a drama in three acts. Act I: the true Forefather, the Abyss, is usurped by the impostor, Jehovah. The author of this act is Valentinus of Alexandria, who abandoned the Great Church in Rome, in the second century of the Common Era, rejecting the sacraments because he had seen that a perfect cognition of the origins was itself more than enough to make us free. Since knowledge alone was salvation, the form of that knowledge, the Gnosis, revealed truly that the Creation had degraded the very Godhead.

Act II: the *Ain-Soph*, infinite Godhead, contracts and withdraws himself, making Creation possible by his self-limitation. The author is Isaac Luria, the *Ari* or lion of Safed in Galilee, in the sixteenth century, founder of a new or diacritical Kabbalah, in which the Gnosis improbably returned to Judaism. This *Zimzum*, or holding-in of the divine breath and being, inaugurated a cataclysmic process that Luria called *Shevirath ha-kelim*, the Breaking of the Vessels, out of which our world emerged, a world from which God himself had exiled himself.

Act III: Urizen, one of the Four Zoas, or primordial men, sickens to a false Creation, repudiating both his wife and his brethren, motivated by jealousy and by a fear of futurity. The author is the Londoner William Blake, writing at the turning between the eighteenth and nineteenth centuries. Creation and Fall again are seen as one event, and the struggle through contraries sets the poet-painter's creation against *the* Creation, in the name of a hope or dream that Blake calls "Vision" or "the real Man the Imagination."

There is a continuity between these three acts of the Demiurge's drama, but it is not a metonymic continuity of cause and effect. Luria had never heard of Valentinus, and the Perpetual Philosophy gang of pseudo-Blakeans have failed to demonstrate that Blake knew anything much of his Gnostic and Kabbalistic precursors. Valentinus came to know that he was not a Catholic, but Luria always thought of himself as a normative rabbinical Jew; and Blake always insisted that he was a Christian, though very much of his own variety, a sect of one. What unites the three prophets is a catastrophe theory of Creation, and what urges me towards them is my growing conviction that any adequate theory of poetic creativity also must be a catastrophe theory. What is called creation, in art, is both a creation *of* catastrophe and a creation *by* catastrophe, and Valentinus, Luria and Blake all are episodes in a history that transcends them, a catastrophic history and history of catastrophes.

But there is truly no first act in the Demiurge's drama. Valentinus so cunningly interprets or strongly misreads the Gospel of John as to arrive at a parody of both the Hebraic Genesis and Plato's *Timaeus*. Yet we cannot judge even Plato's Demiurge to be a true beginner, nor even the Priestly author's breath moving over the Abyss. Who, what is the Demiurge, catastrophic *daemon* who shammed the role of the Father? To what point of origin, or as Freud might say, primal fixation or repression, is the Demiurge to be traced?

Perhaps that point ultimately is in Parmenides, Plato's precursor, or perhaps it is in Pythagoras, Heraclitus or Empedocles. Certainly that point is present *after* Plato, in the middle Platonists who preceded Plotinus. In any case, that point is hardly *in* Plato himself, though most traditional commentators have judged otherwise, down to A. E. Taylor. I am persuaded instead by F. M. Cornford's book *Plato's Cosmology*, where Cornford reminded us that Plato after all was not a Hebraic or Christian monotheist. The Demiurge is divine all right, but equally so is the world he makes, and so are the stars. In this serious (though perhaps also ironic) polytheism, the Demiurge is perhaps not so much a religious figure as he is a mythological workman. Unlike Jehovah (or the Elohim), this workman does not make the world out of nothing, and he is not himself an object of worship, let alone the supreme object. He must work with Necessity and Chaos, even as an Athenian carpenter building the public planetarium must use the materials to hand, and like the Athenian *demiourgos* or public workman he can hope to do only as good a job as is possible within the limitations of his material. The only sense in which the Platonic Demiurge represents divine reason is tropological; he is a synecdoche for what is divine, but so are the earth, the other planets and the stars.

It was a strong misreading of this Demiurge, by the earlier Platonists, that constituted what I would call the truly Primal repression that made possible catastrophe theory of creation and creativity, indeed made possible the rival yet strangely allied modes of Plotinus and the Gnostics. Plato's Demiurge is clearly not a contemplative being. Following an ideal model, he makes a world where none had existed previously. The Demiurge of Plotinus however dwells in a world of transparency, of pure vision, without start or end. There is will and action in Plato; but in Plotinus there is only one giant trope, the figure of emanation, of a Power dividing itself and weakening as it radiates out from center to circumference.

Plato, like the Priestly author, is anthropomorphic in his handling of the *deliberateness* of the Creation. Purged of this willfulness, the Demiurge of Plotinus wanes into creation. Hans Jonas remarks that the Plotinean descensus of Being "proceeds through the autonomous movement of impersonal concept, by an inner necessity that is its own justification." I think we can say that where creation is at once so impersonal and so marked by inwardness, even catastrophe becomes muted, which is why the Plotinean emanation seems a less violent trope than actually it is. For what *is* emanation? Plotinus continually varied the conceptual image, as though the intuition never could find its inevitable trope. A force that is neither personal nor material surges, expands, overflows, like water, yet also like fire. Why does the force rush and radiate out? Because its perfection, fullness and presence are too great, and such greatness must move outwards and downwards. Again, why? The question is curiously like Freud's question "Why does the ego fall in love?" Because otherwise ego-libido would choke and burst on the excess of its delights. Presumably the Plotinean One, unlike the Freudian ego, would not get ill if it failed to emanate, yet what can perfection do except produce its own epiphanies through flaming forth or flooding out? And yet, like the Freudian falling in love, the Plotinean emanation is indeed a fall, and a Creation-Fall at that.

Was it an accident that the rhetoric of emanation in Plotinus led on to the rhetoric of creation and of creativity in his Renaissance followers? Plato's Demiurge was artisan but not artist, because for Plato the artist was mere craftsman turned deceiver, while the Demiurge did an honest if muddled job of work. Plotinus prepared the way for the quite anti-Platonic trope of the poet or sculptor as "creator," as the godlike man giving no bare reproduction of the thing seen but instead going back to the Ideas from which Nature itself derives. But though he was the precursor of this Italian Renaissance trope, Plotinus would have been uneasy with Landino's statement that "although the feigning of the poet is not entirely out of nothing, it nevertheless departs from making and comes very near to creating. And God is the supreme poet, and the world is his poem." By the time the Elizabethan rhetorician Puttenham gets hold of this doctrine, we are out of the high transcendentalism of Plotinus and moving towards High Romanticism, since Puttenham (though "by maner of speech") actually refers to poets as "creating gods."

My concern is not with Plotinus but with his enemies the

Gnostics, yet as enemies they were indeed very close to home for Plotinus. The history of Neoplatonism after Plotinus shows that Gnosticism kept contaminating its increasingly eclectic doctrines; but the contamination is already evident in Plotinus himself, perhaps prompting him to his highly uncharacteristic vehemence as he argues against the Gnosis. For my purpose, which is to track the origin of catastrophe creation, Plotinus needs to be read between the lines even as he concludes his casting-out of the Gnostics:

> This school may lay claim to vision as a dignity reserved to themselves, but they are not any the nearer to vision by the claim—or by the boast that while the celestial powers, bound for ever to the ordering of the Heavens, can never stand outside the material universe, they themselves have their freedom in their death. This is a failure to grasp the very notion of "standing outside," a failure to appreciate the mode in which the All-Soul "cares for the unensouled."
>
> No: it is possible to go free of love for the body; to be clean-living, to disregard death; to know the Highest and aim at that other world; not to slander, as negligent in the quest, others who are able for it and faithful to it; and not to err with those that deny vital motion to the stars because to our sense they stand still—the error which in another form leads this school to deny to the Star-Nature the vision of what lies outside the material universe, only because they do not see that the Star-Soul itself arises in that non-material sphere.

When we listen to Plotinus here, we encounter the speaking of what Angus Fletcher has named "Kosmos: the allegorical image proper":

> It signifies (1) a universe, and (2) a symbol that implies a rank in a hierarchy. As the latter it will be attached to, or associated with, or even substituted for, any object which the writer wants to place in hierarchial position.

Applying Fletcher, we can say that Plotinus wishes to save, from the Gnostics, the prestige of both the demiurgical Creation and of Hellenic rationalism, since the mind's place in regarding the Creation is as much threatened here as is the virtue of the Creation itself. But between the lines we read a wavering in confidence on Plotinus's own part. His vision of emanation has prepared the way for a catastrophic view of the Creation. Hans Jonas remarks that "in what he criticizes, Plotinus shows us one of the roots of our world," the world of Kafka and Heidegger, to which I turn now, by moving from the Demiurge of Plato and Plotinus to the Demiurge of the Gnostics.

Every Gnostic version of the Demiurge is an instance of what I would call "revisionary counterpoint," in which the Hebraic Genesis, the Gospel of John, and Plato's *Timaeus* are intricately "misread" so as to produce a "corrective" new amalgam, which is always a catastrophe. In this amalgam, the elements of catastrophe are gathered all too readily from the innate puzzlements of the orthodox accounts of Creation and after. R. M. Grant, in his *Gnosticism and Early Christianity*, catalogs some of these peculiarities that stimulated Gnostic revisionism: the Creation story of Elohim; the confusing split between Yahweh and Elohim in the account of the Flood; Elohim as an angel at Jacob's blessing; perhaps most shocking, Yahweh's attempt to murder Moses. Yet none of these incongruities was the true scandal for Gnostic revisionists. Their strong misprision of the Priestly author and of the Jahvist turned upon the issue of priority. I quote E. A. Speiser's version of the opening of the Priestly author's account of Creation:

> When God set about to create heaven and earth—the world being then a formless waste, with darkness over the seas and only an awesome wind sweeping over the water—God said, "Let there be light." And there was light. God was pleased with the light that he saw, and he separated the light from the darkness. . . .

Jewish Gnostics, reading this text, brooded upon that "then" prior to God's Creation, upon a "formless waste," *tohu wa-bohu,* unformed and void, over which the awesome breath of the Elohim swept in a belated will-to-power. The Gnostics brooded also upon the "darkness" and the deep sea, *hoshekh* and *tehom,* prior entities that, like *tohu* and *bohu*, had been overcome. Out of these brood-ings rose an alternate account of Beginnings, a conviction that the Abyss and its allies had been usurped by a Demiurge.

The Biblical doctrine of Creation is deliberately free of specula-tions upon origins. Bultmann remarks that the orthodox doctrine is a confession of faith, hence the *creatio ex nihilo*, "a notion utterly inconceivable to the Greek mind." It seems clear that Jewish Gnostics also found it inconceivable, even before Hellenis-tic influences swept Palestine. There are Talmudic warnings against the *Minim* or Jewish Gnostics that center upon warning away those who would speculate upon the origins. Modern schol-arship has not settled the problem of the origins of Gnosticism, but I believe its prime roots to be Jewish, both Palestinian and Alexandrian. As a Jewish heresy, it had to begin at the Beginnings, and thus had to challenge the orthodox doctrine of Creation, for that doctrine fixed man's place. I cite Bultmann again:

> In the last analysis, the Old Testament doctrine of creation expresses a sense of the present situation of man. He is hedged in by the incomprehensible power of Almighty God. . . .

There, swerving away from Bultmann, is where I would place the Gnostic *clinamen*: if you are not to be hedged in by God's incomprehensible power, then you must dissent from the doctrine of Creation. You must learn to speculate about the origins, and the aim of your speculation will have to be a vision of catastrophe, for only a divine catastrophe will allow for your own, your human freedom.

The genesis of the Valentinian Gnosis, most advanced of specu-lations in Gnosticism, is itself still veiled. I myself suspect that Valentinus came out of Alexandrian Jewry, and that he blent to-gether the ethos of the Therapeutae, Jewish contemplatives whom Philo described, with Ophite or Naasene doctrines, before attempt-ing the impossible amalgamation of his vision with that of the Great Church. After he left the Church at Rome, Valentinus seems to have freed himself to mythologize, a turn that opened up an almost unlimited imaginative freedom for his disciples. But even in its earliest version, Valentinus's speculation seems to have centered, with shocking originality, upon the idea of divine degradation, and upon Creation as the catastrophic result of that degradation. Divine error, divine failure, divine catastrophe is the Valentinian formula which traces the descent of being from the Abyss our Forefather down to the Demiurge Error elaborating its own matter in the Void. Here is Theodotus the Valentinian giving us a vision of the final process, mocking the Elohim and also mocking Plato, since this Valentinian Demiurge cannot even understand the ideas or paradigms he wretchedly copies:

> The Demiurge, his nature given to action, believed that he manufactured these things by himself, unaware that the Achamoth worked through him. He made a heaven without knowing "the heaven"; he formed a man without knowing "the man"; he made appear an earth without knowledge of "the earth": throughout he was ignorant of the *ideas* of whatever he created and of the Mother herself and believed himself alone to be everything.

What is the ontological nature of the Valentinian catastrophe? Hans Jonas, the scholar who understands Valentinianism best, gives a Heideggerian interpretation. The Demiurge has thrown us into this cosmos precisely in the sense of Heidegger's *Geworfenheit*, the "having been thrown" which is the fundamental character of *Dasein*, being-in-our-cosmos. Without disputing Jonas, I would modify the interpretation only by remembering that the Valentinian catastrophe is also a creation. Something other than a crisis-point between past and future marks a creation, though *that* does seem to me *the* peculiar mark of creation: the crisis-point or crossing between temporal gulfs, the flashing out of an image of will against the dissolving backgrounds of two ignorances, past and future. The demiurgical will is the Gnostic trope of what it means to sicken to a false creation; but even a false creation is marked by power and by drive.

Plotinus never tired of mocking the Gnostics by repeating the one question: *Why* did the divine degrade itself, and if it did, how could there be a *when* to such degradation? Why should it not have happened *before* it supposedly happened? Plotinus's truer question was: How *could* the divine, by definition, degrade itself? What makes a catastrophe creation possible? Valentinus, subtle as he was, could not have answered these questions. Heidegger's true Gnostic parallel is not Valentinus, but his older Alexandrian contemporary Basilides, who was an even more negative theologian than Valentinus (or than Heidegger, for that matter!). Here is the heresiologist Hippolytus summarizing Basilides on the Creation:

> There was a time, says he, when there was nothing; not even the nothing was there, but simply, clearly, and without any sophistry there was nothing at all. When I say "there was" he says, I do not indicate a being. . . .
>
> Since therefore there was nothing, no matter, no substance, nothing insubstantial, nothing simple, nothing composite, nothing imperceptible (non-subjective), no man, no angel, no god, nothing at all that can be named or can be apprehended by sense-perception, nothing of the mental things and thus (also nothing of all that which can be simply described in even more subtle ways,) the non-existent God . . . without intelligence, without perception, without will, without resolve, without impulse, without desire, wished to make a world. I say "he wished," he says, for want of a word, wish, intelligence, and perception being excluded. By "world" (I mean) not the flat, divisible world which later divided itself, but the world-seed. . . .

I have cited this self-deconstructing rhapsody because it is an epitome of Gnosis, almost indeed a parody of Gnosis. Basilides is so revisionary in regard to the Bible and to Plato that he cannot even attain to creation or catastrophe, or even an amalgam thereof, since the basis of his vision is that nothing exists. To the Leibnizian question to which Heidegger returns us—"Why is there being at all and not much rather non-being?"—Basilides would answer that he favors the "much rather." The divine degradation is the reassertion of non-being, the return of the repressed, the triumph of the Abyss. God is not only beyond naming; he is beyond being, beyond attribute, but also beyond negation. Catastrophe creation brings about a rift or a dualism in the divine, but beyond this dualism is the uncanniness of an authentic nihilism, a vertigo that Greek and Jew alike dreaded. Whether or not Gnosis originated with renegade Jews may always be beyond demonstration. What is more extraordinary is that it came back fourteen centuries after Basilides and Valentinus into the spiritual center of Jewry, the Kabbalah of Isaac Luria. The inevitable commentator upon this transcendental and extraordinary breakthrough is Gershom Scholem, who reads it as the revenge of myth against the normative rabbinicism which had expelled Gnostic myth definitively in the second century of the Common Era:

> . . . It was through this conception of a creation out of nothing over against the conquest of chaos by the Creator-God, that the so-called rational theology of late Rabbinism, going still further than the Biblical position on Creation, tried to break definitively with all vestiges of myth. The substitution of nothingness for chaos seemed to provide a guarantee of the Creator-God's freedom as opposed to all mythical determination by fate. His Creation thus ceases to be a struggle and a crisis and becomes a free act of love. None of this is retained in the Kabbalah, except for the naked formula itself, which is proclaimed with the utmost passion and displayed as a banner. But its meaning has been reversed. . . . If there were a breach, a nothing, in the earliest beginning, it could only be in the very essence of God. . . . It is this abyss within God, coexisting with His infinite fulness, that was overcome in the Creation. . . . We may speak of a productive misunderstanding, by which mythical images were re-discovered. . . .

What Scholem calls a "productive misunderstanding" I would call another catastrophe creation, which like all such creations realizes that the dualistic rift in being is a symptom of a greater nihilism that must be overcome if any transcendental belief is to survive. There is a desperate belatedness in all Gnosis, a nightmare sense of coming *after the event*, of trying to occupy ground where others have stood more significantly. To have come too late *into* the story is necessarily to fear that one is too late in the story.

With regard to both the Bible and Hellenic Creation, the Gnostics were precisely those intellectuals who could tolerate least a crippling sense of belatedness. The contrast between Plotinus and the Alexandrian Gnostics is extraordinarily instructive just here. Plotinus joyously comes after Plato and the Ancients; he presents himself as the true understander of their mysteries, exactly as Philo of Alexandria presents himself in regard to the Septuagint. Plotinus and Philo refuse to see themselves as revisionists. But Basilides and Valentinus, and all other Gnostics, indeed *are* revisionists, and they say that Genesis and Plato got everything that was crucial quite wrong. This is the litany of every Modernism since Alexandria, down to contemporary French varieties of Modernist criticism. That the Kabbalist deconstructors of the later, Gnostic sort should have the melancholy distinction of being the inaugural deconstructors is rather less than they might have hoped for from their heroic battles against belatedness.

The demiurgical creation in Gnosticism, even in Valentinianism, was an undialectical catastrophe, dualistic yet without a systematic explanation. It was the achievement of Isaac Luria to imagine the dialectics of a monistic catastrophe creation, and so to give us a coherent paradigm for some of the designs of revisionist poetry. Luria had as starting points Moses de Leon's *Zohar* and his own teacher Moses Cordovero's *Pardes Rimmon*, yet his most startling departure stems not from Kabbalah at all.

Zimzum, meaning originally "that the Omnipresent God contracts and confines His Shekinah on, or to, a certain spot," according to Arthur Marmorstein's *The Old Rabbinic Doctrine of God* is a creation of the Amoraic Haggadah of the third century c.e. Marmorstein reads this divine contraction and confinement of the Shekinah as a myth of God's exile from his tabernacle, the destroyed temple. Scholem comments: "Here we have the origin of the term *Tsimtsum*, while the thing itself is the precise opposite of this idea: to the Kabbalist of Luria's school *Tsimtsum* does not mean the concentration of God *at* a point, but his retreat *away* from a point."

Scholem's opposition of the thing itself to its idea catches the deconstructive spirit of Lurianic Kabbalah, which is technically (as it were) the most negative of all negative Gnostic theologies. But rather than repeat Scholem on Lurianic negation, or my own aesthetic analogizing of that negation in my *Kabbalah and Criticism*, I am going to leap over Luria himself here in order to trace the catastrophic force of his most original dialectical conception, the Breaking of the Vessels (*Shevirath ha-Kelim*), in a catastrophic disciple he would have disowned, Nathan of Gaza. Luria remains one of the most honored names in Judaic tradition; Nathan has been forgotten except for the labors of Scholem and his school of scholars. Exactly a century after Luria, the frightening movement of the false Messiah Sabbatai Zevi all but wrecked later-seventeenth-century Jewry throughout both Europe and the East. Sabbatai himself was a manic-depressive of no particular creative and/or intellectual talents, but of considerable charisma. His prophet, Nathan of Gaza, though he began his heretical career with a twenty-four-hour ecstatic illumination, was an original and powerful theologian, who transformed the Lurianic vision into a Gnosis akin to that of the second-century Ophites or Naasenes.

In the Lurianic story of Creation, God's contraction first produces a vacancy (*tehiru*). Beholding the vacancy and a residue (*reshimu*) of his light within this original absence, God sends forth a creative ray of greater light which interacts with residual light so as to produce the *sefiroth* or emanations. Amidst the emanations there appears the *Adam Kadmon* or Primal Man, the ontological aspect of God's light when it fills the first absence (*tehiru*). Primal Man has lights bursting forth from him, and these emanations are called *kelim* (containers or vessels) by Luria. Scholem, in his great book on Sabbatai Zevi, illuminates the rhetorical ambiguity of these Lurianic *kelim*:

> The Hebrew *keli* can mean an instrument or tool used by an artisan for a definite purpose, as well as a container or vessel, which contains but also limits that which is inside it. The former meaning was in the minds of the earlier kabbalists when

they spoke of *sefiroth* as "vessels," that is, tools used by the Emanator God in the process of creation. But soon the second meaning asserted itself, particularly since the *sefiroth*—unlike ordinary tools—were not distinct from the essence of the artisan that used them.

Though Scholem, in this passage, is not concerned with the differences between earlier Gnosis and the Lurianic Kabbalah, the ambiguity he comments upon, between artisan's tool and vessel, marks precisely the Judaizing swerve away from Gnosticism in Luria. The artisan's tool suggests the Platonic Demiurge, but the broken vessels that are not distinct from the *Ain-Soph* remind us that Kabbalah contains the contradiction of a Gnostic monism, rather than the dualism of Basilides or Valentinus. Nor could the Kabbalists react to this contradiction with the American Sublime irony of an Emerson, who both celebrated and lamented his Gnosis with his customary uncanny eloquence:

> . . . As a plant in the earth so I grow in God. I am only a form of him. He is the soul of me. . . . Yet why not always so? How came the Individual, thus armed and impassioned, to parricide thus murderously inclined, ever to traverse and kill the Divine Life? Ah, wicked Manichee! Into that dim problem I cannot enter. A believer in Unity, a seer of Unity, I yet behold two. . . .

That parricide, indeed Gnostic deicide, was impossible for the Kabbalists and even for the followers of Sabbatai Zevi after them. Thus the *kelim* as vessels had to break apart, be burst asunder by the divine lights. Falling into the primal vacancy of God's contraction, the glowing fragments of the broken vessels in time created or became the husks or shells of a demonic evil, the *Kelippah*. In this Lurianic Fall or Exile of God, a divine catharsis or sublimation was enacted, according to Isaiah Tishby, who stands next after Scholem among living scholars of Kabbalah. The dangers of elevating sublimation as a defense into the sphere of God were demonstrated not so much in the subsequent development of Lurianic doctrine as in the strong misreading of Luria that was performed by Sabbatai Zevi's prophet, Nathan of Gaza.

The Cossack insurrection of 1648 in Poland and Russia produced a quasi-Holocaust of East European Jewry. In this triumph of the evil husks of the *kelippoth*, the way was prepared for the Messianic advent of Sabbatai Zevi, proclaimed by Nathan in 1665, one year before the widely expected apocalypse. Nathan's *Treatise on the Dragons* is the most formidable tract to survive of the Sabbatian literature. In Nathan's vision, the Lurianic *tehiru*, or vacated space resulting from the *Zimzum*, itself contains in its *reshimu* or residual divine light the roots of the *kelippoth* or evil shells. God's own light, according to Nathan, is of two sorts; "thought-some" and "thought-less" Scholem renders them, but I would prefer to call them respectively the cognitive light and the nihilizing light. The nihilizing light, opposed to creation, Nathan also calls "monstrous," *golem*. In the sphere of the vacated space, the lower half becomes *golem* due to God's unforming light. No breaking of the vessels is necessary therefore in Nathan's version of a catastrophic creation. The *kelippoth* or evil shells are formed directly by God's nihilizing light, and they are formed as dragons or serpents. Nathan's ultimate antinomianism is to situate the soul of the Messiah not in the upper sphere, where the cognitive light plays, but in the *golem* or dragon-world. Here is Nathan directly:

> Know that the soul of the messianic king exists in the lower *golem*. For just as the primal dragon emerged in the vacant space, even so the soul of the messiah was created by the will of God. This soul existed before the creation of the world, and it remains in the great abyss.

Nathan has reversed both ancient Gnosis and Lurianic Kabbalah. The *pneuma* of the Gnostic was a pearl or gold in the mud; it was no part of the demiurgic Creation. Sabbatai Zevi's soul is at once divine and evil, part of the universe of forlorn husks. That universe came into being, according to Luria, because the *kelim* were not strong enough to hold God's light. In Nathan of Gaza,

God's uncreating light directly forms the husks, and the Messiah's soul with them. Out of so nihilistic a formula an apostate Messiah could emerge, not as a paradox, but as the final catastrophe intended by Creation.

If Luria's myth of God's exile represented an ultimate triumph for Gnostic traditions of Creation, then it seems accurate to judge Nathan of Gaza's myth as both the travesty and the tragedy of Gnosis. God is still in exile, but he has sent his true Messiah, who is, however, properly degraded, apostate, and down among the dragons. Yet I would not judge Nathan as having been a mere travesty of belatedness. Sabbatai Zevi was a self-deluded manic-depressive, but Nathan was a catastrophe creator of some genius, and deserves more of our own cognitive light than the purely nihilistic Sabbatai Zevi can be said to merit. Nathan has something to teach us about negative moments in creation and creativity, something of his own and not just the greater and more comprehensive lessons that Valentinus or Luria or Blake teaches us.

In a lecture, *Sabbatianism and Mystical Heresy*, that he delivered more than forty years ago, Scholem made a useful distinction, from a wholly Jewish perspective, between Sabbatai Zevi and the Christian Messiah:

> The paradox of crucifixion and that of apostasy are after all on two altogether different levels. The second leads straight into the bottomless pit; its very idea makes almost anything conceivable. The shock which had to be surmounted in both cases is greater in the case of Sabbatianism. The believer is compelled to furnish even more emotional energy in order to overcome the terrible paradox of an apostate Savior. Death and apostasy cannot possibly evoke the same or similar sentiments, if only because the idea of betrayal contains even less that is positive. Unlike the death of Jesus, the decisive action (or rather, passion) of Sabbatai Zevi furnished no new revolutionary code of values. His betrayal merely destroyed the old. . . .

Scholem emphasizes a passion or suffering that is catastrophic, being wholly negative and destructive. Can we not relate this catastrophe, as Nathan of Gaza implicitly did, to the essence of all Gnosticism, even of an oxymoronic Jewish Gnosticism? Prophecy fails and becomes apocalyptic; apocalyptic fails and becomes Gnosticism; Gnosticism cannot fail because it is wholly antithetical to natural existence, to temporality, even to psychic identity. Bultmann in his *Primitive Christianity* asserted that "Gnosticism is incapable of defining transcendence in positive terms," unlike the Greeks, and unlike Christianity which conceived transcendence in terms of pure futurity. We can say that Bultmann was only partly right, since the Greek conception of the spirit is now wholly alien to all of us, and the notion of a "pure futurity" has little meaning in regard to our own increasingly oppressive sense of temporality. Gnosticism, as the truly first Modernism, sets the pattern even now for all those linguistic problematics that hedge or enclose any available notions of transcendence. We have learned to read psyches, poems, and systems and structures in all the oxymoronic "human sciences," only in terms of their negative moments. I could cite many contemporary theorists, in many disciplines, who work more in the mode and spirit of Nathan of Gaza than in that of Bultmann, but I forbear, as the citations would be redundant.

The coda to my account of divine degradation and catastrophe-creation is in Blake, who never faltered in his conviction that the Accuser was the god of this world. Blake's Demiurge, Urizen, is certainly now more familiar to most readers than is the Demiurge of the Gnostics, let alone the nihilizing or "thought-less" light that Nathan of Gaza added to the Lurianic mythology. But Urizen's very familiarity veils or masks how uncanny a figure he is, and how curiously sympathetic he becomes if we observe him from, say, a truly enlightened Freudian perspective.

As Philip Rieff first observed, Freud formulated a catastrophe-theory of the genesis of drives, both libido and the death drive. I have tried to show elsewhere that Freud held an implicit catastrophe theory of the genesis of creativity. The drives, the defenses against drives, and catastrophe creativity all contaminate one another in Freud's writings until at last the Freudian Sublime or *unheimlich* subsumes them all in a dualistic agon that Freud sets against the whole of Western cultural tradition. I don't seek to degrade Freud by saying that Urizen is Blake's prophetic version of the author of *Beyond the Pleasure Principle.* Here are two great Romantic rationalists, two belated versions of the Demiurge, and if both are parodies of Jahweh Elohim in *Genesis,* both in some respects surpass their original. Freud has a better temper than either Jehovah or Urizen, but then Jung was a less formidable rebel angel than either Satan or Orc.

The Demiurge of Plato had to do the best he could, granted his materials and his tools. Like Jehovah, Urizen and Freud, the Demiurge essentially mapped out the mind, and like his three rival catastrophe creators he marked the mind's limits by the death-drive. All four makers foresee our end in our urge to repose, "to strive toward a state of absence of irritability," as Rieff sums up the Freudian "beyonding" or negative transcendence. Urizen seems to me the most eloquent of all these titanic compass-wielders:

> I have sought for a joy without pain,
> For a solid without fluctuation
> Why will you die O Eternals?
> Why live in unquenchable burnings?

> First I fought with the fire; consum'd
> Inwards, into a deep world within:
> A void immense, wild dark and deep,
> Where nothing was; Nature's wide womb.
> And self balanc'd stretch'd o'er the void
> I alone, even I! the winds merciless
> Bound; but condensing, in torrents
> They fall and fall; strong repell'd
> The vast waves I arose on the waters
> A wide world of solid obstruction.

Though the irony here is directed at Milton's God, that hero of *Paradise Lost,* Book VII, is being viewed as a later version of the Demiurge. Urizen battles the Abyss, "where nothing was," and so he is both Milton's God and Milton's exploring Satan. But the largest irony of Urizen's passion is that, catastrophic to an extreme, it remains creative, indeed constitutes *the* Creation. What are we then? At least as we were made, or broken, by Urizen, we are a huge opacity: "a wide world of solid obstruction." What are we also? Why, the death drive, the repetition compulsion, the "unquenchable burnings" of libido. Blake's wisdom, Gnostic as to Nature, though not as to the human, is to see the Demiurge's heroism as being also the horror and solitude of all belated strong creativity: "self balanc'd stretch'd o'er the void / I alone, even I!" For what is that if it is not *the* Sublime stance, the agonistic glory of Milton *and* of Blake, the final truth of Freud's Psychological Man? Catastrophic in their mutual origins, Romantic and Freudian man amalgamate in an endless contraction from demiurgic injured narcissism, which is identical with the motive for metaphor in every belated creator.

Nowadays, the theorists of negation have replaced the Demiurge by "language," but that is only to transform "language" into the Demiurge. From a Gnostic perspective, anti-mimetic and mimetic theories of creation merely repeat the ancient difference between Stoic and Platonic accounts, a difference that pragmatically makes little difference, as both the anti-mimetic and mimetic theories of aesthetic representation yield themselves up to the tyranny of time, to one or another rhetoric of temporality. Whether language thinks and writes, or whether the subject governs, is exposed by Gnosis as a mock quarrel, a mimic war between two kinds of ironists, neither of whom is willing to press his dualism beyond the final bounds of demiurgic reason.

Freud, though rigorously opposed to every religious formulation, someday may be judged as closer to Gnosis than the overtly Gnosticizing Jung ever was, as we come to comprehend better the consequences of Freud's final dualisms. Gnosis affirms that fantasy must be primary in our belated condition, where every agon has been internalized, as it was by Urizen, and where the drive for freedom becomes also the death drive, where creativity and catastrophe become indistinguishable. Freud affirms the same. Laplanche speaks of Freud's discovery of "a kind of antilife as sexuality, frenetic enjoyment, the negative, the repetition compulsion" by necessity being inscribed within the vital order. The discovery, we can say now, was made before Freud by every belated strong poet from Petrarch onwards and in the ancient world was made initially by the Gnostics.

It is hardly possible to conclude a discourse on catastrophe creation upon an affirmative chord, yet the defense of Gnostic negation, against Bultmann as against lesser orthodox denigrators, must be to argue that a Gnosis of catastrophe creation is a path to freedom. Even Nathan of Gaza, who parodies the Gnosis of Luria, sought to free his Jewish contemporaries from the horrors of a wholly temporal condition, from seeing their human existence as being purely a historical existence and so removed from every hope of transcendence. To argue that we live in a catastrophe is to urge upon our wills a spirit of super-mimesis, by which historical and material catastrophe can be evaded, though of course never reversed nor abolished. The argument against the Demiurge, whether Gnostic, Kabbalistic or Blakean, is conducted always in the name of what makes us free. Against every orthodox or normative account of benign Creation, I end by quoting the Valentinian chant that will not accept any god of *this* world as being the alien god of our true freedom from the catastrophe of the Creation:

> What makes us free is the Gnosis
>   of who we were
>   of what we have become
>   of where we were
>   of wherein we have been thrown
>   of what we are being freed
>   of what birth really is
>   of what rebirth really is

4

Freud and the Sublime:
A Catastrophe Theory
of Creativity

Jacques Lacan argues that Freud "derived his inspiration, his ways of thinking and his technical weapons" from imaginative literature rather than from the sciences. On such a view, the precursors of Freud are not so much Charcot and Janet, Brücke and Helmholtz, Breuer and Fliess, but the rather more exalted company of Empedocles and Heraclitus, Plato and Goethe, Shakespeare and Schopenhauer. Lacan is the foremost advocate of a dialectical reading of Freud's text, a reading that takes into account those problematics of textual interpretation that stem from the philosophies of Hegel, Nietzsche and Heidegger, and from developments in differential linguistics. Such a reading, though it has attracted many intellectuals in English-speaking countries, is likely to remain rather alien to us, because of the strong empirical tradition in Anglo-American thought. Rather like Freud himself, whose distaste for and ignorance of the United States were quite invincible, Lacan and his followers distrust American pragmatism, which to them is merely irritability with theory. Attacks by French Freudians upon American psychoanalysis tend to stress issues of societal adjustment or else of a supposed American optimism concerning human nature. But I think that Lacan is wiser in his cultural vision of Freud than he is in his polemic against ego psychology, interpersonal psychoanalysis or any other American school. Freud's power *as a writer* made him the contemporary not so much of his rivals and disciples as of the strongest literary minds of our century. We read Freud not as we read Jung or Rank, Abraham or Ferenczi, but as we read Proust or Joyce, Valéry or Rilke or Stevens. A writer who achieves what once was called the Sublime will be susceptible to explication either upon an empirical *or* upon a dialectical basis.

The best brief account of Freud that I have read is by Richard Wollheim (1971), and Wollheim is an analytical philosopher, working in the tradition of Hume and of Wittgenstein. The Freud who emerges in Wollheim's pages bears very little resemblance to Lacan's Freud, yet I would hesitate to prefer either Wollheim's or Lacan's Freud, one to the other. There is no "true" or "correct" reading of Freud because Freud is so strong a writer that he *contains* every available mode of interpretation. In tribute to Lacan, I add that Lacan in particular has uncovered Freud as the greatest theorist we have of what I would call the necessity of misreading. Freud's text both exemplifies and explores certain limits of language, and therefore of literature, insofar as literature is a linguistic as well as a discursive mode. Freud is therefore as much the concern of literary criticism as he is of psychoanalysis. His intention was to found a science; instead he left as legacy a literary canon and a discipline of healing.

It remains one of the sorrows, both of psychoanalysis and of literary criticism, that as modes of interpretation they continue to be antithetical to one another. The classical essay on this antithesis is still Lionel Trilling's *Freud and Literature*, first published back in 1940, and subsequently revised in *The Liberal Imagination* (1950). Trilling demonstrated that neither Freud's notion of art's status nor Freud's use of analysis on works of art was acceptable to a literary critic, but nevertheless praised the Freudian psychology as being truly parallel to the workings of poetry. The sentence of Trilling's eloquent essay that always has lingered in my own memory is the one that presents Freud as a second Vico, as another great rhetorician of the psyche's twistings and turnings:

> In the eighteenth century Vico spoke of the metaphorical, imagistic language of the early stages of culture; it was left to Freud to discover how, in a scientific age, we still feel and think in figurative formations, and to create, what psychoanalysis is, a science of tropes, of metaphor and its variants, synecdoche and metonymy.

That psychoanalysis is a science of tropes is now an accepted commonplace in France, and even in America, but we do well to remember how prophetic Trilling was, since the *Discours de Rome* of Jacques Lacan dates from 1953. Current American thinkers in psychoanalysis like Marshall Edelson and Roy Schafer describe psychic defenses as fantasies, not mechanisms, and fantasies are always tropes, in which so-called "deep structures," like desires, become transformed into "surface structures," like symptoms. A fantasy of defense is thus, in language, the recursive process that traditional rhetoric named a trope or "turning," or even a "color," to use another old name for it. A psychoanalyst interpreting a symptom, dream or verbal slip and a literary critic interpreting a poem thus share the burden of having to become conceptual rhetoricians. But a common burden is proving to be no more of an authentic unifying link between psychoanalysts and critics than common burdens prove to be among common people, and the languages of psychoanalysis and of criticism continue to diverge and clash.

Partly this is due to a certain over-confidence on the part of writing psychoanalysts when they confront a literary text, as well as to a certain over-deference to psychoanalysis on the part of various critics. Psychoanalytic over-confidence, or courageous lack of wariness, is hardly untypical of the profession, as any critic can learn by conducting a seminar for any group of psychoanalysts. Since we can all agree that the interpretation of schizophrenia is a rather more desperately urgent matter than the interpretation of poetry, I am in no way inclined to sneer at psychoanalysts for their instinctive privileging of their own kinds of interpretation. A critical self-confidence, or what Nietzsche might have called a will-to-

power over the text-of-life, is a working necessity for a psychoanalyst, who otherwise would cease to function. Like the shaman,
the psychoanalyst cannot heal unless he himself is persuaded by
his own rhetoric. But the writing psychoanalyst adopts, whether
he knows it or not, a very different stance. As a writer he is neither
more nor less privileged than any other writer. He cannot invoke
the trope of the Unconscious as though he were doing more (or
less) than the poet or critic does by invoking the trope of the
Imagination, or than the theologian does by invoking the trope of
the Divine. Most writing psychoanalysts privilege the realm of
what Freud named as "the primary process." Since this privileging,
or valorization, is at the center of any psychoanalytic account of
creativity, I turn now to examine "primary process," which is
Freud's most vital trope or fiction in his theory of the mind.

Freud formulated his distinction between the primary and secondary processes of the psyche in 1895, in his *Project for a Scientific Psychology*, best available in English since 1954 in *The Origins
of Psychoanalysis* (ed. Bonaparte, A. Freud and Kris). In Freud's
mapping of the mind, the primary process goes on in the system
of the unconscious, while the secondary process characterizes the
preconscious-conscious system. In the unconscious, energy is conceived as moving easily and without check from one idea to another, sometimes by displacement (dislocating) and sometimes by
condensation (compression). This hypothesized energy of the
psyche is supposed continually to reinvest all ideas associated with
the fulfillment of unconscious desire, which is defined as a kind of
primitive hallucination that totally satisfies, that gives a complete
pleasure. Freud speaks of the primary process as being marked by
a wandering-of-meaning, with meaning sometimes dislocated onto
what ought to be an insignificant idea or image, and sometimes
compressed upon a single idea or image at a crossing point between a number of ideas or images. In this constant condition of
wandering, meaning becomes multiformly determined, or even
over-determined, interestingly explained by Lacan as being like a
palimpsest, with one meaning always written over another one.

Dreaming is of course the principal Freudian evidence for the primary process, but wishing construed as a primitive phase of desiring may be closer to the link between the primary process and what could be called poetic thinking.

Wollheim calls the primary process "a primitive but perfectly coherent form of mental functioning." Freud expounded a version of the primary process in Chapter VII of his masterwork, *The Interpretation of Dreams* (1900), but his classic account of it is in the essay of 1911, *Formulations on the Two Principles of Mental Functioning.* There the primary process is spoken of as yielding to the secondary process when the person abandons the pleasure principle and yields to the reality principle, a surrender that postpones pleasure only in order to render its eventuality more certain.

The secondary process thus begins with a binding of psychic energy, which subsequently moves in a more systematic fashion. Investments in ideas and images are stabilized, with pleasure deferred, in order to make possible trial runs of thought as so many path-breakings towards a more constant pleasure. So described, the secondary process also has its links to the cognitive workings of poetry, as to all other cognitions whatsoever. The French Freudians, followers of Lacan, speak of the primary and secondary process as each having different laws of syntax, which is another way of describing these processes as two kinds of poetry or figuration, or two ways of "creativity," if one would have it so.

Anthony Wilden observes in his *System and Structure* (1972): "The concept of a primary process or system applies in both a synchronic and a diachronic sense to all systemic or structural theories." In Freudian theory, the necessity of postulating a primary process precludes any possibility of regarding the forms of that process as being other than abnormal or unconscious phenomena. The Lacanian psychoanalyst O. Mannoni concludes his study *Freud* (English translation 1971) by emphasizing the ultimate gap between primary process and secondary process as being the tragic, unalterable truth of the Freudian vision, since "what it reveals profoundly is a kind of original fracture in the way man is constituted, a split that opposes him to himself (and not to reality or society) and exposes him to the attacks of his unconscious."

In his book *On Art and the Mind* (1973), Wollheim usefully reminds us that the higher reaches of art "did not for Freud connect up with that other and far broader route by which wish and impulse assert themselves in our lives: Neurosis." Wollheim goes on to say that, in Freudian terms, we thus have no reason to think of art as showing any single or unitary motivation. Freud first had developed the trope or conceptual image of the unconscious in order to explain repression, but then had equated the unconscious with the primary process. In his final phase, Freud came to believe that the primary process played a positive role in the strengthening of the ego, by way of the fantasies or defenses of introjection and projection. Wollheim hints that Freud, if he had lived, might have investigated the role of art through such figures of identification, so as to equate art "with recovery or reparation on the path back to reality." Whether or not this surmise is correct, it is certainly very suggestive. We can join Wollheim's surmise to Jack Spector's careful conclusion in his *The Aesthetics of Freud* (1972) that Freud's contribution to the study of art is principally "his dramatic view of the mind in which a war, not of good and evil, but of ego, super-ego, and id forces occurs as a secular *psychomachia*." Identification, through art, is clearly a crucial weapon in such a civil war of the psyche.

Yet it remains true, as Philip Rieff once noted, that Freud suggests very little that is positive about creativity as an intellectual process, and therefore explicit Freudian thought is necessarily antithetical to nearly any theory of the imagination. To quarry Freud for theories of creativity, we need to study Freud where he himself is most imaginative, as in his great phase that begins with *Beyond the Pleasure Principle* (1920), continues with the essay *Negation* (1925) and then with *Inhibitions, Symptoms, and Anxiety* (1926, but called *The Problem of Anxiety* in its American edition), and that can be said to attain a climax in the essay *Analysis Terminable and Interminable* (1937). This is the Freud who establishes the priority of anxiety over its stimuli, and who both imagines the origins of consciousness as a catastrophe and then relates that catastrophe to repetition-compulsion, to the drive-towards-death, and to the defense of life as a drive towards agonistic achievement, an agon directed not only against death but against the achievements of anteriority, of others, and even of one's own earlier self.

Freud, as Rieff also has observed, held a catastrophe theory of the genealogy of drives, but *not* of the drive-towards-creativity. Nevertheless, the Freudian conceptual image of a catastrophe-creation of our instincts is perfectly applicable to our will-to-creativity, and both Otto Rank and more indirectly Sandor Ferenczi made many suggestions (largely unacceptable to Freud himself) that can help us to see what might serve as a Freudian theory of the imagination-as-catastrophe, and of art as an achieved anxiety in the agonistic struggle both to repeat and to defer the repetition of the catastrophe of creative origins.

Prior to any pleasure, including that of creativity, Freud posits the "narcissistic scar," accurately described by a British Freudian critic, Ann Wordsworth, as "the infant's tragic and inevitable first failure in sexual love." Parallel to this notion of the narcissistic scar is Freud's speculative discovery that there are early dreams whose purpose is not hallucinatory wish-fulfillment. Rather they are attempts to master a stimulus retroactively by first developing the anxiety. This is certainly a creation, though it is the *creation of an anxiety*, and so cannot be considered a sublimation of any kind. Freud's own circuitous path-breaking of thought connects this creation-of-an-anxiety to the function of repetition-compulsion, which turns out, in the boldest of all Freud's tropes, to be a regressive return to a death-instinct.

Freud would have rejected, I think, an attempt to relate this strain in his most speculative thinking to any theory of creativity, because for Freud a successful repression is a contradiction in terms. What I am suggesting is that any theory of artistic creation that wishes to use Freud must depart from the Freudian letter in order to develop the Freudian spirit, which in some sense is already the achievement of Lacan and his school, though they have had no conspicuous success in speculating upon art. What the Lacanians *have* seen is that Freud's system, like Heidegger's, is a science of anxiety, which is what I suspect the art of belatedness, of the last several centuries, mostly is also. Freud, unlike Nietzsche, shared in the Romantics' legacy of over-idealizing art, of accepting an ill-defined trope of "the Imagination" as a kind of mythology of creation. But Freud, as much as Nietzsche (or Vico, before them both), provides the rational materials for demythologizing our pieties about artistic creation. Reading the later Freud teaches us that our instinctual life is agonistic and ultimately self-destructive and that our most authentic moments tend to be those of negation, contraction and repression. Is it so unlikely that our creative drives are deeply contaminated by our instinctual origins?

Psychoanalytic explanations of "creativity" tend to discount or repress two particular aspects of the genealogy of aesthetics: first, that the creative or Sublime "moment" is a negative moment; second, that this moment tends to rise out of an encounter with someone else's prior moment of negation, which in turn goes back to an anterior moment, and so on. "Creativity" is thus always a mode of repetition *and* of memory and also of what Nietzsche called the will's revenge against time and against time's statement of: "It was." What links repetition and revenge is the psychic operation that Freud named "defense," and that he identified first with repression but later with a whole range of figurations, including identification. Freud's rhetoric of the psyche, as codified by Anna Freud in *The Ego and the Mechanisms of Defense* (1946), is as comprehensive a system of tropes as Western theory has devised. We can see now, because of Freud, that rhetoric always was more the art of defense than it was the art of persuasion, or rather that defense is always *prior* to persuasion. Trilling's pioneering observation that Freud's science shared with literature a reliance upon trope has proved to be wholly accurate. To clarify my argument, I need to return to Freud's trope of the unconscious and then to proceed from it to his concern with catastrophe as the origin of drive in his later works.

"Consciousness," as a word, goes back to a root meaning "to cut or split," and so to know something by separating out one thing from another. The unconscious (Freud's *das Unbewusste*) is a purely inferred division of the psyche, an inference necessarily based only upon the supposed effects that the unconscious has upon ways we think and act that can be *known*, that are available to consciousness. Because there are gaps or disjunctions to be accounted for in our thoughts and acts, various explanatory concepts of an unconscious have been available since ancient times, but the actual term first appears as the German *Unbewusste* in the later eighteenth century, to be popularized by Goethe and by Schelling. The English "unconscious" was popularized by Coleridge, whose theory of a poem as reconciling a natural outside with a human inside relied upon a formula that "the consciousness is so impressed on the unconscious as to appear in it." Freud acknowledged often that the poets had been there before him, as discoverers of the unconscious, but asserted his own discovery as being the scientific *use* of a concept of the unconscious. What he did not assert was his intense narrowing down of the traditional concept, for he separated out and away from it the attributes of creativity that poets and other speculators always had ascribed to it. Originality or invention are not mentioned by Freud as rising out of the unconscious.

There is no single concept of the unconscious in Freud, as any responsible reading of his work shows. This is because there are two Freudian topographies or maps of the mind, earlier and later (after 1920), and also because the unconscious is a dynamic concept. Freud distinguished his concept of the unconscious from that of his closest psychological precursor, Pierre Janet, by emphasizing his own vision of a civil war in the psyche, a dynamic conflict of opposing mental forces, conscious against unconscious. Not only the conflict was seen thus as being dynamic, but the unconscious peculiarly was characterized as dynamic in itself, requiring always a contending force to keep it from breaking through into consciousness.

In the first Freudian topography, the psyche is divided into

Unconscious, Preconscious, and Conscious, while in the second the divisions are the rather different triad of id, ego, and super-ego. The Preconscious, descriptively considered, is unconscious, but can be made conscious, and so is severely divided from the Unconscious proper, in the perspective given either by a topographical or a dynamic view. But this earlier system proved simplistic to Freud himself, mostly because he came to believe that our lives began with all of the mind's contents in the unconscious. This finally eliminated Janet's conception that the unconscious was a wholly separate mode of consciousness, which was a survival of the ancient belief in a creative or inaugurating unconscious. Freud's new topology insisted upon the dynamics of relationship between an unknowable unconscious and consciousness by predicating three agencies or instances of personality: id, ego, super-ego. The effect of this new system was to devaluate the unconscious, or at least to demystify it still further.

In the second Freudian topography, "unconscious" tends to become merely a modifier, since all of the id and very significant parts of the ego and super-ego are viewed as being unconscious. Indeed, the second Freudian concept of the ego gives us an ego which is *mostly* unconscious, and so "behaves exactly like the repressed—that is, which produces powerful effects without itself being conscious and which requires special work before it can be made conscious," as Freud remarks in *The Ego and the Id*. Lacan has emphasized the unconscious element in the ego to such a degree that the Lacanian ego must be considered, despite its creator's protests, much more a revision of Freud than what ordinarily would be accounted an interpretation. With mordant eloquence, Lacan keeps assuring us that the ego, every ego, is essentially paranoid, which as Lacan knows *sounds* rather more like Pascal than it does like Freud. I think that this insistence is at once Lacan's strength and his weakness, for my knowledge of imaginative literature tells me that Lacan's conviction is certainly true if by the ego we mean the literary "I" as it appears in much of the most vital lyric poetry of the last three hundred years, and indeed in all literature that achieves the Sublime. But with the literary idea of "the Sublime" I come at last to the sequence of Freud's texts that I wish to examine, since the first of them is Freud's theory of the Sublime, his essay *The "Uncanny"* of 1919.

The text of *The "Uncanny"* is the threshold to the major phase of Freud's canon, which begins the next year with *Beyond the Pleasure Principle*. But quite aside from its crucial place in Freud's writings, the essay is of enormous importance to literary criticism because it is the only major contribution that the twentieth century has made to the aesthetics of the Sublime. It may seem curious to regard Freud as the culmination of a literary and philosophical tradition that held no particular interest for him, but I would correct my own statement by the modification, no *conscious* interest for him. The Sublime, as I read Freud, is one of his major *repressed* concerns, and this literary repression on his part is a clue to what I take to be a gap in his theory of repression.

I come now, belatedly, to the definition of "the Sublime," before considering Freud as the last great theorist of that mode. As a literary idea, the Sublime originally meant a style of "loftiness," that is of verbal power, of greatness or strength conceived agonistically, which is to say against all possible competition. But in the European Enlightenment, this literary idea was strangely transformed into a vision of the terror that could be perceived both in nature and in art, a terror uneasily allied with pleasurable sensations of augmented power, and even of narcissistic freedom, freedom in the shape of that wildness that Freud dubbed "the omnipotence of thought," the greatest of all narcissistic illusions.

Freud's essay begins with a curiously weak defensive attempt to separate his subject from the aesthetics of the Sublime, which he insists deals only "with feelings of a positive nature." This is so flatly untrue, and so blandly ignores the long philosophical tradition of the negative Sublime, that an alert reader ought to become very wary. A year later, in the opening paragraphs of *Beyond the Pleasure Principle*, Freud slyly assures his readers that "priority and originality are not among the aims that psycho-analytic work sets itself." One sentence later, he charmingly adds that he would be glad to accept any philosophical help he can get, but that none is available for a consideration of the meaning of pleasure and unpleasure. With evident generosity, he then acknowledges G. T. Fechner, and later makes a bow to the safely distant Plato as author of *The Symposium*. Very close to the end of *Beyond the Pleasure Principle*, there is a rather displaced reference to Schopenhauer, when Freud remarks that "we have unwittingly steered our course into the harbor of Schopenhauer's philosophy." The apogee of this evasiveness in regard to precursors comes where it should, in the marvelous essay of 1937, *Analysis Terminable and Interminable*, which we may learn to read as being Freud's elegiac *apologia* for his life's work. There the true precursor is unveiled as Empedocles, very safely remote at two and a half millennia. Perhaps psychoanalysis does not set priority and originality as aims in its *praxis*, but the first and most original of psychoanalysts certainly shared the influence-anxieties and defensive misprisions of all strong writers throughout history, and particularly in the last three centuries.

Anxieties when confronted with anterior powers are overtly the concerns of the essay on the "uncanny." E. T. A. Hoffmann's *The Sand-Man* provides Freud with his text, and for once Freud allows himself to be a very useful practical critic of an imaginative story. The repetition-compulsion, possibly imported backwards from *Beyond the Pleasure Principle* as work-in-progress, brilliantly is invoked to open up what is hidden in the story. Uncanniness is traced back to the narcissistic belief in "omnipotence of thought," which in aesthetic terms is necessarily the High Romantic faith in the power of the mind over the universe of the senses and of death. *Das Heimliche*, the homely or canny, is thus extended to its only apparent opposite, *das Unheimliche*, "for this uncanny is in reality nothing new or foreign, but something familiar and old-established in the mind that has been estranged only by the process of repression."

Freud weakens his extraordinary literary insight by the latter part of his essay, where he seeks to reduce the "uncanny" to either an infantile or a primitive survival in our psyche. His essay knows better, in its wonderful dialectical play on the *Unheimlich* as being subsumed by the larger or parental category of the *Heimlich*. Philip Rieff finely catches this interplay in his comment that the effect of Freud's writing is itself rather uncanny, and surely never more so than in this essay. Rieff sounds like Emerson or even like Longinus on the Sublime when he considers the condition of Freud's reader:

> The reader comes to a work with ambivalent motives, learn-
> ing what he does not wish to know, or, what amounts to the
> same thing, believing he already knows and can accept as his
> own intellectual property what the author merely "articulates"
> or "expresses" for him. Of course, in this sense, everybody
> knows everything—or nobody could learn anything. . . .

Longinus had said that reading a sublime poet ". . . we come to believe we have created what we have only heard." Milton, strong- est poet of the modern Sublime, stated this version of the reader's Sublime with an ultimate power, thus setting forth the principle upon which he himself read, in Book IV of his *Paradise Regained*, where his Christ tells Satan:

> . . . who reads
> Incessantly, and to his reading brings not
> A spirit and judgment equal or superior
> (And what he brings, what needs he elsewhere seek?),
> Uncertain and unsettled still remains. . . .

Pope followed Boileau in saying that Longinus "is himself the great Sublime he draws." Emerson, in his seminal essay *Self- Reliance*, culminated this theme of the reader's Sublime when he asserted that "in every work of genius we recognize our own re- jected thoughts; they come back to us with a certain alienated majesty." The "majesty" is the true, high, breaking light, aura or lustre, of the Sublime, and this realization is at the repressed center of Freud's essay on the "uncanny." What Freud declined to see, at that moment, was the mode of conversion that alienated the "canny" into the "uncanny." His next major text, *Beyond the Pleasure Principle*, clearly exposes that mode as being catastrophe.

Lacan and his followers have centered upon *Beyond the Pleasure Principle* because the book has not lost the force of its shock value, even to Freudian analysts. My contention would be that this shock is itself the stigma of the Sublime, stemming from Freud's literary achievement here. The text's origin is itself shock or aura, the trauma that a neurotic's dreams attempt to master, *after the event.* "Drive" or "instinct" is suddenly seen by Freud as being catastrophic in its origins, and as being aimed, not at satisfaction, but at death. For the first time in his writing, Freud overtly assigns priority to the psyche's fantasizings over mere biology, though this valorization makes Freud uneasy. The pleasure principle produces the biological principle of constancy, and then is converted, through this principle, into a drive back to the constancy of death. Drive or instinct thus becomes a kind of defense, all but identified with repression. This troping of biology is so extreme, really so literary, that I find it more instructive to seek the aid of commentary here from a Humean empiricist like Wollheim than from Continental dialecticians like Lacan and Laplanche. Wollheim imperturbably finds no violation of empiricism or biology in the death-drive. He even reads "beyond," *jenseits,* as meaning only "inconsistent with" the pleasure principle, which is to remove from the word the transcendental or Sublime emphasis that Freud's usage gave to it. For Wollheim, the book is nothing more than the working through of the full implication of the major essay of 1914, *On Narcissism: An Introduction.* If we follow Wollheim's lead quite thoroughly here, we will emerge with conclusions that differ from his rather guarded remarks about the book in which Freud seems to have shocked himself rather more than he shocks Wollheim.

The greatest shock of *Beyond the Pleasure Principle* is that it ascribes the origin of all human drives to a catastrophe theory of creation (to which I would add: "of creativity"). This catastrophe theory is developed in *The Ego and the Id,* where the two major catastrophes, the drying up of ocean that cast life onto land and the Ice Age are said to be repeated psychosomatically in the way the latency period (roughly from the age of five until twelve) cuts a gap into sexual development. Rieff again is very useful when he says that the basis of catastrophe theory, whether in Freud or in Ferenczi's more drastic and even apocalyptic *Thalassa* (1921), "remains Freud's *Todestrieb*, the tendency of all organisms to strive toward a state of absence of irritability and finally 'the death-like repose of the inorganic world.'" I find it fascinating from a literary critical standpoint to note what I think has not been noted, that the essay on narcissism turns upon catastrophe theory also. Freud turns to poetry, here to Heine, in order to illustrate the psychogenesis of Eros, but the lines he quotes actually state a psychogenesis of creativity rather than of love:

> . . . whence does that necessity arise that urges our mental life to pass on beyond the limits of narcissism and to attach the libido to objects? The answer which would follow from our line of thought would once more be that we are so impelled when the cathexis of the ego with libido exceeds a certain degree. A strong egoism is a protection against disease, but in the last resort we must begin to love in order that we may not fall ill, and must fall ill if, in consequence of frustration, we cannot love. Somewhat after this fashion does Heine conceive of the psychogenesis of the creation:

> Krankheit ist wohl der letzte Grund
> Des ganzen Schöpferdrangs gewesen;
> Erschaffend konnte ich genesen,
> Erschaffend wurde ich gesund.

To paraphrase Heine loosely, illness is the ultimate ground of the drive to create, and so while creating the poet sustains relief, and by creating the poet becomes healthy. Freud transposes from the catastrophe of creativity to the catastrophe of falling in love, a transposition to which I will return in the final pages of this chapter.

Beyond the Pleasure Principle, like the essay on narcissism, is a discourse haunted by images (some of them repressed) of catastrophe. Indeed, what Freud verges upon showing is that to be human is a catastrophic condition. The coloring of this catastrophe, in Freud, is precisely Schopenhauerian rather than, say, Augustinian or Pascalian. It is as though, for Freud, the Creation and the Fall had been one and the same event. Freud holds back from this abyss of Gnosticism by reducing mythology to psychology, but since psychology and cosmology have been intimately related throughout human history, this reduction is not altogether persuasive. Though he wants to show us that the daemonic is "really" the compulsion to repeat, Freud tends rather to the "uncanny" demonstration that repetition-compulsion reveals many of us to be daemonic or else makes us daemonic. Again, Freud resorts to the poets for illustration, and again the example goes beyond the Freudian interpretation. Towards the close of section III of *Beyond the Pleasure Principle*, Freud looks for a supreme instance of "people all of whose human relationships have the same outcome" and he finds it in Tasso:

> . . . The most moving poetic picture of a fate such as this is given by Tasso in his romantic epic *Gerusalemme Liberata*. Its hero, Tancred, unwittingly kills his beloved Clorinda in a duel while she is disguised in the armor of an enemy knight. After her burial he makes his way into a strange magic forest which strikes the Crusaders' army with terror. He slashes with his sword at a tall tree; but blood streams from the cut and the voice of Clorinda, whose soul is imprisoned in the tree, is heard complaining that he has wounded his beloved once again.

Freud cites this episode as evidence to support his assumption "that there really does exist in the mind a compulsion to repeat which overrides the pleasure principle." The repetition in Tasso is not just incremental, but rather is qualitative, in that the second wounding is "uncanny" or Sublime, and the first is merely accidental. Freud's citation is an allegory of Freud's own passage into the Sublime. When Freud writes (and the italics are his): "*It seems, then, that a drive is an urge inherent in organic life to restore an earlier state of things*," then he slays his beloved trope of "drive" by disguising it in the armor of his enemy, mythology. But when he writes (and again the italics are his): *"the aim of all life is death,"* then he wounds his figuration of "drive" in a truly Sublime or "uncanny" fashion. In the qualitative leap from the drive to restore pure anteriority to the apothegm that life's purpose is death, Freud himself has abandoned the empirical for the daemonic. It is the literary authority of the daemonic rather than the analytical which makes plausible the further suggestion that

> . . . sadism is in fact a death instinct which, under the influence of the narcissistic libido, has been forced away from the ego. . . .

This language is impressive, and it seems to me equally against literary tact to accept it or reject it on any supposed biological basis. Its true basis is that of an implicit catastrophe theory of meaning or interpretation, which is in no way weakened by being circular and therefore mythological. The repressed rhetorical formula of Freud's discourse in *Beyond the Pleasure Principle* can be stated thus: *literal meaning equals anteriority equals an earlier state of meaning equals an earlier state of things equals death equals literal meaning.* Only one escape is possible from such a formula, and it is a simpler formula: *Eros equals figurative meaning.* This is the dialectic that informs the proudest and most moving passage in *Beyond the Pleasure Principle*, which comprises two triumphant sentences *contra* Jung that were added to the text in 1921, in a Sublime afterthought:

> Our views have from the very first been *dualistic*, and today they are even more definitely dualistic than before—now that we describe the opposition as being, not between ego-instincts and sexual instincts, but between life instincts and death instincts. Jung's libido theory is on the contrary *monistic*; the fact that he has called his one instinctual force "libido" is bound to cause confusion, but need not affect us otherwise.

I would suggest that we read *dualistic* here as a trope for "figurative" and *monistic* as a trope for "literal." The opposition between life drives and death drives is not just a dialectic (though it *is* that) but is a great writer's Sublime interplay between figurative and literal meanings, whereas Jung is exposed as being what he truly was, a mere literalizer of anterior mythologies. What Freud proclaims here, in the accents of sublimity, is the power of his own mind over language, which in this context *is* the power that Hegelians or Lacanians legitimately could term "negative thinking."

I am pursuing Freud as prose-poet of the Sublime, but I would not concede that I am losing sight of Freud as analytical theorist. Certainly the next strong Freudian text is the incomparable *Inhibitions, Symptoms, and Anxiety* of 1926. But before considering that elegant and somber meditation, certainly the most illuminating analysis of anxiety our civilization has been offered, I turn briefly to Freud's essay on his dialectic, *Negation* (1925).

Freud's audacity here has been little noted, perhaps because he packs into fewer than five pages an idea that cuts a considerable gap into his theory of repression. The gap is wide enough so that such oxymorons as "a successful repression" and "an achieved anxiety," which are not possible in psychoanalysis, are made available to us as literary terms. Repressed images or thoughts, by Freudian definition, *cannot* make their way into consciousness, yet their content can, on condition that it is *denied*. Freud cheerfully splits head from heart in the apprehension of images:

> Negation is a way of taking account of what is repressed; indeed, it is actually a removal of the repression, though not, of course, an acceptance of what is repressed. It is to be seen how the intellectual function is here distinct from the affective process. Negation only assists in undoing *one* of the consequences of repression—namely, the fact that the subject-matter of the image in question is unable to enter consciousness. The result is a kind of intellectual acceptance of what is repressed, though in all essentials the repression persists. . . .

I would venture one definition of the literary Sublime (which to me seems always a negative Sublime) as being that mode in which the poet, while expressing previously repressed thought, desire, or emotion, is able to continue to defend himself against his own created image by disowning it, a defense of *un-naming* it rather than *naming* it. Freud's word *Verneinung* means both a grammatical negation and a psychic disavowal or denial, and so the linguistic and the psychoanalytical have a common origin here, as Lacan and his school have insisted. The ego and the poet-in-his-poem both proceed by a kind of "misconstruction," a defensive process that Lacan calls *méconnaissance* in psychoanalysis, and that I have called "misprision" in the study of poetic influence (a notion formulated before I had read Lacan, but which I was delighted to find supported in him). In his essay *Aggressivity in Psychoanalysis* Lacan usefully connects Freud's notion of a "negative" libido to the idea of Discord in Heraclitus. Freud himself brings his essay on *Verneinung* to a fascinating double conclusion. First, the issue of truth or falsehood in language is directly related to the defenses of introjection and projection; a true image thus would be introjected and a false one projected. Second, the defense of introjection is aligned to the Eros-drive of affirmation, "while negation, the derivative of expulsion, belongs to the instinct of destruction," the drive to death beyond the pleasure principle. I submit that what Freud has done here should have freed literary discussion from its persistent over-literalization of his idea of repression. Freud joins himself to the tradition of the Sublime, that is, of the strongest Western poetry, by showing us that negation allows poetry to free itself from the aphasias and hysterias of repression, *without* however freeing the poets themselves from the unhappier human consequences of repression. Negation is of *no* therapeutic value for the individual, but it *can* liberate him into the linguistic freedoms of poetry and thought.

I think that of all Freud's books, none matches the work on inhibitions, symptoms and anxiety in its potential importance for students of literature, for this is where the concept of defense is ultimately clarified. Wollheim says that Freud confused the issue of defense by the "overschematic" restriction of repression to a single species of defense, but this is one of the very rare instances where Wollheim seems to me misled or mistaken. Freud's revised account of anxiety *had* to distinguish between *relatively* non-repressive and the more severely repressive defenses, and I only wish that both Freud and his daughter after him had been even more schematic in mapping out the defenses. We need a rhetoric of the psyche, and here the Lacanians have been a kind of disaster, with their simplistic over-reliance upon the metaphor/metonymy distinction. Freud's revised account of anxiety is precisely at one with the poetic Sublime, for anxiety is finally seen as a technique for mastering anteriority by *remembering* rather than *repeating* the past. By showing us that anxiety is a mode of expectation, closely resembling desire, Freud allows us to understand why poetry, which loves love, also seems to love anxiety. Literary and human romance both are exposed as being anxious quests that could not bear to be cured of their anxieties, even if such cures were possible. "An increase of excitation underlies anxiety," Freud tells us, and then he goes on to relate this increase to a repetition of the catastrophe of human birth, with its attendant trauma. Arguing against Otto Rank, who like Ferenczi had gone too far into the abysses of catastrophe-theory, Freud enunciated a principle that can help explain why the terror of the literary Sublime must and can give pleasure:

> Anxiety is an affective state which can of course be experienced only by the ego. The id cannot be afraid, as the ego can; it is not an organization, and cannot estimate situations of danger. On the contrary, it is of extremely frequent occurrence that processes are initiated or executed in the id which give the ego occasion to develop anxiety; as a matter of fact, the repressions which are probably the earliest are motivated, like the majority of all later ones, by such fear on the part of the ego of this or that process in the id. . . .

Freud's writing career was to conclude with the polemical assertion that "mysticism is the obscure self-perception of the realm outside the ego, of the id," which is a splendid farewell thrust at Jung, as we can see by substituting "Jung" for "the id" at the close of the sentence. The id perceiving the id is a parody of the Sublime, whereas the ego's earliest defense, its primal repression, is the true origin of the Sublime. Freud knew that "primal repression" was a necessary fiction, because without some initial fixation his story of the psyche could not begin. Laplanche and Pontalis, writing under Lacan's influence in their *The Language of Psychoanalysis*, find the basis of fixation

> in primal moments at which certain privileged ideas are indelibly inscribed in the unconscious, and at which the instinct itself becomes fixated to its psychical representative—perhaps by this very process constituting itself *qua* instinct.

If we withdrew that "perhaps," then we would return to the Freudian catastrophe-theory of the genesis of all drives, with fixation now being regarded as another originating catastrophe. How much clearer these hypotheses become if we transpose them into the realm of poetry! If fixation becomes the inscription in the unconscious of the privileged idea of a Sublime poet, or strong precursor, then the drive towards poetic expression originates in an agonistic repression, where the agon or contest is set against the pattern of the precursor's initial fixation upon an anterior figure. Freud's mature account of anxiety thus concludes itself upon an allegory of origins, in which the creation of an unconscious implicitly models itself upon poetic origins. There was repression, Freud insists, before there was anything to be repressed. This insistence is neither rational nor irrational; it is a figuration that knows its own status as figuration, without embarrassment.

My final text in Freud is *Analysis Terminable and Interminable*. The German title, *Die Endliche und die Unendliche Analyse*, might better be translated as "finite or indefinite analysis," which is Lacan's suggestion. Lacan amusingly violates the taboo of discussing how long the analytic session is to be when he asks:

> . . . how is this time to be measured? Is its measure to be that of what Alexander Koyré calls "the universe of precision"? Obviously we live in this universe, but its advent for man is relatively recent, since it goes back precisely to Huyghens' clock— in other words, to 1659—and the *malaise* of modern man does

not exactly indicate that this precision is in itself a liberating factor for him. Are we to say that this time, the time of the fall of heavy bodies, is in some way sacred in the sense that it corresponds to the time of the stars as they were fixed in eternity by God who, as Lichtenberg put it, winds up our sundials?

I reflect, as I read Lacan's remarks, that it was just after Huyghens's clock that Milton began to compose *Paradise Lost*, in the early 1660's, and that Milton's poem is *the* instance of the modern Sublime. It is in *Paradise Lost* that temporality fully becomes identified with anxiety, which makes Milton's epic the most Freudian text ever written, far closer to the universe of psychoanalysis than such more frequently cited works, in Freudian contexts, as *Oedipus Tyrannus* and *Hamlet*. We should remember that before Freud used a Virgilian tag as epigraph for *The Interpretation of Dreams* (1908), he had selected a great Satanic utterance for his motto:

Seest thou yon dreary plain, forlorn and wild,
The seat of desolation, void of light,
Save what the glimmering of these livid flames
Casts pale and dreadful? Thither let us tend
From off the tossing of these fiery waves,
There rest, if any rest can harbour there,
And reassembling our afflicted powers,
Consult how we may henceforth most offend
Our enemy, our own loss how repair,
How overcome this dire calamity,
What reinforcement we may gain from hope;
If not, what resolution from despair.

This Sublime passage provides a true motto for all psychoanalysis, since "afflicted powers" meant "cast-down powers," or as Freud would have said, "repressed drives." But it would be an even apter epigraph for the essay on finite and indefinite analysis than it could have been for the much more hopeful *Interpretation of Dreams*, thirty years before. Freud begins his somber and beautiful late essay by brooding sardonically on the heretic Otto Rank's scheme for speeding up analysis in America. But this high humor gives

way to the melancholy of considering every patient's deepest resistance to the analyst's influence, that "negative transference" in
which the subject's anxiety-of-influence seeks a bulwark. As he re-
views the main outlines of his theory, Freud emphasizes its *economic* aspects rather than the dynamic and topographical points
of view. The *economic* modifies any notion that drives have an
energy that can be measured. To estimate the magnitude of such
excitation is to ask the classical, agonistic question that *is* the Sublime, because the Sublime is always a comparison of two forces or
beings, in which the agon turns on the answer to three queries:
more? equal to? or less than? Satan confronting hell, the abyss,
the new world, is still seeking to answer the questions that he sets
for himself in heaven, all of which turn upon comparing God's
force and his own. Oedipus confronting the Sphinx, Hamlet facing
the mystery of the dead father, and Freud meditating upon repression are all in the same economic stance. I would use this shared
stance to re-define a question that psychoanalysis by its nature
cannot answer. Since there is *no* biological warrant for the Freudian concept of libido, what is the energy that Freud invokes when
he speaks from the economic point of view? Wollheim, always
faithful to empiricism, has only one comment upon the economic
theory of mind, and it is a very damaging observation:

> . . . though an economic theory allows one to rela*t*e the
> damming up of energy or frustration at one place in the psychic
> apparatus with discharge at another, it does not commit one to
> the view that, given frustration, energy will seek discharge along
> all possible channels indifferently. Indeed, if the system is of
> any complexity, an economic theory would be virtually un-
> informative unless some measure of selectivity in discharge was
> postulated. . . .

But since Freud applied the economic stance to sexual drives
almost entirely, no measure of selectivity *could* be postulated. This
still leaves us with Freud's economic obsessions, and I suggest now
that their true model was literary, and not sexual. This would
mean that the "mechanisms of defense" are dependent for their

formulaic coherence upon the traditions of rhetoric, and not upon biology, which is almost too easily demonstrable. It is hardly accidental that Freud, in this late essay which is so much his *summa*, resorts to the textual analogue when he seeks to distinguish repression from the other defenses:

> Without pressing the analogy too closely we may say that repression is to the other methods of defense what the omission of words or passages is to the corruption of a text. . . . For quite a long time flight and an avoidance of a dangerous situation serve as expedients. . . . But one cannot flee from oneself and no flight avails against danger from within; hence the ego's defensive mechanisms are condemned to falsify the inner perception, so that it transmits to us only an imperfect and travestied picture of our id. In its relations with the id the ego is paralysed by its restrictions or blinded by its errors. . . .

What is Freud's motive for this remarkably clear and eloquent recapitulation of his theory of repression and defense (which I take to be the center of his greatness)? The hidden figuration in his discourse here is his economics of the psyche, a trope which is allowed an overt exposure when he sadly observes that the energy necessary to keep such defenses going "proves a heavy burden on the psychical economy." If I were reading this essay on finite and indefinite analysis as I have learned to read Romantic poems, I would be on the watch for a blocking-agent in the poetic ego, a shadow that Blake called the Spectre and Shelley a daemon or *Alastor*. This shadow would be an anxiety narcissistically intoxicated with itself, an anxiety determined to go on being anxious, a drive towards destruction in love with the image of self-destruction. Freud, like the great poets of quest, has given all the premonitory signs of this Sublime terror determined to maintain itself, and again like the poets he suddenly makes the pattern quite explicit:

> The crux of the matter is that the mechanisms of defense against former dangers recur in analysis in the shape of *resistances* to cure. It follows that the ego treats recovery itself as a new danger.

Faced by the patient's breaking of the psychoanalytic compact, Freud broods darkly on the war between his true Sublime and the patient's false Sublime:

> Once more we realize the importance of the quantitative factor and once more we are reminded that analysis has only certain limited quantities of energy which it can employ to match against the hostile forces. And it does seem as if victory were really for the most part with the big battalions.

It is a true challenge to the interpreter of Freud's text to identify the economic stance here, for what is the source of *the energy of analysis*, however limited in quantity it may be? Empiricism, whether in Hume or in Wittgenstein, does not discourse on the measurement of its own libido. But if we take Freud as Sublime poet rather than empirical reasoner, if we see him as the peer of Milton rather than of Hume, of Proust rather than of the biologists, then we can speculate rather precisely about the origins of the psychoanalytical drive, about the nature of the powers made available by the discipline that one man was able to establish in so sublimely solitary a fashion. Vico teaches us that the Sublime or severe poet discovers the origin of his rhetorical drive, the catastrophe of his creative vocation, in *divination*, by which Vico meant both the process of foretelling dangers to the self's survival and the apotheosis of becoming a daemon or sort of god. What Vico calls "divination" is what Freud calls the primal instinct of Eros, or that "which strives to combine existing phenomena into ever greater unities." With moving simplicity, Freud then reduces this to the covenant between patient and analyst, which he calls "a love of truth." But, like all critical idealisms about poetry, this idealization of psychoanalysis is an error. No psychic economy (or indeed *any* economy) can be based upon "a love of truth." Drives depend upon fictions, because drives *are* fictions, and we want to know more about Freud's enabling fictions, which grant to him his Sublime "energy of analysis."

We can acquire this knowledge by a very close analysis of the final section of Freud's essay, a section not the less instructive for being so unacceptable to our particular moment in social and cultural history. The resistance to analytical cure, in both men and women, is identified by Freud with what he calls the "repudiation of femininity" *by both sexes*, the castration complex that informs the fantasy-life of everyone whatsoever: ". . . in both cases it is the attitude belonging to the sex opposite to the subject's own which succumbs to repression." This is followed by Freud's prophetic lament, with its allusion to the burden of Hebraic prophecy. Freud too sees himself as the *nabi* who speaks to the winds, to the winds only, for only the winds will listen:

> . . . At no point in one's analytic work does one suffer more from the oppressive feeling that all one's efforts have been in vain and from the suspicion that one is "talking to the winds" than when one is trying to persuade a female patient to abandon her wish for a penis on the ground of its being unrealizable, or to convince a male patient that a passive attitude towards another man does not always signify castration and that in many relations in life it is indispensable. The rebellious overcompensation of the male produces one of the strongest transference-resistances. A man will not be subject to a father-substitute or owe him anything and he therefore refuses to accept his cure from the physician. . . .

It is again one of Lacan's services to have shown us that this is figurative discourse, even if Lacan's own figurative discourse becomes too baroque a commentary upon Freud's wisdom here. Freud prophesies to the winds because men and women cannot surrender their primal fantasies, which are their poor but desperately prideful myths of their own origins. We cannot let go of our three fundamental fantasies: the primal scene, which accounts for our existence; the seduction fantasy, which justifies our narcissism; and the castration complex, which explains to us the mystery of sexual differentiation. What the three fantasy-scenes share is the fiction of an originating catastrophe, and so a very close relation to the necessity for defense. The final barrier to Freud's heroic labor of healing, in Freud's own judgment, is the human imagination. The original wound in man cannot be healed, as it is in Hegel, by the same force that makes the wound.

Freud became a strong poet of the Sublime because he made the solitary crossing from a realm where effect is always traced to a cause, to a mode of discourse which asked instead the economic and agonistic questions of comparison. The question of how an emptiness came about was replaced by the question that asks: more, less, or equal to? which is the agonistic self-questioning of the Sublime. The attempt to give truer names to the rhetoric of human defense was replaced by the increasing refusal to name the vicissitudes of drive except by un-namings as old as those of Empedocles and Heraclitus. The ambition to make of psychoanalysis a wholly positive *praxis* yielded to a skeptical and ancient awareness of a rugged negativity that informed every individual fantasy.

Lacan and his school justly insist that psychoanalysis has contributed nothing to biology, despite Freud's wistful hopes that it could, and also that the life sciences inform psychoanalysis hardly at all, again in despite of Freud's eager scientism. Psychoanalysis is a varied therapeutic *praxis,* but it is a "science" only in the peculiar sense that literature, philosophy and religion are also *sciences of anxiety.* But this means that no single rhetoric or poetic will suffice for the study of psychoanalysis, any more than a particular critical method will unveil all that needs to be seen in literature. The "French way" of reading Freud, in Lacan, Derrida, Laplanche, and others, is no more a "right" reading than the way of the ego-psychologists Hartmann, Kris, Erikson, and others, which Lacan and his followers wrongly keep insisting is the only "American reading." In this conflict of strong misreadings, partisans of both ways evidently need to keep forgetting what the French at least ought to remember: strong texts become strong by mis-taking all texts anterior to them. Freud has more in common with Proust and Montaigne than with biological scientists, because his interpretations of life and death are mediated always by texts, first by the literary texts of others, and then by his own earlier texts, until at last the Sublime mediation of otherness begins to be performed by his text-in-process. In the *Essays* of Montaigne or Proust's vast novel, this ongoing mediation is clearer than it is in Freud's almost perpetual self-revision, because Freud wrote no definitive, single text; but the canon of Freud's writings shows an increasingly uneasy sense that he had become his own precursor, and that he had begun to defend himself against himself by deliberately audacious arrivals at final positions.

5

Freud's Concepts of Defense
and the Poetic Will

A person tropes in order to tell many-colored rather than white lies to himself. The same person utilizes the fantasies or mechanisms of defense in order to ward off unpleasant truths concerning dangers from within, so that he sees only what Freud called an imperfect and travestied picture of the id. Troping and defending may be much the same process, which is hardly a comfort if we then are compelled to think that tropes, like defenses, are necessarily infantilisms, travesties that substitute for more truly mature perceptions. The potential power of trope necessarily dismisses all such pseudo-compulsion. Yet the analytical tendency in any lover of poetry ought to keep him vulnerable to the audacity of the wit of Thomas Love Peacock, who in *The Four Ages of Poetry* saw poetic trope as a "wallowing in the rubbish of departed ignorance, and raking up the ashes of dead savages to find gewgaws and rattles for the grown babies of the age." Defense in poetry then called up Shelley's reply, A *Defense of Poetry*, where amid so much magnificence, Shelley gave us the finest trope of critical transumption (or troping upon a previous trope) that I know. Speaking of the errors and sins of the men who were the great poets, Shelley grandly adds: "they have been washed in the blood of the mediator and redeemer, time." The reader is thus reminded that the infantilism of the grown baby is of that sort to which Shelley leaps, transcending Christian tropes of salvation and subtly recalling a marvelous figuration by the dark Heraclitus:

> Time is a child playing draughts; the lordship is to the child.

If that is infantilism, then we need not fear a yielding to it. But clearly it is something else, something we want to call poetry, and to whose defense we spring. To defend poetry, which is to say, to defend trope, in my judgment is to defend defense itself. And to discuss Freud's concepts of defense is to discuss also what in Romantic or belated poetry is the poetic will itself, the ego of the poet not as man, but of the poet as poet. Freud's triumph, in an aesthetic rather than a scientific sense, is that the reverse seems more true also. To discuss the poetic will without referring to the ego's defenses is less and less interesting.

But I must begin by defining, as best I can, the poetic will, taking Nietzsche as inescapable point of origin. One day when Nietzsche's Zarathustra crosses over a bridge, he is surrounded by a crowd of cripples. A hunchback, with admirable irony, utters a great challenge to the prophet:

> You can heal the blind and make the lame walk; and from him who has too much behind him you could perhaps take away a little.

Zarathustra refuses, saying that to take away the hump from the hunchback is to rob him of his spirit. Yet in his meditation upon redemption that follows, Zarathustra transcends the hunchback's irony and proceeds to dream a great dream of the will. All of us have too much behind us, and the prophet, though poignantly calling himself "a cripple at this bridge," gives us a vision of the will's limits and of the will's desire beyond limits:

> To redeem those who lived in the past and to re-create all "it was" into a "thus I willed it"—that alone should I call redemption. Will—that is the name of the liberator and joy-bringer; thus I taught you, my friends. But now learn this too: the will itself is still a prisoner. Willing liberates; but what is it that puts even the liberator himself in fetters? "It was"—that

is the name of the will's gnashing of teeth and most secret melancholy. Powerless against what has been done, he is an angry spectator of all that is past. The will cannot will backwards; and that he cannot break time and time's covetousness, that is the will's loneliest melancholy.

A little further on, Zarathustra sums up this wisdom for us:

> This, indeed this alone, is what *revenge* is: the will's resentment against time and time's "it was."

Nietzsche does not mean that this will is itself the poetic or creative will, but the burden here must be taken on by the poet above all persons, since earlier in the Second Part of *Zarathustra* Nietzsche twice attacks the poets, meaning Goethe in particular. In the rhapsody "Upon the Blessed Isles," we are warned that the poets lie too much, and yet the creative will is exalted. Out of the poets, if they cease to lie, will come "ascetics of the spirit," as Zarathustra will prophesy later.

But *can* they cease to lie, and particularly *against* time's "it was"? What is the poetic drive, or instinct to make what can reverse time? Freud ended with a vision of two drives, death drive and Eros or sexual drive, but he posited only a single energy, libido. The poetic drive or will is neither masked death drive nor sublimated sexual drive, and yet I would not assert for it a status alongside the two Freudian drives. Instead I will suggest that the creative will or poetic drive puts the Freudian drives into question, by showing that those drives themselves are defenses, or are so contaminated by defenses as to be indistinguishable from the resistances they supposedly provoke.

It isn't possible to ask coherently what Freud meant to mean by "defense" without deciding first what he meant to mean by a "drive" (*Trieb*). The drive or urge (setting aside the weak translation "instinct") is a dynamic movement that puts pressure upon a person towards some object. Your body and mind are stimulated, whether sexually and towards self-preservation, or towards aggression and death, and your body and mind therefore become tense.

This tension needs resolution, and so the drive or urge moves upon some object so as to end tension. That Freud cannot be talking about merely biological impulses always should have been clear, long before the drives became overtly cosmological and hence mythological in *Beyond the Pleasure Principle*. Freud postulates that the psyche indeed has bodily intentions, or as he finally put it in his *Outline of Psychoanalysis*, drives are "the somatic demands upon mental life." Since psyche and body are conceived as a radical dualism, Freud is justified in seeing the drive as a frontier concept, neither truly mental nor truly physical. "Drive" is thus a dialectical term. Philip Rieff expressed this nicely when he wrote that the drive, to Freud, is "just that element which makes any response inadequate." A dialectical concept necessarily is subject to "vicissitudes," and if it invokes the will, we can be sure that a shadow or blocking-agent will threaten the will, that anteriority will make a stand against desire.

Yet defense, in Freud, is a far less mythological concept than the drive, and also is less dialectical. No one has ever demonstrated to us that drives even exist, but no hour of our lives goes by without reminding us painfully that the entire range of defense mechanisms can be at work unceasingly. Jacques Lacan has insisted that the four fundamental concepts of psychoanalysis are the unconscious, the compulsion to repeat, the transference, and the drive. I am not a psychoanalyst, but as an amateur speculator I would ask whether defense is not *the* most fundamental concept of psychoanalysis, and also the most empirically grounded of all Freud's path-breaking ideas? Repression is the center of Freud's vision of man, and when a revised theory of defense broke open the white light of repression into the multi-colored auras of the whole range of defenses, then Freud had perfected an instrument that even psychoanalysis scarcely has begun to exploit. The theory of defense is now essentially where Freud left it, and it seems to me startling that ego psychology should have done so little to develop what might have been its main resource. Yet it may be inevitable that so agonistic a concept as defense should make Freud's followers wary of entering upon a struggle in which the Founder is doomed always to win.

Freud's earliest notion of defense was very simple; defense was what put an idea out of the range of consciousness. But even that simple a concept is a trope, since the flight or distancing of an idea, putting it out of range, is hardly literal language (whatever *that* may be). And though this first concept of defense was intellectually simple, its figuration was very complex. A sustained meditation upon Freud's rhetoric would have to engage the highly problematic troping of flight as the prime image of repression throughout his work, a troping that he shares with Milton, whether we think of Satan exploring the abyss, Eve's dream of flight, or Milton's own stance in his invocations.

Why Freud, in 1894, chose the word *Abwehr* for this most crucial of all his concepts I do not know, but the choice was in some respects a misleading one. Freud's *Abwehr* is set against *change;* it is in the first place then a stabilizing mechanism. Defense, in war or in sport, seeks more than stability; it seeks victory, or the annihilation of change. Perhaps Freud selected the word *Abwehr* because he intuited even then, back in 1894, that the ego's pleasure in defense was both active and passive, and so an ambiguous concept of ego required a more ambiguous process than mere stabilization in its operations against internal excitations.

Defense, though it be against drive, in actuality works against representations of the drive, and these can be only fantasies, memories, signals, unless a particular situation is interpreted by the ego as fantasy or signal. But defense is so contaminated by drive that defense also becomes fantasy or signal. I merely state the clinical evidence that everyone encounters every day, but this leads to the particular difficulty or inadequacy of Freud's concepts of defense, both early and late. Defense is unique among all central Freudian formulations in that its weaknesses are entirely theoretical, and not at all practical or empirical. Why is there psychic defense anyway? Why should an urge arising from the drive cause unpleasure to any ego whatsoever? I do not believe that Freud ever found a single clear answer to these questions. Later I will suggest that this failing is what compelled Freud to his mythological speculations in *Beyond the Pleasure Principle*.

Defense, for poets, always has been trope, and always has been directed against prior tropes. Drive, for poets, is the urge for immortality, and can be called the largest of all poetic tropes, since it makes even of death, literal death, our death, a figuration rather than a reality. But here I return to the problematic of the poetic will, in order to explore that analogue of the mutual contamination of drive and defense in the Freudian vision.

Following Nietzsche, I have suggested that the poetic will is an argument against time, revengefully seeking to substitute "It is" for "It was." Yet this argument always splits in two, because the poetic will needs to make another outrageous substitution, of "I am" for "It is." Both parts of the argument are quests for priority, and Freud takes his place in a tradition·that goes from Vico to Emerson and Nietzsche whenever the founder of psychoanalysis speculates upon priority, which is so frequent an undersong throughout his writings.

The *psyche*, the image or trope of the self, has an invariable priority, for Freud, over reality or the object-world. Rieff expresses this rhetorical priority of mind over reality in Freud by returning us to the most fundamental of Western synecdoches, man as microcosm and the cosmos as macrocosm: "The self was no alien from the natural world; we were conscious of being not only subjects but objects of nature among other natural objects." The dominant influence upon Freud, here as elsewhere, as noted by so many exegetes from Rank to Rieff, is certainly Schopenhauer, a presence difficult to evade in Freud's Vienna.

Schopenhauer's account of repression emphasized only the derangements of memory, but in his theory of the Sublime the philosopher more authentically can be judged Freud's precursor. If we substitute for Schopenhauer's conscious turning-away Freud's unconsciously purposeful forgetting, then Schopenhauer's story of how the will is made poetic and Sublime becomes Freud's story of repression:

. . . But these very objects, whose significant forms invite us to a pure contemplation of them, may have a hostile relation to the human will in general, as manifested in its objectivity, the human body. They may be opposed to it; they may threaten it by their might that eliminates all resistance, or their immeasurable greatness may reduce it to nought. Nevertheless, the beholder may not direct his attention to this relation to his will which is so pressing and hostile, but, although he perceives and acknowledges it, he may consciously turn away from it, forcibly tear himself from his will and its relations, and, giving himself entirely up to knowledge, may quietly contemplate, as pure, will-less subject of knowing, those very objects so terrible to the will . . . he is then filled with the feeling of the *sublime.* . . .

Repression, like the movement to the Sublime, is a turning operation, away from the drive and towards the heaping up of the unconscious. Pragmatically repression, like Schopenhauer's Sublime, exalts mind over reality, over the hostile object-world, though in Freud's valorization this exaltation is highly dialectical. The unconscious mind is rhetorically an oxymoron, and the augmentation of the unconscious, though it cuts away much of the domain of the object-world, is covertly a parody version of Schopenhauer's contemplation.

I have been following a circuitous path to a declaration that the poetic will, or urge to the Sublime, is just as mythological an entity, no more and no less, as libido or the death-drive. The chiasmus that Laplanche isolates as the rhetorical figure for the relation of Eros to Thanatos appears again in the relation of trope to the poetic will. Freud's concepts of defense are themselves drives, and his difficult notion of the drive itself is a defense. Against what? Lacan, in his lecture *The Deconstruction of the Drive*, calls the drive a fundamental fiction, in Bentham's sense of a "fiction," and so Lacan is able to speak of a constant force, beyond biology: "it has no day or night, no spring or autumn, no rise and fall." Lacan even speaks of the drive as *montage*, meaning that every drive must be partial, and also that the scopic drive becomes the true model for understanding. As Lacan says, in one of his superb breakthroughs: "What one looks at is what cannot be seen." Drive is ambiguous, a synecdoche for that aspect of every ego "who, alternately, reveals himself and conceals himself by means of the pulsation of the unconscious." Whatever Lacan intends here, I read him as interpreting the Freudian synecdoche as being at once the partial drive and its defensive vicissitudes. Drive therefore defends against its own incompleteness, its own need to look at what cannot be seen.

But perhaps what Freud always defended against, until *Beyond the Pleasure Principle*, was the possibility that a monistic vision of human aggression would crowd out the dualistic vision of human sexuality. If this speculation were wholly correct, then the mythology of drives was a perpetual defense against a Nietzschean nihilism, against seeing the will to power as the true center of mankind. It seems clear today that the full range of defenses elaborated by Anna Freud are perfectly coherent entities in the context of aggression, without any necessary recourse to sexual neuroses. As I read the great epilogue-essay *Analysis Terminable and Interminable*, it is Freud's belated valorization of the castration complex, a final attempt to give the theory of sexuality equal privilege with the theory of aggressivity's valorization of the death-drive.

Freud, in my judgment, wrote two texts which truly are High Romantic crisis-poems, *On Narcissism: An Introduction* and *Beyond the Pleasure Principle*. I am going to give a full reading here only to the latter, strictly following the paradigm of the crisis-lyric as I have developed it in some previous books. But to account for the full range of psychic tropes or verbal defenses in *Beyond the Pleasure Principle*, and to illustrate further the mutual contamination of the concepts of drive and defense in Freud, I turn first to the essay, really the prose rhapsody, on narcissism. Though I will dissent implicitly from much that Laplanche says, my reading of this essay is indebted to the fourth chapter of *Life and Death in Psychoanalysis*. The binary rhetoric of Lacan and Laplanche, with its reductive reliance upon Jakobson's metaphor/metonymy pseudo-dialectic, accounts for my principal unhappiness with the "French reading" of Freud, but that is an argument to be conducted else-where.

The concept of narcissism, as we ought never to forget, was the actual engine of change in Freud's theory. In the crisis-year of 1914, Freud's theory at first seemed complete, but the vehement burst of inspiration in Rome, during "seventeen delicious days" with Minna Bernays, changed all that. If Minna was the Muse, the Sublime antagonist was the treacherous Gentile son, Jung, whose appropriation of Freud's earlier version of the ego helped provoke a severe *clinamen* away from that ego. The earlier ego was a kind of Virgilian *logos*, dependent upon repression of the drive, upon the tropological flight of images, memories, thoughts permeated by the ambivalences of drive. This ego is still vulnerable to the devastating critique of J. H. Van den Berg that "the theory of repression . . . is closely related to the thesis that there is sense in everything, which in turn implies that everything is past and there is nothing new. . . ." Van den Berg might well be criticizing Virgil, but not Ovid; and I would venture that the later Freudian ego, the narcissistic ego, is an Ovidian image. The simplistic conflict of drives—ego drives against sexual drives—is over, because the narcissistic ego is not at all an agent directing itself against a sexual drive, an Aeneas defending himself from a Dido of Carthage. From the ambiguous cosmos of the drive we have moved to an Ovidian flowing world of desire and wish, a cosmos where a more radical dualism lurks, the cosmos of Eros and Thanatos, as it will prove to be.

It is always worth recalling that Freud initially followed Ovid, in 1910, when he used the term "narcissism" for the first time, to refer to homosexuals taking themselves as their own sexual object. In the wavering interplay between the ego-libido of self-preservation and object-love, Freud found a more powerful trope for his earlier balancings of the drive as taking place between mind and reality. Captivated by its own bodily image, the Ovidian ego confines libido within the flood-gates of the psychic microcosm, a confinement that allowed Lacan his prime heresy of the mirror-stage.

After 1920, with his second theory of the psyche, Freud was to espouse a more primal heresy, almost a Gnosis, in the absolute dualism that set against all object relations a primary narcissism, a true First Idea, glorying in priority, and solipsistically free of objects, as in Schopenhauer's Sublime. There is no distinction between id and ego, precursor and Ovidian poet, in the curiously sleep-like vision of primary narcissism. The Stevensian image of a child asleep in its own life is precisely applicable to Freud at this single moment. As in Whitman's *Song of Myself*, the distinction between autoeroticism and narcissism wavers and those two states of the psyche uneasily merge.

Lacan and Laplanche, in their different but complementary ways, have shown that Freud placed his concept of libido in a more coherent context after 1914 by hinting that psychic energy truly derives from the "narcissistic passion," and also that the essay on narcissism was able to tie together the two previously disjunctive notions of psychic topography and the theory of drives. Laplanche brilliantly reads the essay's dialectic as: narcissism is a love of the self; narcissism is a love of the ego; this investment of self-love actually *constitutes* the otherwise elusive ego.

At the least, Lacan and Laplanche help explain why the breakthrough of the narcissism essay led Freud on to the writing of *Beyond the Pleasure Principle*. The dialectics of aggression, so long evaded by Freud, follow the realization that narcissistic self-esteem, once badly wounded, must *defend* itself by aggression. Aggression rising up as a defense against the narcissistic scar that everyone suffers during infancy is still the most persuasive account we have for why human aggressivity develops so early. With this link between the theory of narcissism and the aggressive drive firmly kept in mind, I turn now to a full reading of *Beyond the Pleasure Principle*. A revisionary text like *Beyond* should be susceptible to an analysis on the scheme of my "revisionary ratios," if they are to be of any general use in reading difficult works that turn upon issues of crisis and catastrophe.

Beyond the Pleasure Principle is divided into seven chapters of which the last is very brief, and clearly serves as a coda. I will interpret the book here as a dialectical lyric, indeed as a post-Romantic crisis lyric. Such an interpretation must be willing to risk outrageousness. Jacques Derrida warns against any premature classification of *Beyond* as a literary text, but I intend to experiment with such a premature reading anyway. A text self-revisionist to this degree is almost definitive of one central stigma of the literary.

Freud's darkest precursor in *Beyond the Pleasure Principle* is necessarily himself, but Chapter I performs a double *clinamen*, an ironic swerve away both from the pre-1919 Freud and from the visions of Schopenhauer and Nietzsche. What looks like self-contradiction in Chapter I is an irony or allegory, in which Freud says one thing and means another. What he says is that the pleasure principle has priority over the principle of constancy. What he means is that the psychoanalyst need not base his speculations upon the empirical groundings of late-nineteenth-century biology and physics.

The concept of the pleasure principle never changed in Freud, but its hierarchical status in regard to other principles was always unstable. Evidently this resulted from the economic nature of the pleasure principle, which is defined dualistically as a drive that seeks to attain a reduction in the quantity of excitation, while fleeing any increase in such excitation. The reductive quest and the repressive flight are not tropes easily assimilated to one another. Something of a similar rhetorical difficulty appears in the images that define the principle of constancy. The psyche is described as maintaining the quantity of excitation in itself at as low and constant a level as can be achieved. But this level is reached by strikingly mixed images: excessive energy must be discharged, while any further augmentation of excitement must be evaded. If it cannot be evaded, then it must be repressed. Thus both principles —pleasure and constancy—require descriptions antithetical *in themselves but not to one another*. The rhetorical pattern of the two principles is much the same, which may be why Freud begins

Beyond with the apparently self-contradictory notion that the constancy principle "is only another way of stating the pleasure principle." But Freud's own dominant trope here is an irony. Only the repressive element in the two principles verges upon an identity. The active element in the pleasure principle is a reductive nay-saying to every stimulus, but in the constancy principle it is an eruption, a volcanic release. By assigning priority to the negative, Freud prepares for his second topology, his final mapping of the mind. I suggest now that a defensive operation, a reaction-formation, is at work in Freud in this revisionary preparation, which culminates in *The Ego and the Id* (1923) and in *Inhibitions, Symptoms, and Anxiety* (1926). Anna Freud remarks that "reaction-formation secures the ego against the return of repressed impulses from within," and the repressed impulse here is nothing less than Freud's own scientism. I crave the indulgence here of quoting my own *A Map of Misreading:*

> . . . dialectical images of presence and absence, when manifested in a poem rather than a person, convey a saving atmosphere of freshness, however intense or bewildering the loss of meaning.

I would apply this to *Beyond the Pleasure Principle*'s first chapter by saying that its dialectical image of presence is the pleasure principle, and of absence the constancy principle. In order to break with his first topology, Freud will bewilder us by reorienting his dualisms. Against his own drive for scientific authority, he now swerves into a purely speculative authority. Against the dualism of Schopenhauer, which set up the Will or thing-in-itself in opposition to the objective world, the world as representation, Freud now opts for a more drastic dualism, or at least what he must have regarded as the most thoroughgoing of dualisms. Beyond the pleasure principle lies not the world as representation, but what Milton had called the universe of death.

Between the first two chapters of *Beyond*, Freud negotiates what I have called a Crossing of Election, a disjunctive awareness of his own revisionary crisis as founder of psychoanalysis. The crisis-question is not: "Am I still a psychoanalyst when I am at my most speculative?" but rather, "Is not psychoanalysis the only true mode of speculation?" To this question, the text of *Beyond* will render a triumphant and affirmative answer, whether or not the reader is prepared to yield to its authority. But this answer is deferred, and Chapter II instances a new defensive strategy, Freud's own playing-out of the vicissitudes of reversal and of turning against one's own self.

Not only is there a disjunctive gap between Chapters I and II, but Chapter II is highly disjunctive in itself. Its two subjects—traumatic neurosis and children's play—are not only antithetical in regard to one another, but Freud emphasizes their overt disjunction by his extremely abrupt and arbitrary transition between them. Their true connection is rhetorical, by way of Freud's highly characteristic synecdoche of neurosis as mutilated part, and psychic health as macrocosmic unity. Rieff has priority in having described this accurately as Freud's master trope. A neurotic's dreams are seen as belated efforts to master trauma *after* the shock has been inflicted. With the keenest element in his genius, which can be called nothing but uncanny, Freud intuits that the crux here is repetition, and in an addition to the text of *Beyond*, made in 1921, he hints that masochism informs this repetition. Suddenly we are given the narrative concerning Freud's infant grandson, with his ingenious game of the "*fort-da.*" Whereas the neurotic repeated his trauma in nightmare, the healthy baby repeated a distressing experience as a game. Rhetorically, by synecdoche, traumatic nightmare is a failed game, because it lacks the joyful restitution of a "*da.*" But Freud does not make the rhetorical interpretation. Games *and* art, he says, are not his concern. In the higher speculation that is psychoanalysis, the quarry must be "the operation of tendencies *beyond* the pleasure principle, that is, of tendencies more primitive than it and independent of it."

In my reading, Chapter II is a *tessera*, an antithetical completion that fails to complete, and that leaves Freud exposed to the literary equivalent of the vicissitudes of drive, that is, to a certain cognitive and imagistic reversal that is self-wounding. The repetition-compulsion is itself a synecdoche for the wounded condition of Freud's earlier hypotheses when he confronts them in the postwar atmosphere of 1919. He had been repeating only a part of psychoanalysis, he now believes, under the delusion that he has mastered the whole of it. Tacitly, and perhaps unknowingly, his text lets us understand that his own earlier synecdoches were incomplete.

With Chapter III we have what I would call Freud's *kenosis*, an emptying-out of his prior stance (pre-1919) which manifests the one repetitive defense to which he was subject: isolation. Too strong a psyche to suffer regression or undoing, he nevertheless shares with the strongest poets the metonymic defense that burns away context. Isolation separates thoughts from all other thoughts, usually by destroying or injuring temporality. Even as we see Stevens, in *The Auroras of Autumn*, defend his poetic self by an undoing metonymic movement, so in Chapter III we can observe Freud defending his psychoanalytic strength by isolating too rigorously a crucial element in his *praxis*: the transference. What is emptied out of its earlier, hoped-for fullness in Chapter III is precisely an idealized transference, and the first product of this *kenosis* is what Freud grimly calls a "fresh, 'transference neurosis.'" Something intense, which I surmise is his isolating compulsion to repeat, fixates Freud to the frustrating difficulties of transference throughout Chapter III. What ought to have been an exposition of repetition itself becomes an eloquent lament that repeats the noble sorrows of the analyst as he struggles on against the transference neurosis.

The frightening trope of the "narcissistic scar" conveys overtly the infant's first failure in sexual love. Does it covertly carry some sense of Freud's more exalted wound of triumph in his agon with all prior speculations, his own included? The "daemonic" power that psychoanalysis reduces as repetition-compulsion is cited by Freud as being present in what he calls the lives of normal people. Is he, Freud, the first listed of those "whose human relationships have the same outcome"? Whose career is it that is summed up in "the benefactor who is abandoned in anger after a time by each of his *protégés*, however much they may otherwise differ from one another, and who thus seems doomed to taste all the bitterness of ingratitude"?

It would seem then that it is the reign of the pleasure principle "over the course of the processes of excitation in mental life" that is truly emptied out in Chapter III. In Chapter 4 I interpreted Freud's use of Tasso here as an allegory of the founder's Sublime wounding of his fundamental concept of the drive. But nearly every paragraph in Chapter III voids something that Freud earlier had posited. Very much in the mode of the Sublime poet, Freud comes up to what I have called a Crossing of Solipsism in the gap between the end of Chapter III and the start of Chapter IV. The question becomes not the poetic one of the possibility of love for others, but the psychoanalytic one of affective investment (cathexis) in Freud's earlier self and its conceptualizations. Enormous strength flows in again with the *daemonizations* of Chapter IV, as Freud begins to open himself more fully to his own darkest and most powerful speculations.

Yet this is a strength of Freud's own repression, of his flight from vexing memories, indeed even from memories of Chapter I of the very book he is writing! Chapter IV is an indeliberate exercise in the Grotesque, with much of its rhetoric a curious litotes, and with its argument colored by images of depth. Freud represses his new freedom from scientism, and the repression allows a certain bathos its moment in the text:

> Let us picture a living organism in its most simplified possible form as an undifferentiated vesicle of a substance that is susceptible to stimulation. . . . This little fragment of living substance is suspended in the middle of an external world charged with the most powerful energies; and it would be killed by the stimulation emanating from these if it were not provided with a protective shield against stimuli. . . . *Protection against* stimuli is an almost more important function for the living organism than *reception of* stimuli. . . .

Supposedly owing this model to embryology, Freud actually owes it to his own defense against biologism, the biologism that consciously he embraced and never could bear to disavow. This grotesque organism is a kind of time-machine, because its "protective shield" precisely does the work of Nietzsche's revengeful will, substituting a temporality that does not destroy for one that would, if mortal time were not warded off. The repressed movement from scientism to speculation here achieves a curious triumph, and allows Freud to revise fully his views of dreams that occur in traumatic neuroses, or dreams recalling childhood traumas that rise during the course of a psychoanalysis. Here are the accents of rhetorical triumph as Freud acquires a new, more Sublime confidence in the fusion of his speculative powers and psychic realities:

> If there is a "beyond the pleasure principle" it is only consistent to grant that there was also a time before the purpose of dreams was the fulfillment of wishes. This would imply no denial of their later function. But if once this general rule has been broken, a further question arises. May not dreams which, with a view to the psychical binding of traumatic impressions, obey the compulsion to repeat—may not such dreams occur *outside* analysis as well? And the reply can only be a decided affirmative.

What fascinates me here is Freud's astonishing rhetorical authority. In response to so scrupulous, so knowing, so rational a voice, even the wariest reader must yield, though the reader yields only to the author's revisions and reversals of earlier formulations. It is fitting that Chapter V, which follows, should be a sublimation or *askesis* of the crucial and invariably problematic theory of the drives. *How*, Freud asks, is the predicate of being *Triebhaft* related to repetition-compulsion? The answer is a definition of drive that sublimates Freud's earlier account of drive, metaphorically substituting "drive" for the defenses of repetition: undoing, isolating, regressing:

> At this point we cannot escape a suspicion that we may have come upon the track of a universal attribute of drives and per-

haps of organic life in general which has not hitherto been clearly recognized. *It seems then, that a drive is an urge inherent in organic life to restore an earlier state of things* which the living entity has been obliged to abandon under the pressure of external disturbing forces. . . .

Where once we encountered a drive only by embodying defenses against it, now we experience a drive as a regressive defense. But against what? Against life itself would seem to be the answer, or at least against animation. Drives are *détours*, in Freud's new metaphor, "circuitous paths to death." They are not instances of self-destructiveness, which has been the influential but weak misreading popularized by Norman O. Brown. Rather, they remain dialectical and mythological entities which cannot be reduced to clinical examples. In some sense, the "paths to death" prelude Freud's own Crossing of Identification, his willingness to confront death, his own death. Certainly he wished to die and did die only in his own fashion; he followed his own path to death, but only after two more decades of productive life. The disjunctive gap between Chapters V and VI can be seen better if we omit the last, brief paragraph of V, which was added in 1923. We would pass then directly from a long final paragraph in V that bitterly rejects the notion that there is a drive towards perfection in human beings, to an almost equally long opening paragraph in VI that actually asserts a desire to be wrong about an "opposition between the ego or death instincts and the sexual or life instincts." If the hidden burden at the end of V is Freud's own, rare drive towards perfection of the work, then the equally hidden burden at the start of VI is Freud's anxiety that his own final formulations make any drive towards perfection of the life impossible. But *that* is Freud's Crossing, to choose perfection of the work, and so he moves on in Chapter VI to project or cast out a specious immortality and to introject the sublime Necessity of dying. This makes of VI that final movement I have named by the ratio of *apophrades*, which in rhetoric is the mode of transumption, and in poetry is manifested through images of earliness and lateness. Freud's own belatedness is elegantly shrugged off with the remark, "We have unwittingly steered our course into the harbor of Schopenhauer's philosophy." But Freud's more crucial earliness, his originality which transcends that of any other modern speculator, is masterfully traced in an extraordinary narrative history of the theory of the drives. In this history, as I remarked in Chapter 4, the monistic libido theory of Jung is accurately dismissed as literalistic reductiveness, and Freud's own thoroughgoing dualism is rightly appraised as a figuration that allows him to anticipate future theory, even in the absence of clinical evidence:

> . . . I do not dispute the fact that the third step in the theory of the drives, which I have taken here, cannot lay claim to the same degree of certainty as the two earlier ones—the extension of the concept of sexuality and the hypothesis of narcissism.

As Freud remarks, his own observational evidence for his speculative third step is repetition-compulsion, and there is a prodigious leap from that to the death-drive. But even physiological or chemical language is figurative, as he goes on to remind us; and how then should depth psychology presume to a language other than trope? The brief and beautiful coda that is Chapter VII extends the transumption, and gives us the hidden Freudian metalepsis that I summarized in Chapter 4 in this formula: literal meaning equals anteriority equals an earlier state of meaning equals an earlier state of things equals death. Literal meaning, by a metaleptic leap, is therefore death, while figurative meaning is Eros. Reverse this Freudian formula, and you have part of the context in which the poetic will must operate. Death, time's "it was," is literal meaning; Eros or figuration becomes the will's revenge against time.

How shall we sum up the revisionary pattern of *Beyond the Pleasure Principle*, its own individual troping of the tradition of crisis-lyric and catastrophe creation? Laplanche eloquently sees the text as granting fantasy an absolute priority, since it mythologizes "a kind of antilife as sexuality, frenetic enjoyment, the negative, repetition-compulsion." But Laplanche need not have been startled, nor should he expect us to be surprised. Rieff long ago pointed out that the idea of the Primal Scene also grants the priority to fantasy, and we can add that primal repression or originary fixation must have a fantasy basis also, since it posits repression *before there is anything to be repressed.* The peculiar achievement and textual originality of *Beyond,* among Freud's works, must be found elsewhere.

The originality, still unsettling, remains Freud's initial *clinamen* or irony in *Beyond,* which is that the principle of constancy, like the pleasure principle, is transcended by a Schopenhauerian drive to Nirvana. This is Freud's actual "beyonding," as it were, and though it is outrageously speculative, it is *not* in the fantasy mode of the various primal formulations. Catastrophe is alas not a fantasy, but is the macrocosmic synecdoche of which masochism and sadism form microcosmic parts. It is not self-destruction that energizes the death-drive, but rather the turning of aggression against the self. Freud's astonishing originality is that in *Beyond* he sees catastrophe as being itself a defense, and I would add that catastrophe creation is thus a defense also. To answer again the question: defense against what? is to return to everything problematic about the poetic will, with its own mutual contaminations of drive and defense.

From a normative Jewish or Christian point of view, catastrophe is allied to the Abyss, and creation is associated with an order imposed upon the Abyss. But from a Gnostic perspective, catastrophe is true creation because it restores the Abyss, while any order that steals its materials from the Abyss is only a sickening to a false creation. Freud's materialistic perspective is obviously neither that of normative theism nor of Gnosis, yet his catastrophe-theories unknowingly border upon Gnosis. For what is the origin of Freud's two final drives, Eros and Thanatos, if it is not catastrophe? Why should there be urges innate in us to restore an earlier condition, unless somehow we had fallen or broken away out of or from that

condition? The urges or drives act as our defenses against our belated condition, but these defenses are gains (however equivocal)
through change, whereas defenses proper, against the drives, are
losses through change, or we might speak of losses that fear further
change. Change is the key term, and every cosmic origin of change
is seen by Freud as having been catastrophe.

The origin of defense proper, for Freud, is primal fixation, almost an initial catastrophic origin of drives. Can we account for
this very curious speculative principle in Freud, in which there is
flight from the drive before the drive has been instituted? The pattern is: defense, followed by catastrophe, followed by drive, or as
I would trope this triad: limitation, or contraction, followed by
substitution, followed by representation or restitution. I do not for
a moment believe that Freud was following, even unconsciously, a
Gnostic or Kabbalistic paradigm, but I certainly do believe that he
was following, perhaps unconsciously, a similar metaphysical model
from Schopenhauer.

Granting that I merely seem to be playing with figurations, permit me to extend the play for a space. What might it mean to say
that defense is a movement of limitation or withdrawal, and that
the drive is a contrary movement of representation or restitution?
Since I have shown defense and drive as contaminating one another anyway, the distinction of contraries here could only be
relative. Thus, one could speak of Thanatos as a limiting drive and
Eros as a restituting one, but the chiasmic linkage of the two
drives (as Laplanche maps it) also brings about a crossing-over
of their functions. Again, one could say that reaction-formation, the
repetition-compulsions and sublimation are defenses or tropes of
limitation, while turning against the self, repression and the negation that mingles projection and introjection are more nearly defenses of restitution. It is suggestive that Thanatos as a drive thus
would be more closely allied to reaction-formations, compulsions
to repeat, and the "cultural" defense of sublimation, whereas sado-
masochism, repression and introjection become the fantasies of
Eros, the losses engendered by its drive.

Freud, during a few weeks in July and August of 1938, wrote his unfinished *An Outline of Psychoanalysis*. The little book is difficult and rewarding, and has the peculiar authority of being Freud's last writing of any length. Perhaps because of the aggressive stance signaled by Freud's Introductory Note, the dualism of the drives is stated with a singular and positive harshness. Both drives are called conservative, indeed almost regressive forces, and deeply contaminate one another, as when Freud bluntly remarks that "the sexual act is an act of aggression having as its purpose the most intimate union." The darkness of this final vision of the drives emerges most clearly when both self-destructiveness or the death-drive and libido or Eros become outriders on our way to oblivion, allegorical and ironic guides to the last things:

> Some portion of self-destructiveness remains permanently within, until it at length succeeds in doing the individual to death, not, perhaps, until his libido has been used up or has become fixated in some disadvantageous way. . . .

What begins to be clear is that the drives and the defenses are modeled upon poetic rhetoric, whether or not one believes that the unconscious somehow is structured like a language. Eros or libido *is* figurative meaning: the death-drive *is* literal meaning. The defenses *are* tropes, and thus constitute the contaminating aspects of both Eros and the death-drive. Eros and Thanatos take the shape of a chiasmus, but this is because the relation between figurative and literal meaning in language is always a crossing-over.

It is a curious truth that figurative meaning or Eros is "more conspicuous and accessible to study" than literal meaning or the death-drive. If my analogue holds at all, then sadism and masochism are over-literalizations of meaning, failures in Eros and so in the possibilities of figurative language. Or perhaps we might speak of a "regression of libido," a fall into metonymizing, as being due to a loss of faith in the mind's capacity to accept the burden of figuration. Sexual "union" is after all nothing but figurative, since the joining involved is merely a yoking in act and not in essence.

The act, in what we want to call normal sexuality, is a figuration for the unattainable essence. Sado-masochism, as a furious literalism, denies the figurative representation of essence by act.

Freud concluded "that the death drives are by their nature mute and that the clamour of life proceeds for the most part from Eros." Can we interpret this as meaning that wounded narcissism becomes physical aggression because the loss of self-esteem is also a loss in the language of Eros? Wounded narcissism is at the origins of poetry also, but in poetry the blow to self-esteem strengthens the language of Eros, which defends the poetic will through all the resources of troping. Lacking poetry, the sado-masochist yields to the literalism of the death-drive precisely out of a rage against literal meaning. When figuration and sado-masochism are identified, as in Swinburne or Robinson Jeffers, then we find always the obsession with poetic *belatedness* risen to a terrible intensity that plays out the poetic will's revenge against time by the unhappy substitution of the body, another's body or one's own, *for* time. Raging against time, forgetting that only Eros or figuration is a true revenge against time, the sado-masochist over-literalizes his revenge and so yields to the death-drive.

In my reading of *Beyond's* Chapter V as Freud's *askesis*, his own sublimation, I implicitly questioned the coherence of the defense of sublimation even as I centered upon the hidden metaphor of contamination. I return to that metaphor for my conclusion. When drive is viewed as defense, then drive becomes trope or myth, cosmological rhetoric rather than biological instinct. Yet Freud had not waited until 1919, or even until *On Narcissism* in 1915, to reveal this mutual contamination of drive and defense. At least as early as the essay *Taboo and Emotional Ambivalence* in 1912, which was to become the second chapter of *Totem and Taboo*, he had recognized that his fundamental concepts necessarily had contaminated one another by what he called a "mutual inhibition":

> As a result of the repression which has been enforced and which involves a loss of memory—an amnesia—the motives for the prohibition (which is conscious) remain unknown; and all

attempts at disposing of it by intellectual processes must fail, since they cannot find any basis of attack. The prohibition owes its strength and its obsessive character precisely to its unconscious opponent, the concealed and undiminished desire—that is to say, to an internal necessity inaccessible to conscious inspection. The ease with which the prohibition can be transferred and extended reflects a process which falls in with the unconscious desire and is greatly facilitated by the psychological conditions that prevail in the unconscious. The instinctual desire is constantly shifting in order to escape from the *impasse* and endeavors to find substitutes—substitute objects and substitute acts—in place of the prohibited ones. In consequence of this, the prohibition itself shifts about as well, and extends to any new aims which the forbidden impulse may adopt. Any fresh advance made by the repressed libido is answered by a fresh sharpening of the prohibition. The mutual inhibition of the two conflicting forces produces a need for discharge, for reducing the prevailing tension; and to this may be attributed the reason for the performance of obsessive acts. . . .

Here the defense of repression and the drive of Eros are so deeply interlocked as to produce taboo, which is the masterpiece of emotional ambivalence, and is the foundation of all literary allegory or irony. Angus Fletcher, in his seminal study of allegory, relates the poetic will's quest to overcome taboo to the trope of transumption, which I have shown to be the ancient rhetorical equivalent of Freud's *Verneinung*, that negation which mingles the defenses of projection and introjection. I shall conclude here by comparing the introjective aspect of the Freudian negation to its parallel in the poet's transumptive will.

Freudian negation and poetic transumption both are instances of psychical duplicity, and both ultimately depend upon a metaphysical dualism. The Freudian *Verneinung* involves the formulation of a previously repressed feeling, desire or thought, which returns into consciousness only by being affectively disowned, so that defense continues. To carry the truth into the light while still denying it means that one introjects the truth cognitively, while projecting it emotionally. Few insights, even in Freud, are so profound as this vision of negation, for no other theoretical statement at once succeeds as well in tracing the epistemological faculty convincingly to so primitive an origin, or accounts nearly so well for the path by which thought sometimes can be liberated from its sexual past. Since the ego is always a bodily ego, the defenses of swallowing-up and spitting-out, though fantasies, still acknowledge cognitively the ultimate authority of the fact.

I want to contrast to Freud's negation the equivalent process in Vico, for Vico is the great precursor theoretician of the poetic will and of its revisionary ratio that I have called transumption (following Fletcher). What Freud calls the drives, Vico calls "ignorance" or "not understanding the things." Here is Vico on the mingled process of projection and introjection, an ambivalence which for him rises out of the bodily ego, out of a situation in which the ego is ignorant of origins and of the relation between cause and effect:

> . . . man in his ignorance makes himself the rule of the universe, for in the examples cited he has made of himself an entire world. So that, as rational metaphysics teaches that man becomes all things by understanding them, this imaginative metaphysics shows that man becomes all things by *not* understanding them; and perhaps the latter proposition is truer than the former, for when man understands he extends his mind and takes in the things, but when he does not understand he makes the things out of himself and becomes them by transforming himself into them. . . .

Extending the ego to take in the things is not introjection but projection, while the imaginative metaphysics of negation, making "the things out of himself," is a mode of identification, just as introjection is. Not to understand is to suffer drives, and the mind's response is the transformation of defense into a negation that provokes thought. The mutual contamination of drive and defense, of poetic will, with its interplay between literal and figurative, and trope, with its interplay of substitutes, is the common feature linking the speculations of Vico and Freud.

Wallace Stevens, in the closing cantos of his superb crisis-poem *The Auroras of Autumn*, provides me with a coda to my investigation of Freud's own poetic will, which took its revenge against time precisely by contaminating the concepts of defense and of the drive. The trope of transumption, as I have expounded it elsewhere, is the ultimate poetic resource in the will's revenge against time, because transumption undoes the poet's belatedness, the Freudian *Nachträglichkeit*. Stevens, having suffered the anxieties of death-in-life when he first confronted the beautiful menace of the aurora borealis, transumes the northern lights and returns to a vision of earliness, to a Nietzschean and Whitmanian trope of earth's innocence which is *not* a regression, but a true Freudian negation:

> So, then, these lights are not a spell of light,
> A saying out of a cloud, but innocence.
> An innocence of the earth and no false sign
>
> Or symbol of malice. That we partake thereof,
> Lie down like children in this holiness,
> As if, awake, we lay in the quiet of sleep,
>
> As if the innocent mother sang in the dark. . . .

Stevens projects what Freud would have called the drive of Eros figurated by the auroras, its serpentine malice, and simultaneously introjects its literal autumnal aspect, the death-drive, final form of serpentine change. The effect is precisely that of Chapters VI and VII of *Beyond the Pleasure Principle*. A final sublimity is achieved, and though literal death is accepted, the figurative promise of a poetic immortality returns, even as the figurative appears to be cast out. That Freud, more passionately even than the poets, shared in this figurative promise we know from many passages in his works, but never more revealingly than from some belated remarks that he added to an interleaved copy of the 1904 edition of *The Psychopathology of Everyday Life*:

> Rage, anger, and consequently a murderous impulse is the source of superstition in obsessional neurotics: a sadistic com-

ponent, which is attached to love and is therefore directed against the loved person and repressed precisely because of this link and because of its intensity.—My own superstition has its roots in suppressed ambition (immortality) and in my case takes the place of that anxiety about death which springs from the normal uncertainty of life. . . .

Against the literalism and repetition of the death-drive, Freud sets, so early on, the high figuration of his poetic will to an immortality. Perhaps that may seem some day the truest definition of the Freudian Eros: the will's revenge against time's "it was" is to be carried out by the mind's drive to surpass all earlier achievements. Only the strongest of the poets, and Sigmund Freud, are capable of so luminous a vision of Eros.

6

Emerson:
The American Religion

I start from a warning of Lichtenberg's:

> As soon as a man begins to see everything, he generally ex-
> presses himself obscurely—begins to speak with the tongues of
> angels.

But Lichtenberg also wrote, "The itch of a great prince gave us
long sleeves." The lengthened shadow of our American culture is
Emerson's, and Emerson indeed saw everything in everything, and
spoke with the tongue of a daemon. His truest achievement was to
invent the American religion, and my reverie intends a spiraling out
from his center in order to track the circumferences of that religion
in a broad selection of those who emanated out from him, directly
and evasively, celebratory of or in negation to his Gnosis. Starting
from Emerson we came to where we are, and from that impasse,
which he prophesied, we will go by a path that most likely he
marked out also. The mind of Emerson is the mind of America,
for worse and for glory, and the central concern of that mind was
the American religion, which most memorably was named "self-
reliance."

Of this religion, I begin by noting that it is *self*-reliance as opposed to God-reliance, though Emerson thought the two were the
same. I will emphasize this proper interpretation by calling the

doctrine "*self*-reliance," in distinction from Emerson's essay *Self-Reliance*. "Reliance" is not of the essence, but the Emersonian *self* is: "To talk of reliance is a poor external way of speaking. Speak rather of that which relies because it works and is." What "works and is" is the stranger god, or even alien god, within. Within? Deeper than the *psyche* is the *pneuma*, the spark, the uncreated self, distinct from the soul that God (or Demiurge) created. *Self*-reliance, in Emerson as in Meister Eckhart or in Valentinus the Gnostic, is the religion that celebrates and reveres what in the self is before the Creation, a whatness which from the perspective of religious orthodoxy can only be the primal Abyss.

In September 1866, when he was sixty-three, and burned out by his prophetic exultation during the Civil War, Emerson brooded in his Journals on the return of the primal Abyss, which he had named Necessity, and which his descendant Stevens was to hail as "fatal Ananke the common god." Earlier in 1866, pondering Hegel, Emerson had set down, with a certain irony, his awareness of the European vision of the end of speculation:

> Hegel seems to say, Look, I have sat long gazing at the all but imperceptible transitions of thought to thought, until I have seen with eyes the true boundary. . . . I know that all observation will justify me, and to the future metaphysician I say, that he may measure the power of his perception by the degree of his accord with mine. This is the twilight of the gods, predicted in the Scandinavian mythology.

A few months later, this irony at another's apocalyptic egocentricity was transcended by a post-apocalyptic or Gnostic realization:

> There may be two or three or four steps, according to the genius of each, but for every seeing soul there are two absorbing facts,—*I and the Abyss*.

This grand outflaring of negative theology is a major text, however gnomic, of *the* American religion, Emersonianism, which this book aspires to identify, to describe, to celebrate, to join. I am not happy with the accounts of Emersonianism available to me. Of the religions native to the United States, Emersonianism or *our literary religion* remains the most diffuse and diffused, yet the only faith of spiritual significance, still of prophetic force for our future. An excursus upon the religions starting in America is necessary before I quest into the wavering interiors of the American religion proper. Sydney Ahlstrom in his definitive *A Religious History of the American People* (1972) recognizes "that Emerson is in fact the theologian of something we may almost term 'the American religion.' " Who were or could have been Emerson's rivals? Of religious geniuses our evening-land has been strangely unproductive, when our place in Western history is fully considered. We have had one great systematic theologian, in Jonathan Edwards, and something close to a second such figure in Horace Bushnell. But we have only the one seer, Emerson, and the essentially literary traditions that he fostered.

The founders of American heresies that have endured are quite plentiful, yet our major historians of American religion—Ahlstrom, W. W. Sweet, H. R. Niebuhr, M. E. Marty, S. E. Mead, C. E. Olmstead, among others—tend to agree that only a handful are of central importance. These would include Ellen Harmon White of the Seventh Day Adventists, Joseph Smith of the Mormons, Alexander Campbell of the Disciples of Christ, Mary Baker Eddy of Christian Science, and Charles Taze Russell of Jehovah's Witnesses. To read any or all of these is a difficult experience, for the founder's texts lack the power that the doctrines clearly are able to manifest. There is, thankfully, no Emersonian church, yet there are certain currents of Harmonial American religion that dubiously assert their descent from the visionary of *Nature* and the *Essays*. Aside from Mrs. Eddy, who seized on poor Bronson Alcott for an endorsement after the subtle Emerson had evaded her, the "health and harmony" Positive Thinkers notably include Ralph Waldo Trine, author of *In Tune with the Infinite* (1897), and his spiritual descendants Harry Emerson Fosdick and Norman Vincent Peale. We can add to this pseudo-Emersonian jumble the various Aquarian theosophies that continue to proliferate in America a decade after the sixties ebbed out. I cite all these sects and schisms because all of them have failed the true Emersonian test for the American religion, which I will state as my own dogma: *it cannot become the American religion until it first is canonized as American literature.* Though this explicit dogma is mine, it was the genius of Emerson implicitly to have established such a principle among us.

2

What in the nineteenth and twentieth centuries *is* religious writing? What can it be? Which of these passages, setting their polemics aside, is better described as religious writing?

> People say to me, that it is but a dream to suppose that Christianity should regain the organic power in human society which once it possessed. I cannot help that; I never said it could. I am not a politician; I am proposing no measures, but exposing a fallacy, and resisting a pretence. Let Benthamism reign, if men dare no aspirations; but do not tell them to be romantic, and then solace them with glory; do not attempt by philosophy what was once done by religion. The ascendancy of Faith may be impracticable, but the reign of Knowledge is incomprehensible. . . .

> . . . He that has done nothing has known nothing. Vain is it to sit scheming and plausibly discoursing: up and be doing! If thy knowledge be real, put it forth from thee: grapple with real Nature; try thy theories there, and see how they hold out. *Do one thing*, for the first time in thy life do a thing; a new light will rise to thee on the doing of all things whatsoever. . . .

I have taken these passages randomly enough; they lay near by. The distinguished first extract is both truly religious and wonderfully written, but the second is religious writing. Newman, in the first, from *The Tamworth Reading Room* (1841), knows both the truth and his own mind, and the relation between the two. Carlyle, in the second, from *Corn-Law Rhymes* (1832), knows only his own knowing, and sets that above both Newman's contraries, religion and philosophy. *Corn-Law Rhymes* became a precursor text for

Emerson because he could recognize what had to be religious writing for the nineteenth century, and to that recognition, which alone would not have sufficed, Emerson added the American difference, which Carlyle could not ever understand. Subtle as this difference is, another intertextual juxtaposition can help reveal it:

"But it is with man's Soul as it was with Nature: the beginning of Creation is—Light. Till the eye have vision, the whole members are in bonds. Divine moment, when over the tempest-tossed Soul, as once over the wild-weltering Chaos, it is spoken: Let there be Light! Ever to the greatest that has felt such moment, is it not miraculous and God-announcing; even as, under simpler figures, to the simplest and least. The mad primeval Discord is hushed; the rudely-jumbled conflicting elements bind themselves into separate Firmaments: deep silent rock-foundations are built beneath; and the skyey vault with its everlasting Luminaries above: instead of a dark wasteful Chaos, we have a blooming, fertile, heaven-encompassed World."

"Nature is not fixed but fluid, Spirit alters, molds, makes it. The immobility or bruteness of nature is the absence of spirit; to pure spirit it is fluid, it is volatile, it is obedient. Every spirit builds itself a house, and beyond its house a world, and beyond its world a heaven. Know then that the world exists for you. For you is the phenomenon perfect. What we are, that only can we see. . . . Build therefore your own world. As fast as you conform your life to the pure idea in your mind, that will unfold its great proportions. . . . The kingdom of man over nature, which cometh not with observation,—a dominion such as now is beyond his dream of God,—he shall enter without more wonder than the blind man feels who is gradually, restored to perfect sight."

This juxtaposition is central, because the passages are. The first rhapsode is Carlyle's Teufelsdröckh uttering his Everlasting Yea in *Sartor Resartus*; the second is Emerson's Orphic poet chanting the conclusion of *Nature*. Carlyle's seeing soul triumphs over the Abyss, until he can say to himself: "Be no longer a Chaos, but a World, or even Worldkin. Produce! Produce!" The Abyss is bondage, the production is freedom, somehow still "in God's name!" Emerson, despite his supposed discipleship to Carlyle in *Nature*, has his seeing soul proclaim a world so metamorphic and beyond natural metamorphosis that its status is radically *prior* to that of the existent universe. For the earth is only part of the blind man's "dream of God." Carlyle's imagination remains orthodox, and rejects Chaos. Emerson's seeing, beyond observation, is more theosophical than Germanic Transcendental. The freedom to imagine "the pure idea in your mind" is the heretical absolute freedom of the Gnostic who identified his mind's purest idea with the original Abyss. American freedom, in the context of Emerson's American religion, indeed might be called "Abyss-radiance."

I return to the question of what, in the nineteenth century, makes writing *religious*. Having set Carlyle in the midst, between Newman and Emerson, I cite next the step in religious writing beyond even Emerson:

> . . . we have an interval, and then our place knows us no more. Some spend this interval in listlessness, some in high passions, the wisest, at least among "the children of this world," in art and song. For our one chance lies in expanding that interval, in getting as many pulsations as possible into the given time. . . .

Pater, concluding *The Renaissance*, plays audaciously against Luke 16:8, where "the children of this world are in their generation wiser than the children of light." Literalizing the Gospel's irony, Pater insinuates that in his generation the children of this world are the only children of light. Light expands our fiction of duration, our interval or place in art, by a concealed allusion to the Blakean trope that also fascinated Yeats; the pulsation of an artery in which the poet's work is done. Pater sinuously murmurs his credo, which elsewhere in *The Renaissance* is truly intimated to be "a strange rival religion" opposed to warring orthodoxies, fit for "those who are neither for Jehovah nor for His enemies."

To name Emerson and Pater as truly "religious writers" is to call into question very nearly everything that phrase usually implies. More interestingly, this naming also questions that mode of displacement M. H. Abrams analyzes in his strong study *Natural Supernaturalism:* "not . . . the deletion and replacement of religious ideas but rather the assimilation and reinterpretation of religious ideas." I believe that the following remarks of Abrams touch their limit precisely where Carlyle and Emerson part, on the American difference, and also where Carlyle and Ruskin part from Pater and what comes after. The story Abrams tells has been questioned by Hillis Miller, from a Nietzschean linguistic or Deconstructive perspective, so that Miller dissents from Abrams exactly where Nietzsche himself chose to attack Carlyle (which I cite below). But there is a more ancient perspective to turn against Abrams's patterns-of-displacement, an argument as to whether poetry did not inform religion before religion ever instructed poetry. And beyond this argument, there is the Gnostic critique of creation-theories both Hebraic and Platonic, a critique that relies always upon the awesome trope of the primal Abyss.

Abrams states his "displacement" thesis in a rhetoric of continuity:

> Much of what distinguishes writers I call "Romantic" derives from the fact that they undertook, whatever their religious creed or lack of creed, to save traditional concepts, schemes, and values which had been based on the relation of the Creator to his creature and creation, but to reformulate them within the prevailing two-term system of subject and object, ego and non-ego, the human mind or consciousness and its transactions with nature. Despite their displacement from a supernatural to a natural frame of reference, however, the ancient problems, terminology, and ways of thinking about human nature and history survived, as the implicit distinctions and categories through which even radically secular writers saw themselves and their world. . . .

Such "displacement" is a rather benign process, as though the incarnation of the Poetic Character and the Incarnation proper could be assimilated to one another, or the former serve as the reinterpretation of the latter. But what if poetry as such is always a counter-theology, or Gentile Mythus, as Vico believed? Abrams, not unlike Matthew Arnold, reads religion as abiding in poetry, as though the poem were a saving remnant. But perhaps the saving remnant *of poetry* is the only force of what we call theology? And what can theology be except what Geoffrey Hartman anxiously terms it: "a vast, intricate domain of psychopoetic events," another litany of evasions? Poems are the original lies-against-time, as the Gnostics understood when they turned their dialectics to revisionary interpretations not only of the Bible and Plato, but of Homer as well. Gnosticism was the inaugural and most powerful of Deconstructions because it undid all genealogies, scrambled all hierarchies, allegorized every microcosm/macrocosm relation, and rejected every representation of divinity as non-referential.

Carlyle, though he gave Abrams both the scheme of displacement and the title-phrase of "natural supernaturalism," seems to me less and less self-deceived as he progressed onwards in life and work, which I think accounts for his always growing fury. Here I follow Nietzsche, in the twelfth "Skirmish" of *Twilight of the Idols* where he leaves us not much of the supposedly exemplary life of Carlyle:

> . . . this unconscious and involuntary farce, this heroic-moralistic interpretation of dyspeptic states. Carlyle: a man of strong words and attitudes, a rhetor from *need*, constantly lured by the craving for a strong faith and the feeling of his incapacity for it (in this respect, a typical romantic!). The craving for a strong faith is no proof of a strong faith, but quite the contrary. If one has such a faith, then one can afford the beautiful luxury of skepticism; one is sure enough, firm enough, has ties enough for that. Carlyle drugs something in himself with the fortissimo of his veneration of men of strong faith and with his rage against the less simple minded: he *requires* noise. A constant passionate dishonesty against himself—that is his *proprium;* in this respect he is and remains interesting. Of course, in England he is admired precisely for his honesty. Well, that is English; and in view of the fact that the English are the people of consummate cant, it is even as it should be, and not only comprehensible. At bottom, Carlyle is an English atheist who makes it a point of honor not to be one.

It seems merely just to observe, following Nietzsche's formidable wit, that Carlyle contrived to be a religious writer without being a religious man. His clear sense of the signs and characteristics of the times taught him that the authentic nineteenth-century writer had to be religious *qua* writer. The burden, as Carlyle knew, was not so much godlessness as belatedness, which compels a turn to Carlyle (and Emerson) on history.

3

Carlyle, with grim cheerfulness, tells us that history is an unreadable text, indeed a "complex manuscript, covered over with formless inextricably-entangled unknown characters,—nay, which is a Palimpsest, and had once prophetic writing, still dimly legible there. . . ." We can see emerging in this dark observation the basis for *The French Revolution*, and even for *Past and Present*. But that was Carlyle *On History* in 1830, just before the advent of Diogenes Teufelsdröckh, the author of *On History Again* in 1833, where the unreadable is read as Autobiography repressed by all Mankind: "a like unconscious talent of remembering and of forgetting again does the work here." The great instance of this hyperbolic or Sublime repression is surely Goethe, whose superb self-confidence breathes fiercely in his couplet cited by Carlyle as the first epigraph to *Sartor Resartus*:

Mein Vermächtnis, wie herrlich weit und breit!
Die Zeit ist mein Vermächtnis, mein Acker ist die Zeit.

Goethe's splendid, wide and broad inheritance is time itself, the seed-field that has the glory of having grown Goethe! But then, Goethe had no precursors in his own language, or none at least that could make him anxious. Carlyle trumpets his German inheritance: Goethe, Schiller, Fichte, Novalis, Kant, Schelling. His English inheritance was more troublesome to him, and the vehemence of his portrait of Coleridge reveals an unresolved relationship. This unacknowledged debt to Coleridge, with its too-conscious swerve away from Coleridge and into decisiveness and overt courage, pain accepted and work deified, may be the hidden basis for the paradoxes of Carlyle on time, at once resented with a Gnostic passion and worshipped as the seed-bed of a Goethean greatness made possible for the self. It is a liberation to know the American difference again when the reader turns from Carlyle's two essays on history to *History*, placed first of the *Essays* (1841) of Emerson:

> This human mind wrote history, and this must read it. The Sphinx must solve her own riddle. If the whole of history is in one man, it is all to be explained from individual experience. . . .
> . . . Property also holds of the soul, covers great spiritual facts, and instinctively we at first hold to it with swords and laws and wide and complex combinations. The obscure consciousness of this fact is the light of all our day, the claim of claims; the plea for education, for justice, for charity; the foundation of friendship and love and of the heroism and grandeur which belong to acts of self-reliance. It is remarkable that involuntarily we always read as superior beings. . . .
> . . . The student is to read history actively and not passively; to esteem his own life the text, and books the commentary. . . .

So much then for Carlyle on history; so much indeed for history. The text is not interpretable? But there is no text! There is only your own life, and the Wordsworthian light of all our day turns out to be: self-reliance. Emerson, in describing an 1847 quarrel with Carlyle in London, gave a vivid sense of his enforcing the American difference, somewhat at the expense of a friendship that was never the same again:

> Carlyle . . . had grown impatient of opposition, especially when talking of Cromwell. I differed from him . . . in his estimate of Cromwell's character, and he rose like a great Norse giant from his chair—and, drawing a line with his finger across the table, said, with terrible fierceness: "Then, sir, there is a line of separation between you and me as wide as that, and as deep as the pit."

Hardly a hyperbole, the reader will reflect, when he reads what two years later Carlyle printed as *The Nigger Question*. This remarkable performance doubtless was aimed against "Christian Philanthropy" and related hypocrisies, but the abominable greatness of the tract stems from its undeniable madness. The astonished reader discovers not fascism, but a terrible sexual hysteria rising up from poor Carlyle, as the repressed returns in the extraordinary trope of black pumpkin-eating:

> . . . far over the sea, we have a few black persons rendered extremely "free" indeed. . . . Sitting yonder with their beautiful muzzles up to the ears in pumpkins, imbibing sweet pulps and juices; the grinder and incisor teeth ready for ever new work, and the pumpkins cheap as grass in those rich climates: while the sugar-crops rot round them uncut, because labour cannot be hired, so cheap are the pumpkins. . . .
> . . . and beautiful Blacks sitting there up to the ears in pumpkins, and doleful Whites sitting here without potatoes to eat. . . .
> . . . The fortunate Black man, very swiftly does he settle *his* account with supply and demand:—not so swiftly the less fortunate white man of those tropical locations. A bad case, his, just now. He himself cannot work; and his black neighbor, rich in pumpkin, is in no haste to help him. Sunk to the ears in pumpkin, imbibing saccharine juices, and much at his ease in the Creation, he can listen to the less fortunate white man's "demand" and take his own time in supplying it. . . .
> . . . An idle White gentleman is not pleasant to me: though I confess the real work for him is not easy to find, in these our epochs; and perhaps he is seeking, poor soul, and may find at last. But what say you to an idle Black gentleman, with his rum-bottle in his hand (for a little additional pumpkin you can have red-herrings and rum, in Demerara),—rum-bottle in his hand, no breeches on his body, pumpkin at discretion. . . .
> . . . Before the West Indies could grow a pumpkin for any Negro, how much European heroism had to spend itself in obscure battle; to sink, in mortal agony, before the jungles, the putrescences and waste savageries could become arable, and the Devils be in some measure chained there!
> . . . A bit of the great Protector's own life lies there; be-

neath those pumpkins lies a bit of the life that was Oliver Cromwell's. . . .

I have cited only a few passages out of this veritable procession of pumpkins, culminating in the vision of Carlyle's greatest hero pushing up the pumpkins so that unbreeched Blacks might exercise their potent teeth. Mere racism does not yield so pungent a phantasmagoria, and indeed I cannot credit it to Carlyle's likely impotence either. This pumpkin litany is Carlyle's demi-Gnosticism at its worst, for here time is no fair seed-bed but rather devouring time, Kronos chewing us up as so many pumpkins, the time of "Getting Under Way" in *Sartor Resartus*:

> . . . Me, however, as a Son of Time, unhappier than some others, was Time threatening to eat quite prematurely; for, strike as I might, there was no good Running, so obstructed was the path, so gyved were the feet. . . .

Emerson, in truth, did not abide in his own heroic stance towards Time and History. The great declaration of his early intensity comes in the 1838 Journals: "A great man escapes out of the kingdom of time; he puts time under his feet." But the next decade featured ebb rather than influx of the Newness. What matter? The American difference, however ill prepared to combat experience, had been stated, if not established. To come to that stating is to arrive fresh at Emerson's *Nature*, where the *clinamen* from Carlyle, and from Coleridge, is superbly turned.

4

Deconstructing any discourse by Ralph Waldo Emerson would be a hopeless enterprise, extravagantly demonstrating why Continental modes of interpretation are unlikely to add any lustres to the most American of writers. Where there are classic canons of construction, protrusions from the text can tempt an unravelling, but in a text like *Nature* (1836) all is protrusion. Emerson's first book is a blandly dissociative apocalypse, in which everything is a cheerful error, indeed a misreading, starting with the title, which says "Nature" but means "Man." The original epigraph, from Plotinus by way of the Cambridge Platonist Cudworth, itself deconstructs the title:

> Nature is but an image or imitation of wisdom, the last thing of the soul; nature being a thing which doth only do, but not know.

The attentive reader, puzzling a way now through Emerson's manifesto, will find it to be more the American Romantic equivalent to Blake's *The Marriage of Heaven and Hell* than to Coleridge's *Aids to Reflection* (which however it frequently echoes). At the Christological age of thirty-three (as was Blake in the *Marriage*), Emerson rises in the spirit to proclaim his own independent majority, but unlike Blake Emerson cheerfully and confidently proclaims his nation's annunciation also. Unfortunately, Emerson's vision precedes his style, and only scattered passages in *Nature* achieve the eloquence that became incessant from about a year later on almost to the end, prevailing long after the sage had much mind remaining. I will move here through the little book's centers of vision, abandoning the rest of it to time's revenges.

Prospects, and not retrospectives, is the Emersonian motto, as we can see by contrasting the title of the last chapter, "Prospects," to the opening sentences of the Introduction:

> Our age is retrospective. It builds the sepulchres of the fathers. It writes biographies, histories, and criticism. The foregoing generations beheld God and nature face to face; we, through their eyes. Why should we not also enjoy an original relation to the universe?

The "fathers" are not British High Romantics, Boston Unitarians, New England Calvinist founders, but rather an enabling fiction, as Emerson well knows. They are Vico's giants, magic primitives, who invented all Gentile mythologies, all poetries of earth. Emerson joins them in the crucial trope of his first chapter, which remains the most notorious in his work:

> Crossing a bare common, in snow puddles, at twilight, under
> a clouded sky, without having in my thoughts any occurrence of
> special good fortune, I have enjoyed a perfect exhilaration. I am
> glad to the brink of fear. In the woods, too, a man casts off his
> years, as the snake his slough, and at what period soever of life
> is always a child. . . . There I feel that nothing can befall me
> in life,—no disgrace, no calamity (leaving me my eyes), which
> nature cannot repair. Standing on the bare ground,—my head
> bathed by the blithe air and uplifted into infinite space,—all
> mean egotism vanishes. I become a transparent eyeball; I am
> nothing; I see all; the currents of the Universal Being circulate
> through me; I am part or parcel of God. . . .

This is not a "Spiritual Newbirth, or Baphometic Fire-baptism,"
akin to those of Carlyle's Teufelsdröckh or Melville's Ahab, because Emerson's freedom rises out of the ordinary, and not out of
crisis. But, despite a ruggedly commonplace genesis, there is little
that is ordinary in the deliberately outrageous "I become a transparent eyeball." Kenneth Burke associates Emerson's imagery of
transparence with the *crossing* or *bridging* action that is transcendence, and he finds the perfect paradigm for such figuration in the
Virgilian underworld. The unburied dead, confronted by Charon's
refusal to ferry them across Stygia, imploringly "stretched forth
their hands through love of the farther shore." Emersonian transparency is such a stretching, a Sublime crossing of the gulf of solipsism, but *not* into a communion with others. As Emerson remarks: "The name of the nearest friend sounds then foreign and
accidental: to be brothers, to be acquaintances, master or servant,
is then a trifle and a disturbance." The farther shore has no persons upon it, because Emerson's farther shore or beyond is no
part of nature, and has no room therefore for created beings. A
second-century Gnostic would have understood Emerson's "I am
nothing; I see all" as the mode of negation through which the
knower again could stand in the Abyss, the place of original fullness, *before* the Creation.

A transparent eyeball is the emblem of the Primal Abyss regarding itself. What can an Abyss behold in an Abyss?

The answer, in our fallen or demiurgical perspective, can be dialectical, the endless ironic interplay of presence and absence, full-ness and emptiness; in Gnostic vocabulary, Pleroma and Kenoma. But the Emerson of *Nature* was not yet willing to settle for such a deconstruction. Not upon an elevation, but taking his stance upon the bare American ground, Emerson demands Victory, to his senses as to his soul. The perfect exhilaration of a perpetual youth which comes to him is akin to what Hart Crane was to term an improved infancy. Against Wordsworth, Coleridge, Carlyle, the seer Emerson celebrates the American difference of *discontinuity*. "I am nothing" is a triumph of the Negative Way; "I see all" be-cause I am that I am, discontinuously present not wherever but whenever I will to be present. "I am part or parcel of God," yet the god is not Jehovah but Orpheus, and Emerson momentarily is not merely the Orphic poet but the American Orpheus himself.

Poetic Orphism is a mixed and vexed matter, beyond disen-tanglement, and it is at the center of Emerson, even in the rhet-orically immature *Nature*. I will digress upon it, and then rejoin *Nature* at its Orphic vortices.

5

The historian of Greek religion M. P. Nilsson shrewdly remarked that "Orphicism is a book religion, the first example of the kind in the history of Greek religion." Whatever it *may* have been his-torically, perhaps as early as the sixth century B.C.E., Orphism be-came the natural religion of Western poetry. Empedocles, an Em-ersonian favorite, shares Orphic characteristics with such various texts as certain Platonic myths, some odes of Pindar and fragments of poems recovered from South Italian Greek grave-sites. But later texts, mostly Neoplatonic, became the principal source for Emer-son, who did not doubt their authenticity. W. K. C. Guthrie sur-mises a historical Orphism, devoted to Apollo, partly turned against Dionysos, and centered on a "belief in the latent divinity and immortality of the human soul" and on a necessity for con-stant purity, partly achieved through *ekstasis*.

Between the Hellenistic Neoplatonists and the seventeenth-century Cambridge variety, of whom Cudworth mattered most to Emerson, there had intervened the Florentine Renaissance mythologies, particularly Ficino's, which Christianized Orpheus. The baptized Orpheus lingers on in Thomas Taylor, whose cloudy account may have been Emerson's most direct source for Orphism. But from *Nature* on, Emerson's Orpheus is simply Primal Man, who preceded the Creation, and very little occult lore actually gets into Emerson's quite autobiographical projection of himself as American Orpheus. His final Orphic reference, in the 1849 Journals, has about it the authority of a self-tested truth though its burden is extravagant, even for Emerson:

> . . . Orpheus is no fable: you have only to sing, and the rocks will crystallize; sing, and the plant will organize; sing, and the animal will be born.

If Orpheus is fact in Emerson's life and work, this must be fact when seen in the light of an idea. The idea is the Central or Universal Man, the American More-than-Christ who is *to come*, the poet prefigured by Emerson himself as voice in the wilderness. In some sense he arrived as Walt Whitman, and some seventy years later as Hart Crane, but that is to run ahead of the story. In Emerson's mythopoeic and metamorphic conception, Central or Orphic Man is hardly to be distinguished from an Orphic view of language, and so breaks apart and is restituted just as language ebbs and flows:

> . . . In what I call the cyclus of Orphic words, which I find in Bacon, in Cudworth, in Plutarch, in Plato, in that which the New Church would indicate when it speaks of the truths possessed by the primeval church broken up into fragments and floating hither and thither in the corrupt church, I perceive myself addressed thoroughly. They do teach the intellect and cause a gush of emotion; which we call the moral sublime; they pervade also the moral nature. Now the Universal Man when he comes, must so speak. He must recognize by addressing the whole nature.

Bacon's Orpheus was a Baconian philosopher–natural scientist; Cudworth's a Neoplatonic Christian; Plutarch's and Plato's an image of spiritual purification. It is sly of Emerson to bring in the not very Orphic Swedenborgians of the New Church, but he really means his Central Man to be universal. The *sparagmos* of Orpheus is a prime emblem for the American religion, whose motto I once ventured as: *Everything that can be broken should be broken.* Emerson's all-but-everything can be given in a brief, grim list:

> February 8, 1831: death of his first wife, Ellen;
> May 9, 1836: death of his brother, Charles;
> January 27, 1842: death of his first son, Waldo.

These Orphic losses should have shattered the American Orpheus, for all his life long these were the three persons he loved best. As losses they mark the three phases in the strengthening of his self-reliant American religion, an Orphism that would place him beyond further loss, at the high price of coming to worship the goddess Ananke, dread but sublime Necessity. But that worship came late to Emerson. He deferred it by a metamorphic doctrine of Orpheus, best stated in his essay *History*:

> The power of music, the power of poetry, to unfit and as it were clap wings to solid nature, interprets the riddle of Orpheus. . . .

This sentence is strangely flanked in the essay, though since Emerson's unit of discourse tends more to be the sentence than the paragraph, the strangeness is mitigated. Still, the preceding sentence is both occult and puzzling:

> Man is the broken giant, and in all his weakness both his body and his mind are invigorated by habits of conversation with nature.

The Orphic riddle is the dialectic of strength and weakness *in Orpheus himself*. Is he god or man? St. Augustine placed Orpheus at the head of poets called theologians, and then added: "But these theologians were not worshipped as gods, though in some fashion the kingdom of the godless is wont to set Orpheus as head over the rites of the underworld." This is admirably clear, but not sufficient to unriddle Orpheus. Jane Harrison surmised that an actual man, Orpheus, came belatedly to the worship of Dionysus and modified those rites, perhaps partly civilizing them. Guthrie assimilated Orpheus to Apollo, while allowing the Dionysiac side also. E. R. Dodds, most convincingly for my purposes, associates Orpheus with Empedocles and ultimately with Thracian traditions of shamanism. Describing Empedocles (and Orpheus), Dodds might be writing of Emerson, granting only some temporal differences:

> . . . Empedocles represents not a new but a very old type of personality, the shaman who combines the still undifferentiated functions of magician and naturalist, poet and philosopher, preacher, healer, and public counsellor. After him these functions fell apart; philosophers henceforth were to be neither poets nor magicians. . . . It was not a question of "synthesising" these wide domains of practical and theoretical knowledge; in their quality as Men of God they practised with confidence in all of them; the "synthesis" was personal, not logical.

Emerson's Orpheus and Empedocles, like those of Dodds, were mythical shamans, and perhaps Emerson as founder of the American religion is best thought of as another mythical shaman. His Orphism was a metamorphic religion of power whose prime purpose was divination, in what can be called the Vichian sense of god-making. But why Orphism, when other shamanisms were available? The native strain in Emerson rejected any received religion. I am unable to accept a distinguished tradition in scholarship that goes from Perry Miller to Sacvan Bercovitch, and that finds Emerson to have been the heir, however involuntary, of the line that goes from the Mathers to Jonathan Edwards. But I distrust also the received scholarship that sees Emerson as the American disciple of Wordsworth, Coleridge and Carlyle, and thus indirectly a weak descendant of German High Transcendentalism, of Fichte and Schelling. And to fill out my litany of rejections, I cannot find Emerson to be another Perennial Philosophy Neoplatonist, mixing some Swedenborgianism into the froth of Cudworth and Thomas Taylor. Since *Nature* is the text to which I will return, I cite as commentary Stephen Whicher's *Freedom and Fate*, still the best book on Emerson after a quarter-century:

> . . . The lesson he would drive home is man's entire independence. The aim of this strain in his thought is not virtue, but freedom and mastery. It is radically anarchic, overthrowing all the authority of the past, all compromise or cooperation with others, in the name of the Power present and agent in the soul.
>
> Yet his true goal was not really a Stoic self-mastery, nor Christian holiness, but rather something more secular and harder to define—a quality he sometimes called *entirety*, or *self-union*. . . .
>
> This self-sufficient unity or wholeness, transforming his relations with the world about him, is, as I read him, the central objective of the egoistic or transcendental Emerson, the prophet of Man created in the 1830's by his discovery of his own proper nature. This was what he meant by "sovereignty," or "majesty," or the striking phrase, several times repeated, "the erect position." . . .

"This strain in his thought" I would identify as what, starting from Emerson, became the Native Strain in our literature. But why call Orphism a religion of "freedom and mastery," anarchic in overthrowing all the past and all contemporary otherness? The choice is Emerson's, as the final chapter of *Nature* shows, so that the question becomes: Why did Emerson identify his Primal, Central or Universal Man with Orpheus?

Hart Crane, Emerson's descendant through Whitman, provokes the same question at the formal close of *The Bridge*:

> Now while thy petals spend the suns about us, hold
> (O Thou whose radiance doth inherit me)
> Atlantis,—hold thy floating singer late!
>
> So to thine Everpresence, beyond time,
> Like spears ensanguined of one tolling star
> That bleeds infinity—the orphic strings,
> Sidereal phalanxes, leap and converge:
> —One Song, one Bridge of Fire!

The belated floating singer is still the metamorphic Orpheus of Ovid:

> . . . The poet's limbs were scattered in different places, but the waters of the Hebrus received his head and lyre. Wonderful to relate, as they floated down in midstream, the lyre uttered a plaintive melody and the lifeless tongue made a piteous murmur, while the river banks lamented in reply. . . .

But beyond time, upon the transcendental bridge of fire that is his poem, Crane as American Orpheus vaults the problematics of loss even as Brooklyn Bridge vaultingly becomes the Orphic lyre bending, away from America as lost Atlantis, to whatever Crane can surmise beyond earth. If Coleridge could salute *The Prelude* as "an Orphic song indeed," then the American Crane could render the same salute to *The Bridge*. Emerson's Orphic songs, first in *Nature* and later in his essay *The Poet*, are Crane's ultimate paradigm, as he may not have known. To answer the question: Why an American Orpheus? I turn back now to *Nature*.

6

Between "Nature" proper, the little book's first chapter, with its epiphany of the transparent eyeball, and the final chapter "Prospects," with its two rhapsodies of the Orphic poet, intervene six rather inadequate chapters, all of which kindle at their close. I give here only these kindlings:

> A man is fed, not that he may be fed, but that he may work.

> But beauty in nature is not ultimate.

> That which was unconscious truth, becomes, when interpreted and defined as an object, a part of the domain of knowledge—a new weapon in the magazine of power.

> . . . the human form, of which all other organizations appear to be degradations. . . .

> . . . the soul holds itself off from a too trivial and microscopic study of the universal tablet. It respects the end too much to immerse itself in the means. . . .

The world proceeds from the same spirit as the body of man. It is a remoter and inferior incarnation of God, a projection of God in the unconscious. . . .

Perhaps Emerson might have kindled these kernels of his vision into something finer than the six chapters they crown. Their design is clear and impressive. Man's work moves beyond natural beauty through a power-making act of knowledge, which identifies the human form, beyond merely natural evidence, as the incarnation of God, an incarnation not yet elevated to full consciousness. That elevation is the enterprise of the Orphic poet, in the chapter "Prospects."

". . . Man is the dwarf of himself. Once he was permeated and dissolved by spirit. He filled nature with his overflowing currents. Out from him sprang the sun and moon; from man the sun, from woman the moon. The laws of his mind, the periods of his actions externized themselves into day and night, into the year and the seasons. But, having made for himself this huge shell, his waters retired; he no longer fills the veins and veinlets; he is shrunk to a drop. He sees that the structure still fits him, but fits him colossaly. Say, rather, once it fitted him, now it corresponds to him from far and on high. He adores timidly his own work. Now is man the follower of the sun, and woman the follower of the moon. Yet sometimes he starts in his slumber, and wonders at himself and his house, and muses strangely at the resemblance betwixt him and it. He perceives that if his law is still paramount, if still he have elemental power, if his word is sterling yet in nature, it is not conscious power, it is not inferior but superior to his will. It is instinct." Thus my Orphic poet sang.

This "instinct" scarcely can be biological; like the Freudian drives of Eros and Thanatos it can only be mythological. Orphic, Gnostic or even Neoplatonic, it appears now in American colors and tropes. Call the Primal Man American, or even America (as Blake called him Albion, or Shelley, more misleadingly, Prometheus). America was a larger form than nature, filling nature with his emanative excess. Not Jehovah Elohim nor a Demiurge made the cosmos and time, but America, who thereupon shrunk to a drop. When this dwarf, once giant, starts in his sleep, then "gleams of a better light" come into experiential darkness. Very American is Emerson's catalog of those gleams of Reason:

> . . . Such examples are, the traditions of miracles in the earliest antiquity of all nations; the history of Jesus Christ; the achievements of a principle, as in religious and political revolutions, and in the abolition of the slave-trade; the miracles of enthusiasm, as those reported of Swedenborg, Hohenlohe, and the Shakers; many obscure and yet contested facts, now arranged under the name of Animal Magnetism; prayer; eloquence; self-healing; and the wisdom of children.

A contemporary Carlyle might react to this list by querying: "But why has he left out flying saucers?" I myself would point to "eloquence" as the crucial item, fully equal and indeed superior in Emerson's view to "the history of Jesus Christ" or "prayer." Eloquence is the true Emersonian instance "of Reason's momentary grasp of the scepter; the exertions of a power which exists not in time or space, but an instantaneous in-streaming causing power." Eloquence is Influx, and Influx is a mode of divination, in the Vichian or double sense of god-making and of prophecy. Emerson, peculiarly American, definitive of what it is to be American, *uses* divination so as to transform all of nature into a transparent eyeball:

> . . . The ruin or the blank, that we see when we look at nature, is in our own eye. The axis of vision is not coincident with the axis of things, and so they appear not transparent but opaque. The reason why the world lacks unity, and lies broken and in heaps, is because man is disunited with himself. . . .

The American swerve here is from Milton, when in his invocation to Book III of *Paradise Lost* he lamented that to his literal blindness nature appeared a universal blank. But, more subtly, Emerson revises Coleridge's previous swerve from Milton's lament, in the despairing cry of *Dejection: An Ode*, where Coleridge sees literally but not figuratively: "And still I gaze—and with how blank an eye." The American transumption of Emerson's revisionary optics comes late, with the tragic self-recognition of the aged Wallace Stevens in *The Auroras of Autumn*, when Stevens walks the Emersonian-Whitmanian shores of America unable to convert his movements into a freshly American figuration, a new variation upon the tradition: "The man who is walking turns blankly on the sand."

What would it mean if the axis of vision and of things were to coincide? What would a transparent world be, or yield? Wordsworth's *Tintern Abbey* spoke of seeing into the life of things, while Blake urged a seeing *through* rather than *with* the eye. Is Emerson as much reliant upon trope as these British forerunners were, or do his optics prod us towards a pragmatic difference? I suggest the latter, because Emerson as American seer is always the shrewd Yankee, interested in what he called "commodity," and because we ought never to forget that if he fathered Whitman and Thoreau and Frost and (despite that son's evasions) Stevens, his pragmatic strain ensued in William James, Peirce and even John Dewey.

The optics of transparency disturb only the aspect of this text that marks it as a fiction of duration, while the topological residuum of the text remains untroubled. Most tropes, as Emerson knew, have only a spatial rather than a temporal dimension, metaphor proper and synecdoche and metonymy among them. Irony and transumption or metalepsis, which Emerson called the comic trick of language and Nietzsche the Eternal Recurrence, are the temporal as well as spatial modes. The Emersonian transparency or transcendence does not oppose itself to presence or spatial immanence, but to the burden of time and of historical continuity. As the quintessential American, Emerson did not need to transcend *space*, which for him as for Whitman, Melville and Charles Olson was the central fact about America. Transparency is therefore an agon with time, and not with space, and opacity thus can be re-defined, in Emersonian terms, as being fixed in time, being trapped in continuity. What Nietzsche called the will's revenge against time's "it was" Emerson more cheerfully sees as a transparency.

Pragmatically this did not mean, for Emerson, seeing things or people as though they were ectoplasm. It meant not seeing the fact except as an epiphany, as a manifestation of the God within the self-reliant seer:

> . . . We make fables to hide the baldness of the fact and conform it, as we say, to the higher law of the mind. But when the fact is seen under the light of an idea, the gaudy fable fades and shrivels. . . .

Why should Orpheus be incarnated again in America? Because he is the authentic prophet-god of discontinuity, of the breaking of tradition, and of re-inscribing tradition as a perpetual breaking, mending and then breaking again. The Orphic seer says of and to time: *It must be broken.* Even so, Emerson's own Orphic poet ends *Nature* by chanting a marvelous breaking:

> Nature is not fixed but fluid. Spirit alters, molds, makes it. The immobility or bruteness of nature is the absence of spirit; to pure spirit it is fluid, it is volatile, it is obedient. Every spirit builds itself a house, and beyond its house a world, and beyond its world a heaven. Know then that the world exists for you. For you is the phenomenon perfect. What we are, that only can we see. All that Adam had, all that Caesar could, you have and can do. Adam called his house, Rome; you perhaps call yours, a cobbler's trade; a hundred acres of ploughed land; or a scholar's garret. Yet line for line and point for point your dominion is as great as theirs, though without fine names. Build therefore your own world. . . .

The metaphoric-mobile, fluid, volatile is precisely the Orphic stigma. I discussed this passage in section 2, above, in terms of Abyss-radiance, but return to it now to venture a more radical interpretation. Pure spirit, or influx, is a remedial force not akin to what moved over the Abyss in merely demiurgical Creation, but rather itself the breath of the truly Primal Abyss. "Build therefore your own world" cannot mean that you are to emulate demiurgical creativity by stealing your material from the origin. Every man his own Demiurge hardly can be the motto for the Emersonian freedom. If seeing ranks above having, for Emerson, then knowing stands beyond seeing:

> The kingdom of man over nature, which cometh not with observation,—a dominion such as now is beyond his dream of God,—he shall enter without more wonder than the blind man feels who is gradually restored to perfect sight.

The crucial words are "now" and "gradually." If the dream of God were to be an Orphic and Gnostic dream of one's own occult self, then the reliance or religion would come now, and with great wonder. Emerson's curiously serene faith, as he closes *Nature*, is that gradually we will be restored to the perfect sight of our truly knowing self.

7

Emerson's theology of being an American, his vision of *self*-reliance, has nothing much in common with historical Gnosticism. In Gnosticism, this world *is* hell, and both man's body and man's soul are the work of the Demiurge who made this world. Only the *pneuma* or spark within the Gnostic elect is no part of the false and evil Creation. Emerson's monism, his hope for the American new Adam, and his Wordsworthian love of nature all mark him as a religious prophet whose God, however internalized, is very distinct from the alien God or Primal Abyss of Gnosticism.

I speak therefore not of Emerson's Gnosticism but of his Gnosis, of his way of knowing, which has nothing in common with philosophic epistemology. Though William James, Peirce and Dewey, and in another mode, Nietzsche, all are a part of Emerson's progeny, Emerson is not a philosopher, nor even a speculator with a philosophic theology. And though he stemmed from the mainstream Protestant tradition in America, Emerson is not a Christian, nor even a non-Christian theist in a philosophic sense.

But I am not going to continue this litany of what our central man is not. Rather I will move directly to an account of Emerson's Gnosis, of that which he was and is, founder of *the* American religion, fountain of our literary and spiritual elite.

I will begin and end with my own favorite Emersonian sentence, from the first paragraph of the essay *Self-Reliance:*

> In every work of genius we recognize our own rejected thoughts; they come back to us with a certain alienated majesty.

Emerson says "rejected" where we might use the word "repressed," and his Gnosis begins with the reader's Sublime, a Freudian Negation in which thought comes back but we are still in flight from the emotional recognition that there is no author but ourselves. A strong reading indeed is the only text, the only revenge against time's "it was" that can endure. Self-estrangement produces the uncanniness of "majesty," and yet we do "recognize our own." Emerson's Gnosis rejects all history, including literary history, and dismisses all historians, including literary historians who want to tell the reader that what he recognizes in Emerson is Emerson's own thought rather than the reader's own Sublime.

A discourse upon Emerson's Gnosis, to be Emersonian rather than literary historical, itself must be Gnosis, or part of a Gnosis. It must speak of a knowing in which the knower himself is known, a reading in which he is read. It will not speak of epistemology, not even deconstructively of the epistemology of tropes, because it will read Emerson's tropes as figures of will, and not figures of knowledge, as images of voice and not images of writing.

"Why then do we prate of self-reliance?" is Emerson's rhetorical question, halfway through that essay. Falling back, with him, upon power as agent and upon a rich internal "way of speaking," I repeat his injunction: "Speak rather of that which relies because it works and is." "Works" as an Emersonian verb has Carlyle's tang to it. Prate not of happiness, but work, for the night cometh. But Emerson's *clinamen* away from Europe, away even from Coleridge and Carlyle, is to be heard in "that which relies because it works and is." In the American swerve, tradition is denied its last particle of authority, and the voice that is great within us rises up:

> Life only avails, not the having lived. Power ceases in the instant of repose; it resides in the moment of transition from a past to a new state, in the shooting of the gulf, in the darting of an aim. . . .

There is no power in what already has been accomplished, and Emerson has not come to celebrate a new state, a gulf crossed, an aim hit. Power is an affair of crossings, of thresholds or transitional moments, evasions, substitutions, mental dilemmas resolved only by arbitrary acts of will. Power is in the traversing of the black holes of rhetoric, where the interpreter reads his own freedom to read. Or, we are read only by voicing, by the images for power we find that free us from the *already said*, from being one of the secondary men, traces of traces of traces.

I am suggesting that what a Gnosis of rhetoric, like Emerson's, prophetically wars against is every philosophy of rhetoric, and so now against the irony of irony and the randomness of all textuality. The Emersonian self, "that which relies because it works and is," is voice and not text, which is why it must splinter and destroy its own texts, subverting even the paragraph through the autonomy of sentences, the aggressivity of aphorisms. The sudden uncanniness of voice is Emerson's prime image for vocation, for the call that his Gnosis answers, as here in *Spiritual Laws*:

> Each man has his own vocation. The talent is the call. . . .
> . . . It is the vice of our public speaking that it has not abandonment. Somewhere, not only every orator but every man should let out the length of all the reins; should find or make a frank and hearty expression of what force and meaning is in him. . . .

Of this Emersonian spark or *pneuma*, this Gnostic true or antithetical self, as opposed to *psyche* or soul, we can observe that as an aggressive image of voice it will resist successfully all deconstruction. For this image is not a fiction *produced by* the original breaking-apart of the vessels of language but rather itself *tropes for* that primal breaking-apart. Emerson's image of voice is precisely a prophetic transumption of his son Nietzsche's image of truth as an army of figures of speech on the march, a march for which Heidegger gives us "language" or Derrida "writing" as a trope. The march keeps breaking up as voice keeps flowing in again, not as the image of presence but of Gnostic aboriginal absence, as here again in *Spiritual Laws* where the *thrownness* of all Gnosis returns in a forward falling:

> . . . When the fruit is ripe, it falls. When the fruit is despatched, the leaf falls. The circuit of the waters is a mere falling. The walking of man and all animals is a falling forward. All our manual labor and works of strength, as prying, splitting, digging, rowing and so forth, are done by dint of continual falling, and the globe, earth, moon, comet, sun, star, fall forever and ever.
>
> . . . Place yourself in the middle of the stream of power and wisdom which flows into you as life, place yourself in the full centre of that flood, then you are without effort impelled to truth, to right, and a perfect contentment. . . .

I gloss these Emersonian passages by the formula: every fall is a *fall forward*, neither fortunate nor unfortunate, but *forward*, without effort, impelled to the American truth, which is that the stream of power and wisdom flowing in as life is eloquence. Emerson *is* the fountain of our will because he understood that, in America, in the evening-land, eloquence *had* to be enough. The image of voice is the image of influx, of the Newness, but always it knowingly is a broken image, or image of brokenness. Whitman, still Emerson's strongest ephebe, caught the inevitable tropes for this wounded image of American voice:

> —and from this bush in the dooryard,
> With delicate-color'd blossoms and heart-shaped leaves of rich green,
> A sprig with its flower I break.
>
> In the swamp in secluded recesses,
> A shy and hidden bird is warbling a song.

Solitary the thrush,
The hermit withdrawn to himself, avoiding the settlements,
Sings by himself a song.

Song of the bleeding throat,
Death's outlet song of life, (for well dear brother I know,
If thou wast not granted to sing thou would'st surely die.)

The breaking of the tally, of the sprig of lilac, is one with the
wounding of the hermit thrush's throat, the breaking of voice, of
the call, of prophetic vocation. Because it is broken, castrated, it
remains an image of voice and of life, not the unbroken image of
writing and of death. Whitman *knows*, even *in extremis*, because
his father Emerson *knew*, and both knowings are fallings forward.
What any philosophical knowing necessarily is or isn't I scarcely
know, but I can read Emerson because every knowing I do know
is part of a thrownness, a synecdoche for what Emerson wanted to
call "victory" or "freedom." Was it not Emerson's peculiar strength
that what to me seems catastrophe was to him—by the mad law of
Compensation—converted to victory? What made him free was his
Gnosis, and I move now into its center, his center, the image of
voice that *is self*-reliance, at the high place of that rhapsody:

> . . . It must be that when God speaketh he should com-
> municate, not one thing, but all things; should fill the world
> with his voice; should scatter forth light, nature, time, souls,
> from the center of the present thought; and new date and new
> create the whole. Whenever a mind is simple and receives a
> divine wisdom, old Things pass away,—means, teachers, texts,
> temples fall; it lives now, and absorbs past and future into the
> present hour. All things are made sacred by relation to it,—one
> as much as another. All things are dissolved to their center by
> their cause. . . .

Let us apply Whitman, since he was the strongest of the Emer-
sonians. In *Specimen Days* he wrote:

> . . . The best part of Emersonianism is, it breeds the giant
> that destroys itself. Who wants to be any man's mere follower?
> lurks behind every page. No teacher ever taught, that has so

provided for his pupil's setting up independently—no truer evolutionist.

Emerson also then is a teacher and a text that must pass away if you or I receive the Newness, a fresh influx of the image of voice. On Emerson's precept, no man's Gnosis can be another's, and Emerson's images of voice are fated to become yet more images of writing. Surely this is part of the lesson of the Middle or Skeptical Emerson, warning us against all idolatries, including my own deep temptation to idolize Emerson. Here is the admonition of his greatest essay, *Experience*:

> . . . People forget that it is the eye which makes the horizon, and the rounding mind's eye which makes this or that man a type or representation of humanity, with the name of hero or saint. Jesus, the "providential man," is a good man on whom many people are agreed that these optical laws shall take effect. . . .

Emerson, unlike Whitman, hoped to evade the American version of that "providential man." If no two disciples can agree upon Emerson's doctrine, and they cannot, we can grant the success of his evasion. Yet there is the center: evasion. Emersonianism, indeed like any Gnosis, moves back and forth between negation and extravagance, and always by way of evasion rather than by substitution. I will digress from Gnosis to Gnosticism, before shuttling back to Emerson's passage through *Experience* to *Fate*, middle and late essays no less modes of Gnosis than *Self-Reliance* is.

The way of evasion for the Gnostics meant freedom, and this was freedom from the god of this world, from time, from text, and from the soul and the body of the universe. Such freedom was both knowledge and salvation, since the knowledge of saving self involved was one with the knowledge of the alien true God and the Primal Abyss. How could so large a knowing be known? Only by an image or trope of the self that transgressed language through the most positive of negative moments. What Coleridge, in his orthodox nightmare, dreads as the Positive Negation of *Limbo* is known by the Gnostics as a being-there in the Pleroma, in the Place of Rest. Coleridge's negative moment loses the self without compensation. Emerson, in his 1838 Journal, slyly turning away from Coleridge, achieves a Gnostic Sublime, a negative moment that is all gain and no loss, the truly American moment of *self*-reliance:

> In the highest moments, we are a vision. There is nothing that can be called gratitude nor properly joy. The soul is raised over passion. It seeth nothing so much as Identity. It is a Perceiving that Truth and Right ARE. Hence it becomes a perfect Peace out of the *knowing* that all things will go well. Vast spaces of nature the Atlantic Ocean, the South Sea; vast intervals of time years, centuries, are annihilated to it; this which I think and feel underlay that former state of life and circumstances, as it does underlie my present, and will always all circumstance, and what is called life and what is called death [my italics].

This passage is not so much an example of Gnostic rhetoric as it is part of a Gnosis of rhetoric, anti-epistemological without being vulnerable to the charge that it simply reverses an epistemological dilemma. In a transcendental hyperbole we mount beyond Coleridgean joy of the Secondary imagination because *we see nothing*. Instead, "we are a vision" and we know the identity between ourselves and our knowledge of ourselves. Space, time and mortality flee away, to be replaced by "the knowing." As always in Emerson, the knowing bruises a limit of language, and the impatient Seer transgresses in order to convey his "Perceiving that Truth and Right ARE," which compels the "ARE" to break through in capital letters. In its extravagance, this passage is nothing but tropological, yet its persuasive rhetoric achieves persuasion by the trick of affirming identity with a wholly discontinuous self, one which *knows* only the highest moments in which it *is* a vision. Emerson evades philosophy and chooses his Gnosis instead precisely because he is wary of the epistemological pitfalls that all trope risks. An image of voice is a fine tangle, well beyond logic, but it can testify only to the presence of things not seen, and its faith is wholly in the Optative Mood.

Yet if we move on from *Self-Reliance* first to *Experience* and then to *Fate*, we pass out of the Optative Mood and into the evidence of that world where men descend to meet, and where they cease to be a vision. But even in *Experience*, and then even more in *Fate*, we read not philosophy but Gnosis, a chastened knowing that is not chastened *as* knowing. Here is a single recovery from *Experience*:

> . . . The partial action of each strong mind in one direction is a telescope for the objects on which it is pointed. But every other part of knowledge is to be pushed to the same extravagance, ere the soul attains her due sphericity. . . .
>
> . . . And we cannot say too little of our constitutional necessity of seeing things under private aspects, or saturated with our humors. And yet is the God the native of these bleak rocks. That need makes in morals the capital virtue of self-trust. We must hold hard to this poverty, however scandalous, and by more rigorous self-recoveries, after the sallies of action, possess our axis more firmly.

Rather than comment upon this in isolation, I juxtapose it first with a more scandalous poverty of *Fate*:

> . . . A man speaking from insight affirms of himself what is true of the mind: seeing its immortality, he says, I am immortal; seeing its invincibility, he says, I am strong. It is not in us, but we are in it. It is of the maker, not of what is made. . . .

The fragment of *Experience* makes imaginative need, epistemological lack, itself into potential Gnosis, the potentia of power. But the resting-point of *Fate* is a more drastic Gnosis, for there the mind and the self have dissociated, in order to win the compensation of the self as spark of the uncreated. And in a coda to this discourse I now abandon Emerson for the giant of Emersonianism, for the question that is a giant himself. What does Emersonianism teach us about an American Gnosis, and what is it which makes that Gnosis still available to us?

The primary teaching of any Gnosis is to deny that human existence is a historical existence. Emerson's American Gnosis denies our belatedness by urging us not to listen to tradition. If you listen hard to tradition, as Walter Benjamin said Kafka did, then you do not see, and Emersonianism wants you to *see*. See what? That is the wrong question, for Gnosis directs *how* to see, meaning to *see earliest*, as though no one had ever seen before you. Gnosis directs also in stance, in taking up a place from which to see earliest, which is one with the place of belated poetry, which is to say, American poetry in particular.

In poetry, a "place" is *where* something is *known*, while a figure or trope is *when* something is willed or desired. In belated poetry, as in any other Gnosis, the place where knowing is located is always a name, but one that comes by negation; an unnaming yields this name. But to un-name in a poem, you first mime and then over-mime and finally super-mime the name you displace. Emerson and Gnosticism alike seek the terrible burden of a super-mimesis. The American poet must overthrow even Shakespeare, a doomed enterprise that shadows *Moby Dick*, despite our generous overpraise of the crippling of Melville's greatness by *King Lear*. Whitman must be the new Adam, the new Moses, and the new Christ, impossible aspirations that astonishingly he did not disappoint wholly. An imaginative literature that stems from a Gnosis, rather than a philosophy, is both enhanced and ruined by its super-mimetic teleologies. In every work of genius—in the Bible, Shakespeare, Spenser, Milton, Wordsworth—just there Hawthorne, Melville, Whitman, Thoreau, Dickinson, Henry James learned to recognize their own rejected thoughts. Frost, Stevens, Hart Crane, Faulkner and so many more later encountered their rejected thoughts coming back to them with a certain alienated majesty, when they read their American nineteenth-century precursors. Plato entered the agon with Homer to be the mind of Greece, but here in America we had no Homer. The mind of America perhaps was Emersonian even before Emerson. After him, the literary, indeed the religious mind of America has had no choice, as he cannot be rejected or even deconstructed. He *is* our rhetoric as he is our Gnosis, and I take it that his sly evasion of both Hegel and Hume deprived us of our philosophy. Since he will not conclude haunting us, I evade concluding here, except for a single hint. He was an interior orator, and not an instructor; a vitalizer and not an historian. We will never know our own knowing, through or despite him, until we learn the lesson our profession refuses. I end therefore by quoting against us an eloquence from the essay *History*, which the seer rightly chose to lead off his essays:

> . . . Those men who cannot answer by a superior wisdom these facts or questions of time, serve them. Facts encumber them, tyrannize over them, and make the men of routine, the men of *sense*, in whom a literal obedience to facts has extinguished every spark of that light by which man is truly man. . . .

That, in one dark epiphany, is Emerson's Gnosis.

7
Whitman's Image of Voice: To the Tally of My Soul

Where does the individual accent of an American poetry begin? How, then and now, do we recognize the distinctive voice that we associate with an American Muse? Bryant, addressing some admonitory lines, in 1830, *To Cole, the Painter, Departing for Europe,* has no doubts as to what marks the American difference:

> Fair scenes shall greet thee where thou goest—fair,
>   But different—everywhere the trace of men,
> To where life shrinks from the fierce Alpine air.
>   Gaze on them, till the tears shall dim thy sight,
>   But keep that earlier, wilder image bright.

Only the Sublime, from which life shrinks, constitutes a European escape from the trace of men. Cole will be moved by that Sublime, yet he is to keep vivid the image of priority, an American image of freedom, for which Emerson and Thoreau, like Bryant before them, will prefer the trope of "wildness." The wildness triumphs throughout Bryant, a superb poet, always and still undervalued, and one of Hart Crane's and Wallace Stevens's legitimate ancestors. The voice of an American poetry goes back before Bryant, and can be heard in Bradstreet and Freneau (not so much, I think, in Edward Taylor, who was a good English poet who happened to be living in America). Perhaps, as with all origins, the American poetic voice cannot be traced, and so I move from my first to my second opening question: how to recognize the Muse of America. Here is Bryant, in the strong opening of his poem *The Prairies*, in 1833:

> These are the gardens of the Desert, these
> The unshorn fields, boundless and beautiful,
> For which the speech of England has no name—
> The Prairies. I behold them for the first
> And my heart swells, while the dilated sight
> Takes in the encircling vastness. . . .

Bryant's ecstatic beholding has little to do with what he sees. His speech swells most fully as he intones "The Prairies," following on the prideful reflection that no English poet could name these grasslands. The reflection itself is a touch awkward, since the word after all is French, and not Amerindian, as Bryant knew. No matter; the beholding is still there, and truly the name is little more important than the sight. What *is* vital is the dilation of the sight, an encircling vastness more comprehensive even than the immensity being taken in, for it is only a New England hop, skip and a jump from this dilation to the most American passage that will ever be written, more American even than Huck Finn telling Aunt Polly that he lies just to keep in practice, or Ahab proclaiming that he would strike the sun if it insulted him. Reverently I march back to where I and the rest of us have been before and always must be again, crossing a bare common, in snow puddles, at twilight, under a clouded sky, in the company of our benign father, the Sage of Concord, teacher of that perfect exhilaration in which, with him, we are glad to the brink of fear:

> . . . Standing on the bare ground,—my head bathed by the blithe air and uplifted into infinite space,—all mean egotism vanishes. I become a transparent eyeball; I am nothing; I see all; the currents of the Universal Being circulate through me; I am part or parcel of God. . . .

Why is this ecstasy followed directly by the assertion: "The name of the nearest friend sounds then foreign and accidental . . ."? Why does the dilation of vision to the outrageous point of becoming a transparent eyeball provoke a denaturing of even the nearest name? I hasten to enforce the obvious, which nevertheless is crucial: the name is not forgotten, but loses the sound of immediacy; it becomes foreign or out-of-doors, rather than domestic; and accidental, rather than essential. A step beyond this into the American Sublime, and you do not even forget the name; you never hear it at all:

> And now at last the highest truth on this subject remains unsaid; probably cannot be said; for all that we say is the far-off remembering of the intuition. That thought by what I can now nearest approach to say it, is this. When good is near you, when you have life in yourself, it is not by any known or accustomed way; you shall not discern the footprints of any other; you shall not see the face of man; you shall not hear any name;—the way, the thought, the good, shall be wholly strange and new. . . .

"This subject" is self-reliance, and the highest truth on it would appear to be voiceless, except that Emerson's voice does speak out to tell us of the influx of the Newness, in which no footprints or faces are to be seen, and no name is to be heard. Unnaming always has been a major mode in poetry, far more than naming; perhaps there cannot be a poetic naming that is not founded upon an unnaming. I want to leap from these prose unnamings in Emerson, so problematic in their possibilities, to the poem in which, more than any other, I would seek to hear Emerson's proper voice for once in verse, a voice present triumphantly in so many hundreds of passages throughout his prose:

> Pour, Bacchus! the remembering wine;
> Retrieve the loss of me and mine!
> Vine for vine be antidote,
> And the grape requite the lote!
> Haste to cure the old despair,—
> Reason in Nature's lotus drenched,
> The memory of ages quenched;
> Give them again to shine;
> Let wine repair what this undid;

And where the infection slid,
A dazzling memory revive;
Refresh the faded tints,
Recut the aged prints,
And write my old adventures with the pen
Which on the first day drew,
Upon the tablets blue,
The dancing Pleiads and eternal men.

But why is Bacchus named here, if you shall not hear any name? My question would be wholly hilarious if we were to literalize Emerson's splendid chant. Visualize the Sage of Concord, gaunt and spare, uncorking a bottle in Dionysiac abandon, before emulating the Pleiads by breaking into a Nietzschean dance. No, the Bacchus of Ralph Waldo is rather clearly another unnaming. As for voice, it is palpably absent from this grand passage, its place taken up not even by writing, but by rewriting, by that revisionary pen which has priority, and which drew before the tablets darkened and grew small.

I am going to suggest shortly that rewriting is an invariable trope for voicing, within a poem, and that voicing and reseeing are much the same poetic process, a process reliant upon unnaming, which rhetorically means the undoing of a prior metonymy. But first I am going to leap ahead again, from Emerson to Stevens, which is to pass over the great impasse of Whitman, with whom I have identified always Hart Crane's great trope: "Oval encyclicals in canyons heaping / The impasse high with choir." Soon enough this discourse will center upon Whitman, since quite simply he *is* the American Sublime, he *is* voice in our poetry, he *is* our answer to the Continent now, precisely as he was a century ago. Yet I am sneaking up on him, always the best way for any critic to skulk near the Sublime Walt. His revisionism, of self as of others, is very subtle; his unnamings and his voices come out of the Great Deep. Stevens's are more transparent:

Throw away the lights, the definitions,
And say of what you see in the dark

That it is this or that it is that,
But do not use the rotted names.

*   *   *

Phoebus is dead, ephebe. But Phoebus was
A name for something that never could be named.
There was a project for the sun and is.

There is a project for the sun. The sun
Must bear no name, gold flourisher, but be
In the difficulty of what it is to be.

*   *   *

This is nothing until in a single man contained,
Nothing until this named thing nameless is
And is destroyed. He opens the door of his house

On flames. The scholar of one candle sees
An Arctic effulgence flaring on the frame
Of everything he is. And he feels afraid.

What have these three unnaming passages most in common? Well, what are we doing when we give pet names to those we love, or give no names to anyone at all, as when we go apart in order to go deep into ourselves? Stevens's peculiar horror of the commonplace in names emerges in his litany of bizarre, fabulistic persons and places, but though that inventiveness works to break casual continuities, it has little in common with the true break with continuity in poets like Lewis Carroll and Edward Lear. Stevens, *pace* Hugh Kenner, is hardly the culmination of the poetics of Lear. He may *not* be the culmination of Whitman's poetics either, since that begins to seem the peculiar distinction of John Ashbery. But like Whitman, Stevens does have a link to the Lucretian Sublime, as Pater the Epicurean did, and such a Sublime demands a deeper break with commonplace continuities than is required by the evasions of nonsense and fantasy. The most authentic of literary Sublimes has the Epicurean purpose of rendering us discontented with easier pleasures in order to prepare us for the ordeal of more difficult pleasures. When Stevens unnames he follows, however unknowingly, the trinity of negative wisdom represented by Emerson, Pater and Nietzsche. Stevens himself acknowledged only Nietzsche, but the unfashionable Emerson and Pater were even stronger in him, with Emerson (and Whitman) repressedly the strongest of strains. Why not, after all, use the rotted names? If the things were things that never could be named, is not one name as bad anyway as another? Stevens's masterpiece is not named *The Somethings of Autumn*, and not only because the heroic desperation of the Emersonian scholar of one candle is not enough. Whether you call the auroras flames or an Arctic effulgence or call them by the trope now stuck into dictionaries, auroras, you are giving your momentary consent to one arbitrary substitution or another. Hence Emerson's more drastic and Bacchic ambition; write your *old* adventures, not just your new, with the Gnostic pen of our forefather and foremother, the Abyss. I circle again the problematic American desire to merge voicing and revisionism into a single entity, and turn to Whitman for a central text, which will be the supposed elegy for Lincoln, *When Lilacs Last in the Dooryard Bloom'd*. So drastic is the amalgam of voicing, unnaming and revisionism here that I take as prelude first Whitman's little motto poem, *As Adam Early in the Morning*, so as to set some of the ways for approaching what is most problematic in the great elegy, its images of voice and of voicing.

What can we mean when we speak of the *voice* of the poet, or the voice of the critic? Is there a pragmatic sense of voice, in discussing poetry and criticism, that does not depend upon the illusions of metaphysics? When poetry and criticism speak of "images of voice," what is being imaged? I think I can answer these questions usefully in the context of my critical enterprise from *The Anxiety of Influence* on, but my answers rely upon a post-philosophical pragmatism which grounds itself upon what has worked to make up an American tradition. Voice in American poetry always necessarily must include Whitman's oratory, and here I quote from it where it is most economical and persuasive, a five-line poem that centers the canon of our American verse:

As Adam early in the morning,
Walking forth from the bower refresh'd with sleep,
Behold me where I pass, hear my voice, approach,
Touch me, touch the palm of your hand to my body as I pass,
Be not afraid of my body.

What shall we call this striding stance of the perpetually passing Walt, prophetic of Stevens's singing girl at Key West, and of Stevens's own Whitman walking along a ruddy shore, singing of death and day? Rhetorically the stance is wholly transumptive, introjecting earliness, but this is very unlike the Miltonic transuming of tradition. Walt is indeed Emerson's new Adam, American and Nietzschean, who can live as if it were morning, but though he is *as* the Biblical and Miltonic Adam, that "as" is one of Stevens's "intricate evasions of as." The Old Adam was not a savior, except in certain Gnostic traditions of Primal Man; the new, Whitmanian Adam indeed is Whitman himself, more like Christ than like Adam, and more like the Whitmanian Christ of Lawrence's *The Man Who Died* than like the Jesus of the Gospels.

Reading Whitman's little poem is necessarily an exercise both in a kind of repression and in a kind of introjection. To read the poem strongly, to voice its stance, is to transgress the supposed boundary between reading or criticism, and writing or poetry. "As" governs the three words of origins—"Adam," "early" and "morning"—and also the outgoing movement of Whitman, walking forth refreshed from a bower (that may be also a tomb), emerging from a sleep that may have been a kind of good death. Whitman placed this poem at the close of the *Children of Adam* division of *Leaves of Grass*, thus positioning it between the defeated American pathos of *Facing West from California's Shores* and the poignant *In Paths Untrodden* that begins the homoerotic *Calamus* section. There is a hint, in this contextualization, that the astonished reader needs to cross a threshold also. Behold Whitman as Adam; do not merely regard him when he is striding past. The injunctions build from that "behold" through "hear" and "approach" to "touch," a touch then particularized to the palm, as the resurrected Walt passes, no phantom, but a risen body. "Hear my voice" is the center. As Biblical trope, it invokes Jehovah walking in Eden in the cool of the day, but in Whitman's American context it acquires a local meaning also. Hear my voice, and not just my words; *hear me as voice*. Hear me, as in my elegy for President Lincoln, I hear the hermit thrush.

Though the great elegy finds its overt emblems in the lilac-bush and the evening star, its more crucial tropes substitute for those emblems. These figures are the sprig of lilac that Whitman places on the hearse and the song of the thrush that floods the western night. Ultimately these are one trope, one image of voice, which we can follow Whitman by calling the "tally," playing also on a secondary meaning of "tally," as double or agreement. "Tally" may be Whitman's most crucial trope or ultimate image of voice. As a word, it goes back to the Latin *talea* for twig or cutting, which appears in this poem as the sprig of lilac. The word meant originally a cutting or stick upon which notches are made so as to keep count or score, but first in the English and then in the American vernacular it inevitably took on the meaning of a sexual score. The slang words "tallywoman," meaning a lady in an illicit relationship, and "tallywhack" or "tallywags," for the male genitalia, are still in circulation. "Tally" had a peculiar, composite meaning for Whitman in his poetry, which has not been noted by his critics. In the odd, rather luridly impressive death-poem *Chanting the Square Deific*, an amazing blend of Emerson and an Americanized Hegel, Whitman identifies himself with Christ, Hermes and Hercules and then writes: "All sorrow, labor, suffering, I, tallying it, absorb it in myself." My comment would be: "Precisely *how* does he tally it?" and the answer to that question, grotesque as initially it must seem, would be: "Why, first by masturbating, and then by writing poems." I am being merely accurate, rather than outrageous, and so I turn to *Song of Myself*, section 25, as first proof-text:

Dazzling and tremendous how quick the sun-rise would kill me,
If I could not now and always send sun-rise out of me.

We also ascend dazzling and tremendous as the sun,
We found our own O my soul in the calm and cool of the daybreak.
My voice goes after what my eyes cannot reach,
With the twirl of my tongue I encompass worlds and volumes of
   worlds.

Speech is the twin of my vision, it is unequal to measure itself,
It provokes me forever, it says sarcastically,
Walt you contain enough, why don't you let it out then?

Come now I will not be tantalized, you conceive too much of
   articulation,
Do you not know O speech how the buds beneath you are folded?
Waiting in gloom, protected by frost,
The dirt receding before my prophetical screams,
I underlying causes to balance them at last,
My knowledge my live parts, it keeping tally with the meaning of
   all things,
Happiness, (which whoever hears me let him or her set out in search
   of this day.)

My final merit I refuse you, I refuse putting from me what I really am,
Encompass worlds, but never try to encompass me,
I crowd your sleekest and best by simply looking toward you.

Writing and talk do not prove me,
I carry the plenum of proof and every thing else in my face,
With the hush of my lips I wholly confound the skeptic.

At this, almost the mid-point of his greatest poem, Whitman is
sliding knowingly near crisis, which will come upon him in the
crossing between sections 27 and 28. But here he is too strong,
really too strong, and soon will pay the price of that over-strength,
according to the Emersonian iron Law of Compensation, that
nothing is got for nothing. Against the sun's mocking taunt: "See
then whether you shall be master!" Whitman sends forth his own
sunrise, which is a better, a more Emersonian answer than what
Melville's Ahab threatens when he cries out, with surpassing
Promethean eloquence: "I'd strike the sun if it insulted me!" As
an alternative dawn, Whitman crucially identifies himself as a
voice, a voice overflowing with presence, a presence that is a sexual

self-knowledge: "My knowledge my live parts, it keeping tally with the meaning of all things." His knowledge and sexuality are one, and we need to ask: how does that sexual self-knowing keep tally with the meaning of all things? The answer comes in the crisis sequence of sections 26–30, where Whitman starts with listening and then regresses to touch, until he achieves both orgasm and poetic release through a Sublime yet quite literal masturbation. The sequence begins conventionally enough with bird song and human voice, passes to music, and suddenly becomes very extraordinary, in a passage critics have admired greatly but have been unable to expound:

> The orchestra whirls me wider than Uranus flies,
> It wrenches such ardors from me I did not know I possess'd them,
> It sails me, I dab with bare feet, they are lick'd by the indolent waves,
> I am cut by bitter and angry hail, I lose my breath,
> Steep'd amid honey'd morphine, my windpipe throttled in fakes of death,
> At length let up again to feel the puzzle of puzzles,
> And that we call Being.

This Sublime antithetical flight (or repression) not only takes Whitman out of nature, but makes him a new kind of god, ever-dying and ever-living, a god whose touchstone is of course voice. The ardors wrenched from him are operatic, and the cosmos becomes stage machinery, a context in which the whirling bard first loses his breath to the envious hail, then sleeps a drugged illusory death in uncharacteristic silence, and at last is let up again to sustain the enigma of Being. For this hero of voice, we expect now a triumphant ordeal by voice, but surprisingly we get an equivocal ordeal by sexual self-touching. Yet the substitution is only rhetorical, and establishes the model for the tally in the Lincoln elegy, since the sprig of lilac will represent Whitman's live parts, and the voice of the bird will represent those ardors so intense, so wrenched from Whitman, that he did not know he possessed them.

After praising his own sensitivity of touch, Whitman concludes section 27 with the highly equivocal line: "To touch my person to some one else's is about as much as I can stand." The crisis section proper, 28, centers upon demonstrating that to touch his own person is also about as much as Whitman can stand. By the time he cries out: "I went myself first to the headland, my own hands carried me there," we can understand how the whole 1855 *Song of Myself* may have grown out of an early notebook jotting on the image of the headland, a threshold stage between self-excitation and orgasm. Section 28 ends with frankly portrayed release:

> You villain touch! what are you doing? my breath is tight
>   in its throat,
> Unclench your floodgates, you are too much for me.

The return of the image of breath and throat, of voice, is no surprise, nor will the attentive reader be startled when the lines starting section 29 take a rather more affectionate view of touch, now that the quondam villain has performed his labor:

> Blind loving wrestling touch, sheath'd hooded sharp-tooth'd
>   touch!
> Did it make you ache so, leaving me?

Since Whitman's "rich showering rain" fructifies into a golden, masculine landscape, we can call this sequence of *Song of Myself* the most productive masturbation since the ancient Egyptian myth of a god who masturbates the world into being. I suggest now (and no Whitman scholar will welcome it) that a failed masturbation is the concealed reference in section 2 of the *Lilacs* elegy:

> O powerful western fallen star!
> O shades of night—O moody, tearful night!
> O great star disappear'd—O the black murk that hides the star!
> O cruel hands that hold me powerless—O helpless soul of me!
> O harsh surrounding cloud that will not free my soul.

The cruel hands are Whitman's own, as he vainly seeks relief from his repressed guilt, since the death of Father Abraham has rekindled the death, a decade before, of the drunken Quaker carpenter-father, Walter Whitman, Senior. Freud remarks, in *Mourning and Melancholia*, that

> . . . there is more in the content of melancholia than in that of normal grief. In melancholia the relation to the object is no simple one; it is complicated by the conflict of ambivalence. This latter is either constitutional, i.e. it is an element of every love-relation formed by this particular ego, or else it proceeds from precisely those experiences that involved a threat of losing the object. . . . Constitutional ambivalence belongs by nature to what is repressed, while traumatic experiences with the object may have stirred to activity something else that has been repressed. Thus everything to do with these conflicts of ambivalence remains excluded from consciousness, until the outcome characteristic of melancholia sets in. This, as we know, consists in the libidinal cathexis that is being menaced at last abandoning the object, only, however, to resume its occupation of that place in the ego whence it came. So by taking flight into the ego love escapes annihilation. . . .

Both conflicts of ambivalence are Whitman's in the *Lilacs* elegy, and we will see love fleeing into Whitman's image of voice, the bird's tallying chant, which is the last stance of his ego. Freud's ultimate vision of primal ambivalence emphasized its origin as being the dialectical fusion/defusion of the two drives, love and death. Whitman seems to me profounder even than Freud as a student of the interlocking of these antithetical drives that darkly combine into one Eros and its shadow of ruin, to appropriate a phrase from Shelley. Whitman mourns Lincoln, yes, but pragmatically he mourns even more intensely for the tally, the image of voice he cannot as yet rekindle into being, concealed as it is by a "harsh surrounding cloud" of impotence. The miraculous juxtaposition of the two images of the tally, sprig of lilac and song of the hermit thrush, in sections 3 and 4 following, points the possible path out of Whitman's death-in-life:

3
In the dooryard fronting an old farm-house near the
    white-wash'd palings,

Stands the lilac-bush tall-growing with heart-shaped leaves
    of rich green,
With many a pointed blossom rising delicate, with the
    perfume strong I love,
With every leaf a miracle—and from this bush in the dooryard,
With delicate-color'd blossoms and heart-shaped leaves of
    rich green,
A sprig with its flower I break.

    4
In the swamp in secluded recesses,
A shy and hidden bird is warbling a song.

Solitary the thrush,
The hermit withdrawn to himself, avoiding the settlements,
Sings by himself a song.

Song of the bleeding throat,
Death's outlet song of life, (for well dear brother I know,
If thou wast not granted to sing thou would'st surely die.)

Whitman breaks the *talea*, in a context that initially suggests a ritual of castration, but the image offers more than a voluntary surrender of manhood. The broken lilac sprig is exactly analogous to the "song of the bleeding throat," and indeed the analogy explains the otherwise baffling "bleeding." For what has torn the thrush's throat? The solitary song itself, image of wounded voice, is the other *talea*, and has been broken so that the soul can take count of itself. Yet why must these images of voice be broken? Whitman's answer, a little further on in the poem, evades the "why" much as he evades the child's "What is the grass?" in *Song of Myself* 6, for the *why* like the *what* is unknowable in the context of the Epicurean-Lucretian metaphysics that Whitman accepted. Whitman's answer comes in the hyperbolic, daemonic, repressive force of his copious over-breaking of the tallies:

Here, coffin that slowly passes,
I give you my sprig of lilac.

    7
(Nor for you, for one alone,
Blossoms and branches green to coffins all I bring,

For fresh as the morning, thus would I chant a song for you
    O sane and sacred death.

All over bouquets of roses,
O death, I cover you over with roses and early lilies,
But mostly and now the lilac that blooms the first,
Copious I break, I break the sprigs from the bushes,
With loaded arms I come, pouring for you,
For you and the coffins all of you O death.)

Why should we be moved that Whitman intones: "O sane and
sacred death," rather than: "O insane and obscene death," which
might seem to be more humanly accurate? "Death" here is a trope
for the sane and sacred Father Abraham, rather than for the actual
father. Whitman's profuse breaking of the tallies attempts to extend this trope, so as to make of death itself an ultimate image of
voice or tally of the soul. It is the tally and not literal death, our
death, that is sane and sacred. But that returns us to the figuration
of the tally, which first appears in the poem as a verb, just before
the carol of death:

And the charm of the carol rapt me,
As I held as if by their hands my comrades in the night,
And the voice of my spirit tallied the song of the bird.

"My knowledge my live parts, it keeping tally with the meaning
of all things" now transfers its knowledge from the vital order to
the death-drive. I am reminded that I first became aware of Whitman's crucial trope by pondering its remarkable use by Hart Crane,
when he invokes Whitman directly in the "Cape Hatteras" section
of *The Bridge:*

O Walt!—Ascensions of thee hover in me now
As thou at junctions elegiac, there, of speed,
With vast eternity, dost wield the rebound seed!
The competent loam, the probable grass,—travail
Of tides awash the pedestal of Everest, fail
Not less than thou in pure impulse inbred
To answer deepest soundings! O, upward from the dead
Thou bringest tally, and a pact, new bound
Of living brotherhood!

Crane's allusion is certainly to the *Lilacs* elegy, but his interpretation of what it means to bring tally "upward from the dead" may idealize rather too generously. That Walt's characteristic movement is ascension cannot be doubted, but the operative word in this elegy is "passing." The coffin of the martyred leader passes first, but in the sixteenth and final section it is the bard who passes, still tallying both the song of the bird and his own soul. That the tally is crucial, Crane was more than justified in emphasizing, but then Crane was a great reader as well as a great writer of poetry. Flanking the famous carol of death are two lines of the tally: "And the voice of my spirit tallied the song of the bird" preceding, and "To the tally of my soul" following. To tally the hermit thrush's carol of death *is* to tally the soul, for what is measured is the degree of sublimity, the agonistic answer to the triple question: more? less? equal? And the Sublime answer in death's carol is surely "more":

> *Come lovely and soothing death,*
> *Undulate round the world, serenely arriving, arriving,*
> *In the day, in the night, to all, to each,*
> *Sooner or later delicate death.*
>
> *Prais'd be the fathomless universe,*
> *For life and joy, and for objects and knowledge curious,*
> *And for love, sweet love—but praise! praise! praise!*
> *For the sure-enwinding arms of cool-enfolding death.*
>
> *Dark mother always gliding near with soft feet,*
> *Have none chanted for thee a chant of fullest welcome?*
> *Then I chant it for thee, I glorify thee above all,*
> *I bring thee a song that when thou must indeed come,*
> *   come unfalteringly.*
>
> *Approach strong deliveress,*
> *When it is so, when thou hast taken them I joyously sing*
> *   the dead,*
> *Lost in the loving floating ocean of thee,*
> *Laved in the flood of thy bliss O death.*

If this grand carol, as magnificent as the Song of Songs which is Solomon's, constitutes the tally or image of voice of the soul, then we ought now to be able to describe that image. To tally, in Whitman's sense, is at once to measure the soul's actual and potential sublimity, to overcome object-loss and grief, to gratify one's self sexually by one's self, to compose the thousand songs at random of *Leaves of Grass*, but above all, as Crane said, to bring a new covenant of brotherhood, and here that pact is new bound with the voice of the hermit thrush. The bird's carol, which invokes the oceanic mother of Whitman's *Sea-Drift cosmos*, is clearly not its tally but Whitman's own, the transgressive verbal climax of his own family romance. When, in the elegy's final section, Whitman chants himself as "Passing the song of the hermit bird and the tallying song of my soul," he prepares himself and us for his abandonment of the image of the lilac. And, in doing so, he prepares us also for his overwhelming refusal or inability to yield up similarly the darker image of the tally:

> Yet each to keep and all, retrievements out of the night,
> The song, the wondrous chant of the gray-brown bird,
> And the tallying chant, the echo arous'd in my soul. . . .

The tally is an echo, as an image of voice must be, yet truly it does not echo the carol of the hermit thrush. Rather, it echoes the earlier Whitman, of *Out of the Cradle Endlessly Rocking*, and his literary father, the Emerson of the great *Essays*. But here I require an *excursus* into poetic theory in order to explain image of voice and its relation to echo and allusion, and rather than rely upon as recondite a theorist as myself, I turn instead to a great explainer, John Hollander, who seems to me our outstanding authority upon all matters of lyrical form. Here is Hollander upon images of voice and their relation to the figurative interplay I have called "transumption," since that is what I take "tally" to be: Whitman's greatest transumption or introjection or Crossing of Identification, his magnificent overcoming both of his own earlier images of poetic origins and of Emerson's story of how poetry comes into being, particularly American poetry. First Hollander, from his forthcoming book, *The Figure of Echo*:

. . . we deal with diachronic trope all the time, and yet we have no name for it as a class. . . . the echoing itself makes a figure, and the interpretive or revisionary power which raises the echo even louder than the original voice is that of a trope of diachrony. . . .

I propose that we apply the name of the classical rhetoricians' trope of *transumption* (or *metalepsis* in its Greek form) to these diachronic, allusive figures. . . .

Proper reading of a metaphor demands a simultaneous appreciation of the beauty of a vehicle and the importance of its freight. . . . But the interpretation of a metalepsis entails the recovery of the transumed material. A transumptive style is to be distinguished radically from the kind of conceited one which we usually associate with baroque poetic, and with English seventeenth-century verse in particular. It involves an ellipsis, rather than a relentless pursuit, of further figuration. . . .

Hollander then names transumption as the proper figure for interpretive allusion, to which I would add only the description that I gave before in *A Map of Misreading*: this is the trope-undoing trope, which seeks to reverse imagistic priorities. Milton crowds all his poetic precursors together into the space that intervenes between *himself and the truth*. Whitman also crowds poetic anteriority—Emerson and the Whitman of 1855–1860—into a little space between the carol of death and the echo aroused in the soul of the elegist of *Lilacs*. Emerson had excluded the questions of sex and death from his own images-of-voice, whether in a verse chant like *Bacchus* or a prose rhapsody like *The Poet*. The earlier Whitman had made of the deathly ocean at night his maternal image of voice, and we have heard the hermit thrush in its culmination of that erotic cry. Whitman's tally transumes the ocean's image of voice, by means of what Hollander calls an ellipsis of further figuration. The tally notches a restored Narcissism and the return to the mode of erotic self-sufficiency. The cost is high as it always is in transumption. What vanishes here in Whitman is the presence of others and of otherness, as object-libido is converted into ego-libido again. Father Abraham, the ocean as dark mother, the love of comrades, and even the daemonic *alter ego* of the hermit thrush all fade away together. But what is left is the authentic American image of voice, as the bard brings tally, alone there in the night among the fragrant pines except for his remaining comrades, the knowledge of death and the thought of death.

In 1934 Wallace Stevens, celebrating his emergence from a decade's poetic silence, boldly attempted a very different transumption of the Whitmanian images of voice:

> It was her voice that made
> The sky acutest at its vanishing.
> She measured to the hour its solitude.
> She was the single artificer of the world
> In which she sang. . . .

The tally, in *The Idea of Order at Key West*, becomes the "ghostlier demarcations, keener sounds" ending the poem. A year later, Stevens granted himself a vision of Whitman as sunset in our evening-land:

> In the far South the sun of autumn is passing
> Like Walt Whitman walking along a ruddy shore.
> He is singing and chanting the things that are part of him,
> The worlds that were and will be, death and day.
> Nothing is final, he chants. No man shall see the end.
> His beard is of fire and his staff is a leaping flame.

It is certainly the passing bard of the end of *Lilacs*, but did he chant that nothing is final? Still, this is Walt as Moses and as Aaron, leading the poetic children of Emerson through the American wilderness, and surely Whitman was always proudly provisional. Yet, the tally of his soul had to present itself as a finality, as an image of voice that had achieved a fresh priority and a perpetually ongoing strength. Was that an American Sublime, or only another American irony? Later in 1935, Stevens wrote a grim little poem called *The American Sublime* that seems to qualify severely his intense images of voice, of the singing girl and of Whitman:

> But how does one feel?
> One grows used to the weather,

The landscape and that;
And the sublime comes down
To the spirit itself,

The spirit and space,
The empty spirit
In vacant space.
What wine does one drink?
What bread does one eat?

The questions return us full circle to Emerson's *Bacchus*, nearly
a century before:

We buy ashes for bread;
We buy diluted wine. . . .

This is not transumptive allusion, but a repetition of figurations,
the American baroque defeat. But that is a secondary strain in
Stevens, as it was in Emerson and in Whitman. I leap ahead, past
Frost and Pound, Eliot and Williams, past even Hart Crane, to
conclude with a contemporary image-of-voice that is another strong
tally, however ruefully the strength regards itself. Here is John Ashbery's *The Other Tradition*, the second poem in his 1977 volume,
Houseboat Days:

They all came, some wore sentiments
Emblazoned on T-shirts, proclaiming the lateness
Of the hour, and indeed the sun slanted its rays
Through branches of Norfolk Island pine as though
Politely clearing its throat, and all ideas settled
In a fuzz of dust under trees when it's drizzling:
The endless games of Scrabble, the boosters,
The celebrated omelette au Cantal, and through it
The roar of time plunging unchecked through the sluices
Of the days, dragging every sexual moment of it
Past the lenses: the end of something.
Only then did you glance up from your book,
Unable to comprehend what had been taking place, or
Say what you had been reading. More chairs
Were brought, and lamps were lit, but it tells
Nothing of how all this proceeded to materialize

Before you and the people waiting outside and in the next
Street, repeating its name over and over, until silence
Moved halfway up the darkened trunks,
And the meeting was called to order.
                                        I still remember
How they found you, after a dream, in your thimble hat,
Studious as a butterfly in a parking lot.
The road home was nicer then. Dispersing, each of the
Troubadours had something to say about how charity
Had run its race and won, leaving you the ex-president
Of the event, and how, though many of these present
Had wished something to come of it, if only a distant
Wisp of smoke, yet none was so deceived as to hanker
After that cool non-being of just a few minutes before,
Now that the idea of a forest had clamped itself
Over the minutiae of the scene. You found this
Charming, but turned your face fully toward night,
Speaking into it like a megaphone, not hearing
Or caring, although these still live and are generous
And all ways contained, allowed to come and go
Indefinitely in and out of the stockade
They have so much trouble remembering, when your forgetting
Rescues them at last, as a star absorbs the night.

I am aware that this charming poem urbanely confronts, absorbs
and in some sense seeks to overthrow a critical theory, almost a
critical climate, that has accorded it a canonical status. Stevens's
Whitman proclaims that nothing is final and that no man shall
see the end. Ashbery, a Whitman somehow more studiously casual
even than Whitman, regards the prophets of belatedness and cheerfully insists that his forgetting or repression will rescue us at last,
even as the Whitmanian or Stevensian evening star absorbs the
night. But the price paid for this metaleptic reversal of American
belatedness into a fresh earliness is the yielding up of Ashbery's
tally or image of voice to a deliberate grotesquerie. Sexuality is
made totally subservient to time, which is indeed "the end of
something," and poetic tradition becomes an ill-organized social
meeting of troubadours, leaving the canonical Ashbery as "ex-
president / Of the event." As for the image of voice proper, the

Whitmanian confrontation of the night now declines into: "You found this / Charming, but turned your face fully toward night, / Speaking into it like a megaphone, not hearing / Or caring." Such a megaphone is an apt image for Paul de Man's deconstructionist view of poetic tradition, which undoes tradition by suggesting that every poem is as much a random and gratuitous event as any human death is.

Ashbery's implicit interpretation of what he wants to call *The Other Tradition* mediates between this vision of poems as being totally cut off from one another and the antithetical darkness in which poems carry over-determined relationships and progress towards a final entropy. Voice in our poetry now tallies what Ashbery in his *Syringa*, a major Orphic elegy in *Houseboat Days*, calls "a record of pebbles along the way." Let us grant that the American Sublime is always also an American irony, and then turn back to Emerson and hear the voice that is great within us somehow breaking through again. This is Emerson in his journal for August 1859, on the eve of being burned out, with all his true achievement well behind him; but he gives us the true tally of his soul:

> *Beatitudes of Intellect.*—Am I not, one of these days, to write consecutively of the beatitude of intellect? It is too great for feeble souls, and they are over-excited. The wineglass shakes, and the wine is spilled. What then? The joy which will not let me sit in my chair, which brings me bolt upright to my feet, and sends me striding around my room, like a tiger in his cage, and I cannot have composure and concentration enough even to set down in English words the thought which thrills me—is not that joy a certificate of the elevation? What if I never write a book or a line? for a moment, the eyes of my eyes were opened, the affirmative experience remains, and consoles through all suffering.

8

Clinamen:
Towards a Theory of Fantasy

I intend to offer here only the opening move or swerve of what might become a theory of literary fantasy, or perhaps might join itself to some existent theories of that mode. As motto or epigraph I take from my personal favorite among modern fantasies the plangent sentence spoken by Nightspore to Krag over the corpse of the Promethean quester, Maskull: "Why was all this necessary?" to which Krag replies with his customary angry abruptness: "Ask Crystalman. His world is no joke." "All this" is nothing less than the most Sublime and spiritually terrifying death-march in all of fantastic literature, in some respects even overgoing similar journeys from Dante on to Browning's *Childe Roland to the Dark Tower Came*. David Lindsay's *A Voyage to Arcturus*, first published in 1920 in England, is a very unevenly written book, varying in tone from preternatural eloquence to quite tedious bathos. Yet I will assert for it a greatness that few contemporary critics might grant, and part of that greatness is the book's near-perfection in a particular kind of romance invention, as once it would have been called—that kind we have agreed to call fantasy.

I am moved by Eric Rabkin's insight when, in his recent anthology of fantasy, he places *A Voyage to Arcturus* together with *Alice in Wonderland* in his "range (10)" category of fantasy, meaning the outer limit of the mode, after which I suppose we would pass into a strange new Scripture, a revelation like that of the Gnostic Valentinus or of Joachim of Flora. The deepest affinities of Lindsay's mad sport of a book are with Lewis Carroll's apocalyptic release of fantastic energies and desires, though what emerges as purified wonder in Carroll manifests itself as horror and torment in Lindsay. Try to imagine *Through the Looking Glass* as it might have been written by Thomas Carlyle, and you will not be far from the verbal cosmos of David Lindsay.

I invoke Carlyle deliberately, because he is the tutelary spirit who informs Lindsay's frightening romance, which is a direct descendant of *Sartor Resartus*. Indeed Carlyle himself, I take it, is the perhaps unconscious model for the god or demi-god Krag, just as Walter Pater and his disciple Oscar Wilde served Lindsay as repressed models for Krag's adversary, Crystalman or Shaping. But I will postpone an account of the Carlyle-Pater agon in *A Voyage to Arcturus* until I have explored some opening aspects of my *clinamen* or ironic swerve into a beginning for a theory of fantasy. "Why was all this necessary?" is the question that, with Nightspore, we must put to the elaborate inventions of any particular fantasy, if we wish to apply those high standards of inevitability in figuration and design that traditionally have been applied to literary romance.

Fantasy is a literary sub-genre, by which I do not mean to deprecate it, but rather to state this formula: what is good in fantasy *is* romance, just as anything good in verse *is* poetry. Historically, the eighteenth century, and subsequently Romanticism, replaced the heroic genre by romance, even as the concept of the Sublime replaced theology. If Freud, as I now believe, extended and rationalized Romanticism rather than replaced it, we can aver that the literary element in dream, as expounded by Freud, is always romance. In the anxiety of belatedness that the eighteenth-century waning of the Enlightenment passed on to Romanticism (and to Freud) can be found the repressed source of modern literary fantasy, because fantasy beckons as a release to any sense of belatedness.

The course of nineteenth-century romance had to ensue in the sub-mode of fantasy, first for children and then for adults, because romance, in reclaiming itself, discovered that it had ceased to be in competition with its Oedipal child, the novel. I would cite here not so much Novalis and Hoffmann, though I will say something of them later, but rather Hans Christian Andersen and Lewis Carroll, who seem to me the most inventive of nineteenth-century romance fantasists. What releases itself in Andersen and Carroll is what I would call a natural Gnosticism, or perhaps only a natural religion that is a kind of Gnosis.

Gnosticism, largely an Alexandrian invention, I take as being uniquely the religion of belatedness, and Gnosis as a mode of knowing seems to me, as it did to Emerson, finally the knowing of what is oldest and so earliest in oneself, and so the true counter-force to a sense of having arrived too late. Prose romance, particularly in its late version of fantasy, attempts an end run around belatedness, and so must skirt the dangers of appearing childish and silly, just as the jealous child of romance, the novel, must skirt instead the dangers of appearing prosaic and expository. I am going to begin now upon a theory of fantasy by dividing the fantasy from the novel on the basis of Freud's two principles of mental functioning, yielding the reality principle to the novel, and claiming the pleasure/pain principle as the domain of fantasy. But I cannot effect such a division without first expounding and also criticizing the Freudian account of the two principles.

Though Freud assigns temporal priority to the pleasure/pain principle, I will discuss the reality principle first, precisely because of its high irrelevance to any theory of fantasy. Freud's principle of reality modifies, dominates and regulates the pleasure/pain principle, and so compels the human urges for fulfillment to go by detours and postponements, obstacles set by the external universe and society. I would say that Freud, in his writing, takes three very different rhetorical stances towards the reality principle: economic, topographical and dynamic. In the economic tonality, free energy is transmuted into bound energy by the reality principle. From a topographical viewpoint, the reality principle finds its home in the preconscious-conscious system of the psyche, as opposed to the unconscious. To a dynamic stance, the reality principle relies for its enabling energy upon urges or drives supposedly in the service of the ego, a very dubious notion even in terms of Freud's own later ideas.

Clearly, such views of the reality principle are more consonant with the fictive universe of George Eliot than with that of Lewis Carroll, and Freud's pragmatic exaltation of the reality principle is a psychological version of the displacement of the romance by the novel. Freud needed to provide what no novelist could hope to invent, a rational account of how the pleasure/pain principle yielded its priority to the disenchantment of the reality principle. With marvelous significance for any theory of fantasy which is not content with mere formalism or structuralism, Freud hypothesized that as infants we begin by living in fantasy. But when fantasy ceases to bring actual satisfaction, then infantile hallucinations end, and the reality-principle begins to enter, together with a lengthening of attention-span, judgment, and the first sense of memory. In this curiously genetic psychology, really rather uncharacteristic of Freud, the infant's cathexis or investment in his own freedom of fantasy is displaced, and energy begins to become bound. Yet the pleasure/pain principle retains its sway over fantasy, a word which for Freud refers to the unconscious and to its primary-process workings.

It will be clear already that I dissent absolutely from those theorists of literary fantasy who wish to separate vigorously their subject from psychological processes of fantasy; but a theorist of influence anxieties and of agonistic misprisions takes up Freudian stances towards fantasy only with some strong misprisions all his own. Freud himself tells us that the drive for ego-preservation provides the dynamic for the onward march of reality-testing, but that the sexual drives are educated by reality only partially and belatedly, thus making for an apparently thoroughgoing dualism between the ego and the unconscious. But Freud, though the greatest and most adroit of modern explainers, cannot explain why as infants we don't all just choose to stay hallucinated. Nor can he ever explain precisely what reality-testing is, which leads me to surmise that finally it is Freud's own displaced version of a kind of Platonizing transcendentalism, a moral vision masking itself as an evidentiary science. We all live and are trapped in time, so I am in no way impressed by the anti-Freudian shibboleth that Freud's "reality" is only a limited nineteenth-century Darwinian or Helmholzian scientism; but I am very disturbed that Freud's reality-principle may be only an idealized and idealizing good in itself, one more thing-in-itself that Nietzsche's dialectic can destroy with great ease. Do we possess the Freudian reality-principle as we possess art, only in order not to perish from the nihilizing truth?

No such question is tempted by the pleasure/pain principle, which Freud usually called just the Pleasure Principle, but which in fact he had begun by naming the Unpleasure Principle. It is difficult to quarrel with a purely economic principle, since it defines pleasure as a reduction in the quantities of any excitation, and pain as an increase in such quantities. These perfectly and outrageously minimalistic definitions Freud never sought to modify, yet he could not ever fix the pleasure/pain principle in regard to the rest of his theories. Temporality as to pleasure and pain alike baffled him, nor could he work out the qualitative difference between pleasure and pain upon his own reductive premises. Yet Freud could not let go of the pleasure/pain principle because uniquely it worked for both conscious and unconscious psychic agencies. Still, this shrewdest of all modern theorists never clarified the relation even between the pleasure/pain principle and his cherished principle of constancy: ought energy to be maintained at a minimal level or at a constant level to avoid unpleasure? The rather desperate attempt to identify the constancy and pleasure/pain principles is the opening move in Freud's beautiful exercise in catastrophe-theory, *Beyond the Pleasure Principle*, which I will cite at the end of my discourse, but here I want to turn to consider Freud's own anxieties about fantasy, both personal and literary, by way of his essay on Hoffmann's magnificent story *The Sandman*.

As one of the strongest literary fantasies, *The Sandman* simply casts off the economics, topography and dynamics of the reality principle, and I pause here to cast off, with amiable simplicity, the theory of fantasy set forth by Todorov. We do *not* hesitate between trope and the uncanny in reading Hoffmann or David Lindsay or Lewis Carroll or *The Tin Drum*, and indeed we can say that here the reader who hesitates *is* lost and *has* lost that moment which is the agonistic encounter of deep, strong reading. Where literary fantasy is strong, the trope itself introjects the uncanny, as Freud rather involuntarily both sees and shows in his anxiously strong reading of *The Sandman*.

Freud's *Sandman* is unquestionably his strongest reading of any literary text, but its strength is in its allegorization of the story as being an overwhelming instance of repetition-compulsion, of the castration complex, and most complexly as the Freudian version of the Sublime, which is the "uncanny." As I remarked earlier, the concerns of Hoffmann are thus swerved into what is at once the great strength and the great weakness of literary fantasy: anxieties when confronted with anterior powers. Though Freud hardly could or would acknowledge it, these were his anxieties also, in him specifically anxieties relating to authority and to transference. Uncanniness in Hoffmann is related to the narcissistic belief in the "omnipotence of thought," which in aesthetic terms *is* the Miltonic and High Romantic faith in the power of the mind over the universe of death. *Das Heimliche*, the cannny or homely, is identified with its merely apparent opposite, *das Unheimliche*, or as Freud says, "this uncanny is in reality nothing new or foreign, but something familiar and old-established in the mind that has been estranged only by the process of repression."

As a formulaic reading of Hoffmann's literary fantasy, this could have been superb, yet Freud applies it rather oddly. Canny and uncanny, familiarity and estrangement, are dialectical entities, rather than ambivalent dualities, but Freud reads a pattern of psychic ambivalence right through the story. Coppelius becomes the castrating bad father who destroys the good father, and who ruins every erotic possibility for Nathanael. Fixated upon Coppelius as the representation of the dead father, the psychically castrated Nathanael is incapable of loving a woman. But surely Freud cannot, as a reader, persuasively give us a *Sandman* whose pattern is at once dialectical and self-contradictory, at once Sublime and castrating. I think though that we can learn from Freud here, as everywhere, because Freud has stumbled brilliantly, in one of his errors that are also grand insights. What he has uncovered is what I would name as the *clinamen* or opening Lucretian swerve of a theory of literary fantasy, and I phrase it in this formula: *fantasy, as a belated version of romance, promises an absolute freedom from belatedness, from the anxieties of literary influence and origination, yet this promise is shadowed always by a psychic over-determination in the form itself of fantasy, that puts the stance of freedom into severe question.* What promises to be the least anxious of literary modes becomes much the most anxious, and this anxiety specifically relates to anterior powers, that is, to what we might call the genealogy of the imagination. The cosmos of fantasy, of the pleasure/pain principle, is revealed in the shape of nightmare, and not of hallucinatory wish-fulfillment.

My formulaic swerve and immediate subsequent remarks may give the impression that I am deprecating literary fantasy, or at least describing its apparent strength as its implicit weakness, but my intention is exactly the reverse; I speak descriptively, but indeed of fantasy's true strength, and of its use for the literary mind in our belated age. To illustrate my formula, and the role of fantasy as a belated Sublime, I turn at last to David Lindsay's *A Voyage to Arcturus*, recalling as I turn that the Sublime originally meant a style of "loftiness," of verbal power conceived agonistically, against all rivals. But in the Enlightenment, this literary idea was psychologized negatively, into a vision of terror in both art and nature, an oxymoronic terror uneasily allied with pleasurable sensations of augmented strength and indeed of narcissistic freedom. This freedom is what Emerson was to call the American stance of "wildness" and what Freud named "the omnipotence of thought," the narcissistic illusion at its height. Freud's own Sublime constituted his true Narcissism, the pride of an originator who could say "I invented psychoanalysis because it had no literature," or even more ironically: "I am not fond of reading."

Criticism begins in the lived experience of a text, meaning both the fondness of reading, and the ambivalences that such fondness calls forth, including those ambivalences that play through relationships between texts in many of the ways they play through human relationships. In regard to Lindsay's *A Voyage to Arcturus*, I have experienced a relationship marked by a wild fondness and an endless ambivalence, itself productive of my own first attempt at literary fantasy, published in 1979 as *The Flight to Lucifer*, a book very much in the Arcturan shadow. Shadow is the great closing trope of Lindsay's book, as Nightspore, the *pneuma* or spark of the dead Promethean, Maskull, confronts the Demiurge Crystalman, from the standing-point of a tower beyond death:

> The shadow-form of Crystalman had drawn much closer to him, and filled the whole sky, but it was not a shadow of darkness, but a bright shadow. It had neither shape, nor colour, yet it in some way suggested the delicate tints of early morning. It was so nebulous that the sphere could be clearly distinguished through it; in extension, however, it was thick. The sweet smell emanating from it was strong, loathsome, and terrible. . . .

This demiurgic shadow has a profound literary anteriority, and historically can be identified with the Aesthetic Movement in England (circa 1870–1900), which we associate with Swinburne, Whistler, Beardsley, the young Yeats, but above all others, with Pater and Wilde. Crystalman's bright shadow, with its delicate tints of early morning, has its clear source in the high purple of Pater's vision of the Renaissance, as here in the famous "Conclusion":

> To such a tremulous wisp constantly reforming itself on the stream, to a single sharp impression, with a sense in it, a relic more or less fleeting, of such moments gone by, what is real in our life fines itself down. It is with movement, with the passage and dissolution of impressions, images, sensations, that analysis leaves off—that continual vanishing away, that strange, perpetual weaving and unweaving of itself.

It might well be a more powerful and subtle version of Lindsay's Crystalman or Gangnet speaking to Maskull, as they wait for the blue sun of Alppain to rise, bringing Maskull's death. Lindsay, like Pound and Stevens, must have read Pater's first essay *Diaphaneite*, where the artist is called a crystal man, transparent and Apollonian, more than human in his perfection. Against Crystalman as Paterian Demiurge, Lindsay sets his most imaginative creation, the grotesque but stalwart god of redemptive pain, strikingly named Krag in what I take to be a tribute to Carlyle's isolated hill farm in Dumfriesshire, the rugged Craigenputtoch, where *Sartor Resartus* was written, it being the book from which the religious vision of *A Voyage to Arcturus* is quarried. In *Sartor Resartus*, the post-Calvinist Lindsay found most of the ingredients of his Gnostic myth, presented by Carlyle however with his characteristic German High Romantic irony and parodistic frenzy of despair. Carlyle's outrageous ontological fable has the humor that Lindsay could not attain, yet it lacks the final frenzy of absolute literary fantasy, which past all opening swerves must stage its own death-march beyond the pleasure/pain principle. We can cite here Carlyle's own Professor Teufelsdröckh's quotation from Friedrich Schlegel: "*Fantasy* is the organ of the Godlike," and on that basis prepare to turn again to Lindsay's quest for fantasy's simultaneous stance of freedom and over-determination.

Carlyle had insisted that the poet's work was to *see*, a willed seeing that would dissolve the cosmos of the pleasure/pain principle for the sake of the high purpose of bringing the reader under the reign of the reality principle. But Pater, and Wilde after him, subverted Carlyle's and Ruskin's moral, post-Calvinist emphasis upon willed seeing as a royal road to reality. Pater's Crystal or Aesthetic Man swerves away from a seeing that is a reality-testing to an Epicurean perceptiveness that dissolves external realities into a concourse of sensations. David Lindsay, following the northern vision of Carlyle, oddly achieves a fantastic world that indeed is Crystalman's or Pater's flux of sensations, but this is a world that Lindsay loathes, and names Tormance, a sado-masochistic amalgam of torment and of romance. The Carlyle-like demigod Krag remarks, with his customary bitterness, that once for all there is nothing worth seeing upon Tormance, an amazing remark that belies both the reader's experience of the book and also Lindsay's fantastic achievement. This paradox between disavowal and representation, in my own view, actually constitutes the aesthetic dynamism of literary fantasy.

Indeed this discursive paradox, at once exalting the *design* of romance, and yet rejecting all romantic *designs*, seems to me a clinching version of my formulaic swerve that begins a theory of literary fantasy by stating the simultaneous presence and absence of freedom, or the rhetorical stances of freedom, and of absence and presence of bondage, of an all but total psychic overdetermination. Other readers, friends and students, whom I have urged to read *A Voyage to Arcturus*, have tended to be severely divided in their reaction to the book, and to literary fantasy in general. When, in my disappointment, I have probed the negative reactions of readers I trust, I have found that they do center uncannily upon what I take to be the true critical issue here: why do books promising aesthetic freedom (and I know no fantasy wilder than *A Voyage to Arcturus*) seem to labor under such apparent aesthetic bondage? Why might a sensitive reader come to believe that Lindsay's book is a vivid nightmare, at best, rather than the absolute vision that I keep discovering in it?

A Voyage to Arcturus begins rather weakly, I would concede, as a kind of parody of science fiction, more or less in the mode of Jules Verne. Yet even in that hopeless first chapter, "The Seance," the Uncanny enters the book with the leaping advent of Krag. Still, it is not until Chapter VI, when Maskull wakes up on Tormance, that the Sublime proper begins as in this book it must: by, through and in suffering. Shelley suggested, as Longinus had, that the Sublime existed in order to induce the reader to abandon easier pleasures for more difficult pleasures. In Lindsay's savage fantasy, the Sublime has passed through Carlyle's Everlasting No and Centre of Indifference, leapfrogged over his Everlasting Yea, and then culminated by turning his Natural Supernaturalism inside out, to produce a Supernatural version of a Darwinian Naturalism. Lindsay seems to have invested himself in the most peculiar chapter of *Sartor Resartus*, "Symbols," and to have taken literally Carlyle's grand injunction there:

> A Hierarch, therefore, and Pontiff of the World will we call him, the Poet and inspired Maker; who Prometheus-like, can shape new Symbols, and bring new Fire from Heaven to fix it there. . . .

That Fire from Heaven Lindsay names Muspel-fire, taking the name "Muspel," I suspect, from *Sartor Resartus* again, where Carlyle writes of "the Adam-Kadmon, or Primeval Element, here strangely brought into relation with the *Nifl* and *Muspel* (Darkness and Light) of the antique North." Carlyle's juxtaposition is of the Kabbalistic Primal Man with the Niflheim or mist-home, the northern night, and with Muspelheim or bright-home, the southern realm of light. Lindsay reverses these mythological *topoi*, in one of his many instances of a kind of natural Gnosticism. It may be, though, that here Lindsay followed Novalis, who in Chapter 9, "Klingsohr's Tale," of *Heinrich von Ofterdingen*, placed the realm of King Arcturus in a northern region of light. Maskull lands on Tormance in its south, and always goes due north, but dies just before the gateway of Muspel, which he then enters in his spiritual form as Nightspore. But that raises the issues both of quest and questers in this daemonic fantasy, and I need to remark on those issues before I can relate the narrative patterns of *A Voyage to Arcturus* to my incipient theory of literary fantasy.

Novalis and Shelley are the two greatest masters of High Romantic fantasy-quest, and Lindsay descended from both of them, like the James Thomson of *The City of Dreadful Night* who called himself "Bysshe Vanolis." Writing to Friedrich Schlegel, Novalis described his own *Klingsohr's Fairy Tale* in terms precisely applicable to Lindsay's book:

> The antipathy between Light and Shadow, the yearning for clear, hot, penetrating aether, the Unknown-Holy, the Vesta in

Sophia, the mingling of the romantic of all ages, petrifying and petrified Reason, Arcturus, Chance, the spirit of life, individual strokes merely as arabesques,—this is the way to look upon my Fairy Tale.

This would also be the way to look upon Lindsay's fantasy, except that Lindsay's remorseless death-drive is so much darker than anything in Novalis, even than the *Hymns to the Night*. Shelley is the closer prototype for Maskull's drive beyond the pleasure/pain principle, a prototype that begins in *Alastor*, proceeds through *Prometheus Unbound* and *Epipsychidion*, and culminates in *Adonais* and *The Triumph of Life*. The protagonists of Shelleyan quest are all antithetical beings, set against nature and every merely natural value or affection. I venture the surmise that Shelley's verse-romances had much to do with establishing the theoretical pattern for most of the prose-fantasies that move in the Promethean tradition, from Mary Shelley's *Frankenstein* on to Lindsay's *Arcturus*. I would call this pattern a narcissistic one, in both the Ovidian and the Freudian sense, because the assimilation to one another of the unlikely duo of Narcissus and Prometheus is central to this internalized kind of fantastic quest-romance. Indeed, that curious assimilation, ensuing in a narcissistic Prometheus or Promethean narcist, is the direct cause of what I have been calling the *clinamen* or opening swerve, or ironic reaction-formation, of a theory of literary fantasy. The aggressivity of Promethean quest, turned quite destructively inwards against the self, results from a narcissistic scar, a scar inflicted by nature upon the questing antithetical will. One consequence of this scar is the aesthetic bafflement of literary fantasy, its ironic or allegorical conflict between a stance of absolute freedom and a hovering fear of total psychic over-determination. Shelley's Poet in *Alastor*, like his wife's Victor Frankenstein, is haunted by his *daemon* or dark double, in Frankenstein's case the creature he has made. The Shelleyan wandering Poet, and Frankenstein, and Lindsay's Maskull are all unable to get beyond self-destruction because their profound Narcissism is indistinguishable from their Prometheanism. Like Ovid's Narcissus, every protagonist of fantasy, even the greatest among them, say Don Quixote and Lewis Carroll's Alice, concludes by crying out: "My image no longer deceives me" and "I both kindle the flames and endure them." To state this another way, the Shelleyan quester, the Don, Alice, Maskull, Frankenstein, any true hero or heroine of literary fantasy discovers at last that the only fire they can steal is already and originally their own fire.

I offer this as a theoretical defense of fantasy and science fiction alike, against the eloquent strictures of the philosopher Stanley Cavell in his recent masterwork, *The Claim of Reason:*

> Dr. Faust's descendant Dr. Frankenstein is generally more childish, or more patently adolescent, in comparison with his ancestor. This is due, it would seem, to his more superficial narcissism, and his more obvious sense of guilt, as well as to his assumptions that what you know is fully expressed by its realization in what you can make. . . . It would be nice to understand, in connection with the declension from the damnation of Faust to the damnable Frankenstein, why there is a parallel declension in the genres they have inspired—why one of them is the subject of one of the great poetic epics of the modern world and the other of them is a classic, even a staple, of the literature (I include cinema) of the fantastic. . . .
>
> . . . we . . . need to articulate the difference between what we might call a thought experiment and what we might call a piece of science fiction. . . . a fictional tale is a history over which the teller has absolute authority, call it the power to stipulate the world from beginning to end. . . .
>
> . . . I . . . assert my sense that science fiction cannot house tragedy because in it human limitations can from the beginning be by-passed. . . .

What Cavell does not see is that Frankenstein, as a Shelleyan, High Romantic quester, has a Narcissism more profound than Faust's, and a sense of guilt not so much obvious as it is Promethean. The compounding of Narcissism and Prometheanism produces the swerve that begins literary fantasy, a swerve that calls into question Cavell's notion that a fictional tale is a history over which the teller has absolute authority. Neither narcist nor Promethean can transcend human limitations, and the story of Narcissus is as much the tragedy of human sexuality as Prometheus is of human aspiration. Technically, of course, Cavell is correct, because Milton's Satan is doubtless the paradigm of Narcissus confounded with Prometheus, and Milton does not allow Satan to become a tragic figure. But fantasy *can* become a tragic mode, if we shift perspectives; and yet again I turn back to read *A Voyage to Arcturus* as a fantasy that triumphantly becomes a narcissistic yet Promethean tragedy.

All through this discourse I keep verging upon an entrance into Lindsay's Tormance, and find great difficulty in negotiating that threshold, so I will allow myself to become more personal even than usual, in order to account for my difficulties on a cognitive as well as an affective basis. Reading Lindsay's book (and I have read it literally hundreds of times, indeed obsessively I have read several copies of it to shreds) is for me at once an experience of great freedom and of tormented psychic over-determination or nightmare. I know of no book that has caused me such an anxiety of influence, an anxiety to be read everywhere in my fantasy imitating it, *The Flight to Lucifer*. I have a vivid recall still of the surprise and shock I felt when it was republished in 1963, and my friend John Hollander gave me the book to read, quietly telling me it was written for me. Repeated readings have confirmed my initial sense that no other fictional work inflicts such spiritual violence upon its audience. E. H. Visiak, himself the author of a violently effective fantasy in his *Medusa*, accurately observed this strange tonality of *A Voyage to Arcturus:*

> This effect, whatever may be the cause or peculiar subconscious energy that was involved, is violently disturbing. The reader's very intellect is assailed; his imagination is appalled. . . .

I would go a step further than Visiak, and say that Lindsay's violence directly assaults what Freud called the bodily ego, the self's or personality's investment of libido in its own ego, which perhaps by such investment creates the narcissistic ego. Like Blake, Lindsay's aim is precisely apocalyptic: our relation to the natural world and to ourselves as natural men and women is to be broken, once and for all. No book, be it Blake's *Jerusalem* or *A Voyage to Arcturus*, can achieve so Sublime an aim; our natural defenses properly are aroused, and we resent so palpable a design upon us. It is Lindsay's astonishing achievement that, like Blake, he can persuade many attentive readers of the universal aspect of his personal nightmare. And, after many palpable evasions, I now will devote the remainder of this discourse to Lindsay's terrifying fantasy, except for a coda upon my anxious misprision of Lindsay in my own first venture into fantasy fiction.

The four central beings of Lindsay's narrative are Krag, whose hidden name is Surtur; Crystalman, whose other name is Shaping; Maskull, the Promethean quester; and Nightspore, who so mysteriously is Maskull's friend upon earth, but who on Tormance cannot come into existence until Maskull dies. As a fourfold, these have their rather precise equivalents in the mythologies of Blake, Shelley, Yeats and Freud, and to list the equivalents is highly instructive. Krag is Blake's Los, or what Yeats in *A Vision* calls Creative Mind, or Freud the achieved ego, beyond the narcissistic investment, and so in touch with the reality principle, or what Shelley's Prometheus will become only after he is unbound. Crystalman is Blake's Satanic Urizen, or Yeats's Will, the Freudian super-ego or the Jupiter of *Prometheus Unbound*. Maskull is Blake's Orc, and rather fascinatingly his name in Yeats's *Vision* is also the Mask, at once the Freudian narcissistic libido and the Shelleyan Promethean. Nightspore, perhaps Lindsay's most surprising personage, is akin to the driving instinctual force or urge that Blake calls Tharmas, Yeats the Body of Fate, Shelley Demogorgon, and Freud the id, agency of the unconscious. But further allegorization of Lindsay's narrative must wait until I have clarified its weird shape as narrative.

Yeats, in the note he added to Lady Gregory's *Cuchulain of Muirthemme*, in 1903, spoke of that traditional element in romance where "nobody described anything as we understood description" because all was figurative: "One was always losing oneself in the unknown, and rushing to the limits of the world." This is certainly the world of Tormance, where every antagonist to Maskull's Promethean quest is only another pleasure, another rejected otherness that ensnares Maskull briefly, intensely and to no purpose. A narrative that is nothing but a remorseless drive to death, beyond the pleasure/pain principle, can proceed only by a systematic assault upon the reader's sensibilities, because the reader *is* the antagonist, whose motive for reading at least begins in pleasure, and desires to end in pleasure. Lindsay audaciously sets as many obstacles for the reader to break through as his master Carlyle did, but the reader who persists will be rewarded, albeit somewhat belatedly.

After the rather unconvincing opening seance, the narrative is puzzlingly inconclusive until the moment that Maskull wakes up in the Arcturan night, to find his companions gone. He will never see Nightspore again, because Nightspore is his own spiritual form, who cannot function upon Tormance until his natural aspect, embodied in Maskull, has died. And there is not the slightest doubt but that Maskull is doom-eager, in the mode of Shelley's Poet in *Alastor*, or of Ovid's Narcissus. He is also astonishingly violent, and awesomely capable of enduring the really unbearable climates, regions and beings of the accursed world of Tormance. The typical inhabitant of Tormance is summed up in the description of one particular ogre as someone "who passed his whole existence in tormenting, murdering, and absorbing others, for the sake of his own delight." Since Maskull is hardly interested in his own delight, but only in his own possible sublimity, a very curious narrative principle goes to work as soon as Maskull starts walking due north upon Tormance. It is that singular kind of nightmare some of us dream obsessively, in which you encounter a series of terrifying faces, and only gradually do you come to realize that these faces *are terrified*, and that *you* are the cause of the terror. Maskull himself is at once the most remarkable and most frightening consciousness upon Tormance, and Maskull after all is technically a lost traveler, cut off in space and time. His truest precursor, as I will suggest later, may be Browning's Childe Roland, who is himself far darker than the dark tower he searches out.

Lindsay's narrative thus has the shape of a destructive fire seeking for a kindlier flame, but finding nothing because it burns up everything in its path. As we discover only in the book's last scene, after Maskull is dead, there is no Muspel or divine flame anyway, because Nightspore's true encounter with the Sublime, beyond death, results in his beautiful realization "that Muspel consisted of himself and the stone tower on which he was sitting. . . ." By then, the exhausted reader has transferred his identification from Maskull to Nightspore, from Prometheus-Narcissus to what Blake called "the real Man the imagination." It is the progressive exhaustion of the reader, through violence and through identification with Maskull, which is the true plot of Lindsay's narrative, as I will demonstrate by breaking into the text at Chapter XIV, which is Maskull's third morning on Tormance.

By then, Maskull has had a career of endless catastrophe, having suffered four murderous enchantments the previous day, and having been instrumental in at least four murders. Once we get away from the beings completely entranced by Crystalman, the Pater- or Wilde-like aesthetes Panawe and Joiwind, Maskull plunges into the problematic world of Ifdawn, where he breaks the neck of the hideous Crimtyphon, fails to prevent the murder of Oceaxe by Tydomin, is saved by Krag from being sorbed by Tydomin, himself sorbs Digrung, and then needlessly executes Tydomin and Spadevil. This sequence of disaster is followed by Maskull's vision in the Wombflash Forest, where he sees himself murdered by Krag and then is shocked unconscious when he attempts to follow Nightspore. When the reader stands with Maskull in the subsequent idyll of the encounter with the gentle fisherman Polecrab and his uncanny wife Gleameil, the reader, like Maskull, badly needs a rest. And, for a very few pages, we are rested, but only to be set up for an extraordinary violence, unlike any other narrative effect I have known. With daemonic cunning, even a kind of narrative cruelty, Lindsay introduces children for the first and only time in his book, and they are presented as being the least narcissistic beings upon Tormance, in another reversal of earth-psychology. Each child's ego seems wholly unparanoid, and in no way formed by the self's narcissistic investment. Confronted by children who have never known a narcissistic scar, and whose reactions to their mother's voluntary departure and almost certain death are so much more dignified than any earthly child could manifest, the reader is lulled into an ontological security, a delusive sense that the book's worst violence is past.

This sense is literally detonated upon Swaylone's Island, where the Paterian dictum that all the arts aspire to the condition of music is answered by a vision of music as the most destructive of all the arts. After Earthrid's music has murdered Gleameil, and failed to rid Tormance of Maskull, the quester from earth plays his own music upon the circular lake called Irontick. Maskull forces the Muspel-light to appear, but strains too hard to contract it into a solid form. His intention is to compel Surtur, the true or alien God who actually is Krag, to appear; but if he were successful, surely he would materialize Nightspore, his own spark or *pneuma*, as the Gnostics would have said. Despite the dangerous power of his extraordinary will, Maskull's success is limited. His music kills Earthrid, yet his fire destroys the lake, Earthrid's instrument. When the Muspel-light vanishes, it is because the waters of the lake have fallen through, thus breaking the instrument, the waters in their descent having met Maskull's fire. The category of the aesthetic and the reader's response to the final pastoral element in the narrative have been broken together. Maskull, and the reader, are left exhausted, waiting for the fourth daybreak upon Tormance.

That exhaustion, and the textual violence provoking it, are the uncanny or Sublime splendor of Lindsay's book, and place it, I would argue, at the very center of modern fantasy, in contrast to the works of the Neochristian Inklings which despite all their popularity are quite peripheral. Tolkien, Lewis and Williams actually flatter the reader's Narcissism, while morally softening the reader's

Prometheanism. Lindsay strenuously assaults the reader's Narcissism, while both hardening the reader's Prometheanism and reminding the reader that Narcissism and Prometheanism verge upon an identity. Inkling fantasy is soft stuff, because it pretends that it benefits from a benign transmission both of romance tradition and of Christian doctrine. Lindsay's savage masterpiece compels the reader to question both the sources of fantasy, *within the reader*, and the benignity of the handing-on of tradition. Fantasy is shown by Lindsay to be a mode in which freedom is won, if at all, by a fearful agon with tradition, and at the price of the worst kind of psychic over-determination, which is the sado-masochistic turning of aggressivity against the self.

Reluctantly, I forbear further commentary upon Maskull's misadventures, and move on to the instructive moment of his death: instructive, particularly in regard to a theory of fantasy, but highly problematic as to its meaning in the book. The ultimate romance model is certainly the curious wasting-away into death of Shelley's Poet in *Alastor*, yet that death seems a less equivocal triumph than Maskull's ebbing-away into sublimity. With Crystalman, barely disguised as the Oscar Wildean Gangnet, on one side of him, and the glowering Krag hammering away on the other, Maskull stands for the dignity of the Promethean human caught between contending divinities. But Lindsay negates the Promethean by an occult triumph, crucial for his dialectic:

> "What is this Ocean called?" asked Maskull, bringing out the words with difficulty.
> "Surtur's Ocean."
> Maskull nodded, and kept quiet for some time. He rested his face on his arm.
> "Where's Nightspore?" he asked suddenly.
> Krag bent over him, with a grave expression.
> "You are Nightspore."
> The dying man closed his eyes, and smiled. Opening them again, a few moments later, with an effort, he murmured, "Who are you?"
> Krag maintained a gloomy silence.

Shortly afterwards a frightful pang passed through Maskull's
heart, and he died immediately.
Krag turned his head round. "The night is really past at last,
Nightspore; . . . The day is here."
Nightspore gazed long and earnestly at Maskull's body.
"Why was all this necessary?"
"Ask Crystalman," replied Krag sternly. "His world is no
joke. He has a strong clutch . . . but I have a stronger.
. . . Maskull was his, but Nightspore is mine."

I quoted the end of this great passage at the beginning of my
discourse, and come full circle back to it now, but in, I trust, the
finer tone of a *clinamen,* a swerve into the start of a theory of literary fantasy. What kills Maskull? In an earlier vision, he had seen
Krag murdering him, whereas Krag, at the start of the final voyage,
prophesies that Crystalman as Gangnet will be the cause of Maskull's death. Lindsay equivocates, as he has to. Every other corpse
in this book of endless corpses has the vulgar Crystalman grin
upon it, even that of the beautiful High Romantic Sullenbode,
who has died for love of Maskull. But Maskull's corpse disappears,
without our knowing what final expression it carried. Krag speaks
two utterly contradictory truths: to Maskull: "You are Nightspore," and to Nightspore: "Maskull was his." In death, Maskull
becomes Nightspore; in life the Narcissus in him kept him Crystalman's. The discursive contradiction is at the heart of the fantasy mode: Promethean freedom or striving for freedom implicates
quester, writer and reader more deeply in the bondage of Narcissus, and a form that promises under-determination takes on both
the strength and the nightmare quality of over-determination.

I cannot leave *A Voyage to Arcturus,* even for the brief coda of
a glance at my loving but uneasy tribute to it in *The Flight to Lucifer,* without a few words of sheer praise for a book that has affected me personally with more intensity and obsessiveness than
all the works of greater stature and resonance of our time. Nothing
else in English since Blake and Shelley, that I know of, has found
its way back so surely to that early romance world where gods and
men meet and struggle as equals or near-equals. It is Lindsay,

about whom C. S. Lewis was ambivalent, rather than George Macdonald, who justifies the odd principle as to literary fantasy that Lewis brought forth on behalf of Macdonald:

> The texture of his writing as a whole is undistinguished, at times fumbling. . . . But this does not dispose of him even for the literary critic. What he does best is fantasy—fantasy that hovers between the allegorical and the mythopoeic. . . . It begins to look as if there were an art, or a gift, which criticism has largely ignored. It may even be one of the greatest arts; for it produces works which give us (at the first meeting) as much delight and (on prolonged acquaintance) as much wisdom and strength as the works of the greatest poets. . . . It gets under our skin, hits us at a level deeper than our thoughts or even our passions, troubles oldest certainties till all questions are reopened, and in general shocks us more fully awake than we are for most of our lives . . .

I am not certain that Lewis is making a critical statement, but I do recognize the reading experience he describes, except that I know it far more strongly from *A Voyage to Arcturus* than from *Lilith* or *Phantastes* or *At the Back of the North Wind*. And that is where I would locate Lindsay's great power, strangely akin to that of more genial masters of fantasy—Carroll, Andersen, Borges— and related also to Kafka's preternatural gifts. Carroll's Alice is after all as much a compound of Narcissus and Prometheus as Maskull is, because that "evilly compounded, vital I," as Wallace Stevens called it, is the ego of the hero or heroine of belated romance or literary fantasy. Lewis hints at a mode that strikes us beneath the level of discursive contradictions, because like our fantasy lives it eddies between the polarities of bondage and freedom, total psychic over-determination and total changeling-like independence of the family romance, which is after all finally indistinguishable from romance itself, or its belated but beautiful child, the literary fantasy of the nineteenth and twentieth centuries.

I turn, as a personal coda, to my own book, *The Flight to Lucifer: A Gnostic Fantasy*, which had its genesis in my obsession with Lindsay's book, just as my fantasy-in-progress, *The Lost Traveller's Dream*, has a double genesis in my inability to get my broodings away from two remarkable semi-fantasies or "realistic" romances, the Elizabethan Thomas Nashe's *The Unfortunate Traveller* and Nathanael West's apocalyptic *Miss Lonelyhearts*. I recall that Allen Tate once wrote an essay upon his own *Ode to the Confederate Dead*, and called it *Narcissus as Narcissus*. I will attempt to be consistent with my own theory, and so I will try to be both Prometheus *and* Narcissus as I comment briefly upon the theoretical aspects of *The Flight to Lucifer*.

I don't know how many narratives have had their genesis in a reader so loving a story that a sequel is desired, and not found, and so the reader proceeds to write the lacking sequel. If my own theories about influence-anxieties are at all relevant or useful, then any really intense love for a story or a poem has its ambivalent elements, however repressed they may be. Psychic ambivalence, as Angus Fletcher reminded us in his superb, path-breaking book *Allegory*, does *not* mean mixed feelings but rather a mixture of diametrically opposed feelings, usually related to a concept of taboo. If the extreme degree of ambivalence is, as Fletcher said, irony *or* allegory, we need to remember that for Freud the masterpiece of psychic ambivalence was the Oedipal conflict. This conflict emerged for Freud most vividly both in the taboo and in the psychoanalytical transference, but I think that Freud always repressed his rather shady basing of the structure of the transference upon the structure of the taboo. Fletcher acutely notes the presence of heightened emotive ambivalence in the literary Sublime, in Gnosticism and in the Freudian dialectic of negation, and also in really fierce satire. I quote Fletcher at his most sublimely illuminating:

> In a way Freud's term "negation" names the process by which, unconsciously, the mind selects terms to express its ambivalence. Extreme dualism must cause symbolic antiphrases. One gets the impression sometimes that the most powerful satirists are dualists, users of "negation," to the point that they become naive gnostics. They, like Gnostics, hover on an edge

of extreme asceticism which can drop off absolutely into an extreme libertinism. . . .

As I think Fletcher implies, it is aesthetically superior to be a "naive gnostic" than it is to be a Gnostic proper, which is only one of many reasons why *A Voyage to Arcturus* is a much more powerful literary fantasy than its anxious imitation, *The Flight to Lucifer*. Lindsay probably did not even know that he was creating a kind of Gnostic heresy all his own, despite *his* anxious debts to Carlyle. The hapless author of *The Flight to Lucifer* set out to assimilate Lindsay's characters and narrative patterns to the actual, historical cosmology, theology and mythology of second-century Gnosticism. But being a disciple of Walter Pater, and not of Thomas Carlyle, he sought to exalt Narcissus as well as Prometheus, or more simply to accept psychic over-determination as fantasy's price for freedom. Though a violent narrative, freely plagiarized by misprision of endless fantasy-sources from Spenser to Kafka, *The Flight to Lucifer* has too much trouble getting off the ground, not because it knows too well what it is about, but because it is rather too interested in the ground, which is to say, too interested in the pleasure/pain principle. If *A Voyage to Arcturus* reads as though Thomas Carlyle was writing *Through the Looking Glass*, then *The Flight to Lucifer* reads as though Walter Pater was writing *Star Wars*.

Still, I do not deny the book *all* merit. It does get better as it goes along, and towards its close can be called something of a truly weird work, as its protagonist Perscors engages in a final battle with the Demiurge himself. I wish to conclude by using the book not as a finality in itself, but as another commentary upon the mode of fantasy, another step towards a critical swerve into a more comprehensive theory of fantasy. Clearly I am neither formalist nor structuralist, nor would any psychoanalytic critic accept me as a brother. I write a kind of Gnostic or Kabbalistic criticism even as I write a Gnostic narrative, or as I would now say, I am a fantastic or Romantic critic of fantasy. For here also, in criticism as in story, the uncanny identity of Narcissus and Prometheus asserts itself. The stance of freedom, critical or creative, is not more nor less catastrophic than the stance of fate, of critical as well as creative psychic over-determination. Literary fantasy, creative or critical, is the mode where pleasure/pain principle and reality principle become most inextricably blended, even as the mode appears to proclaim a negation of the reality principle. As taboo and transference mutually contaminate one another in Freud, even so literary fantasy contaminates fate and freedom in its own texts. Perscors, my American version of Maskull, goes into battle against Saklas, the ancient Gnostic version of Crystalman, convinced that he fights as Prometheus against Narcissus, but his pathos is that he is mistaken, and he dies in the Ovidian narcissistic or high Shelleyan vision that always beautifully deludes the hero of fantasy:

> The will to follow the maimed Demiurge ebbed in Perscors. He felt neither pain nor desire but only the peace of exhaustion. After a few moments, a fire broke forth from his own loins. When he realized that it was indeed his own fire, he smiled in contentment. Triumph was his final thought as his head became the fire.

9

The Sublime Crossing
and the Death of Love

Reflected light, according to Cordovero (*Pardes* 15), fulfills a
great task in the consolidation of the potencies and *behinot* of
judgment (*din*) in each *Sefirah*, for it functions through a
process of restrictive contraction rather than free expansion.
. . . The face of one *Sefirah* turns toward another and conse-
quently there develops between them a "channel" (*zinnor*) of
influence which is not identical with actual emanation. . . .

It is not clear to what extent there is any identity between
the symbols of reflected light and channels nor, if there is
none at all, what their relationship is. Any interruption in the
return of influx from below to above is called a Breaking of the
Channels. . . .

SCHOLEM, *Kabbalah*

Poems, like people, tend to change two ways, sometimes gradually,
but perhaps more often suddenly, by fits and starts. Sudden
changes partake of catastrophe, and crisis-poems (which are now
our norm) tend to re-imagine their own origins as having been
catastrophic. I read post-Wordsworthian (which is to say "modern") poetry as tending to a pattern of three crossings or crisis-
points, a pattern I have sketched in the coda to a book on Stevens.
The middle crossing or channel, which I have named the Crossing
of Solipsism, or topologically the Death of Love, is my concern in
this chapter. I shall propose that the breaking of this middle

channel is the making of the modern moment of what once was called the Sublime.

Here is a random cento of textual instances:

> . . . other gifts
> Have followed; for such loss, I would believe,
> Abundant recompense. For I have learned
> To look on nature, not as in the hour
> Of thoughtless youth; but hearing oftentimes
> The still, sad music of humanity. . . .

> As if his whole vocation
> Were endless imitation.

> Thou, whose exterior semblance doth belie
> Thy soul's immensity. . . .

> No shrine, no grove, no oracle, no heat
> Of pale-mouthed prophet dreaming.

> O brightest! though too late for antique vows,
> Too, too late for the fond believing lyre. . . .

> How dull it is to pause, to make an end,
> To rust unburnished, not to shine in use!
> As though to breathe were life. Life piled on life
> Were all too little, and of one to me
> Little remains: but every hour is saved
> From that eternal silence. . . .

The Crossings of Solipsism, in these extracts, can be located quite precisely, in the disjunctions between experiential loss and rhetorical gain. "To look on nature" leads to a repression of the seen which yields a visionary sound; leads to a pathos, a *potentia*, a power. A despairing sense that a child's true calling always is reduced to a repetitive mimesis is replaced by the grotesque strength of a curious litotes, in which the child's outside is interpreted as a lie against his inward authority. The blind mouth of a belated poet-priest suddenly is shuttled aside for a hyperbolical brightest, a goddess whose fictive lateness is the warrant of her ever-early candor. A hero turns from his lament for lost brightness, through a refusal to accept the metonymy of breath for life, and substitutes a heaping-up of every hour remaining that can be rammed with life. All these are solitary crossings, passages to the Sublime, and all rely upon a movement *from* a place where effect is traced to a cause, a movement which is also a movement *to* a place of comparison. The question of how an emptiness came about is replaced by the question that asks: more, less, or equal to? which is the agonistic self-questioning of the Sublime. When we suffer the effect of loss, and know too well the cause of that effect, we need to abandon the fiction of causation, in order to make a turning into some renewed sense of our own power. A loss of love is a loss also to the self that makes figurations, or if you prefer, to the figuration that we call the self. Erotic loss is self-loss, because it is a loss in solipsistic transport. The pain of loss is the pain of returning to otherness, an otherness in which the quest for lost selfhood turns into a sounding of the chasm of the Sublime.

In sounding that chasm, we transgress necessarily, because the Sublime moment in poetry has its nearest psychic analogue in the defense Freud named repression, a defense frequently manifested as hysteria. But that manifestation is in the text-of-life; the gap between life and art is revealed again by the verbal glory of the Sublime in the life-of-the-text. The Sublime is an un-naming accomplished by a purposeful forgetting, a forgetting of anterior texts. Where repression is an unconsciously purposeful forgetting, in and by the psyche, a poetic text does curious tricks, odd turnings, that render the unconscious only another trope as the poem both forgets to remember and remembers to forget. Repression, in a Sublime poem, or in a poem's Sublime turning, is evidenced just as much in and by the words present as by the words absent. I give here two contemporary instances:

The hawk comes.

His wing
Scythes down another day, his motion

Is that of the honed steel-edge, we hear
The crashless fall of stalks of Time.

The head of each stalk is heavy with the gold of our error.

Look! look! he is climbing the last light
Who knows neither Time nor error, and under
Whose eye, unforgiving, the world, unforgiven, swings

Into shadow. . . .

They were the players, and we who had struggled at the game
Were merely spectators, though subject to its vicissitudes
And moving with it out of the tearful stadium, borne on shoulders, at
   last.
Night after night this message returns, repeated
In the flickering bulbs of the sky, raised past us, taken away from us,
Yet ours over and over until the end that is past truth,
The being of our sentences, in the climate that fostered them,
Not ours to own, like a book, but to be with, and sometimes
To be without, alone and desperate.
But the fantasy makes it ours.

In the first of these two Sublime passages, the hawk is troped as
death-the-reaper, and also as a divinity whose immanent force represses all knowledge of time, error and forgiveness. What is being
repressed is that the hawk remains the image of poetry itself, of
the poems the poet still hopes to write. The cost of this rhetorical
gain is the poet's affective self-distancing from any sympathy or
forgiveness with the beautiful oxymoron of our experiential loss:
"The head of each stalk is heavy with the gold of our error."
Again we have a crossing from a love of others to a solitary transport, un-named because there is no human name for the immanent
thrust of the hawk's outward movement as he climbs the last
light.

In the second passage, there is a gentler sublimity, almost a discursive one, closely related to the Whitmanian "we," both in and
out of the game, as Whitman said. The Sublime sense here is an
endless dialectic of absence and presence, an ironized catachresis

of hyperbole, as the message both abandons us and keeps returning to us in the ontology of our own speech, and in the solitary
desperation of our fantasies. What is repressed here, our own sublimity, keeps returning waveringly, only to be repressed anew. The
critical question I want to ask is: can there be a theory of a modern Sublime that will illuminate everything that is both problematic and strong in all of my extracts, which were, in sequence,
Wordsworth's *Tintern Abbey* and his *Intimations of Immortality*
ode; Keats's *Ode to Psyche*; Tennyson's *Ulysses*; Robert Penn
Warren's *Evening Hawk*; John Ashbery's *Soonest Mended*. What
Gershom Scholem, elucidating Moses Cordovero, expounded as a
Breaking of the Channels is an image of what remains our modern
Sublime, an image of an "interruption in the return influx from
below to above" of a certain light we all of us continue to pursue.

2

Neil Hertz, in the course of his profound analysis of Longinus,
strikingly compares the theorist of the Sublime to

> . . . the modern critic whom he most resembles, Walter
> Benjamin. Both would seem, at moments, to be writing out of
> a deep nostalgia directed ambiguously towards certain great
> literary works and towards the traditional culture out of which
> they spring. . . . Each finds a word richly equivocal enough
> to locate the peculiar quality of the texts they admire in some
> relation to something beyond literature: so Longinus' word for
> the sublime, *hupsos*, is linked . . . with cosmic Nature itself,
> just as Benjamin's *aura* is made to participate in the ritual
> values of a lost culture. . . .

Hertz goes on to show that the Sublime turning, in both Longinus and Benjamin, tends to associate itself with catastrophe,
with a figurative movement of disintegration and subsequent reconstitution that, according to Hertz, is essentially a rhetorical
problematic masking itself as cultural history or as psychic ambivalence. Hertz thus joins himself to such conceptual rhetoricians as

Jacques Derrida and Paul de Man, and his deconstruction of Longinus and Benjamin therefore proceeds to uncover the method of writing in both critics as

> . . . the more or less violent fragmentation of literary bodies into "quotations," in the interests of building up a discourse of one's own, a discourse which, in its turn, directs attention to passages that come to serve as emblems of the critic's most acute, least nostalgic sense of what he is about. . . .

Though I am going to dispute Hertz's deconstruction of the Sublime turning, I am indebted to him for his brilliant linking of the *hupsos* of Longinus to the *aura* of Benjamin, a linking to which I am going to add the word that does the same work in Emerson, which is *lustre*. "I read for the lustres," Emerson said, and like Longinus before him, and Benjamin after him, he tended to fragment all anterior texts into "quotations," so as to keep the continuity of his own literary discourse going. I will show later in my own discourse that the poetic Sublime itself, as well as its criticism, is produced through quotation, but repressed quotation in the case of poetry. First I want to center on Benjamin's *aura* in a rather full discussion, partly because Benjamin is necessarily closer to us than Longinus and Emerson can be, and partly because there is a repressed element in Benjamin's notion of the *aura* that I think is central to the modern Sublime.

The *aura* is a conceptual image hovering almost everywhere in Benjamin's work, including his essays on Leskov and on Proust, but it is particularly dominant in two of his most famous essays, *The Work of Art in the Age of Mechanical Reproduction* and *On Some Motifs in Baudelaire*. In the first of these, *aura* is defined as loss, since the *aura* of the work of art is that which withers in the age of mechanical reproduction. Illustrating his concept of *aura*, Benjamin identifies it with distance, with unapproachability, and by implication with an estrangement of the object-world. The *Baudelaire* essay offers a more complex notion of *aura*, one which manifests a curious and cunning play between *aura* and the etymologically unrelated "aureole," the bright halo of god or saint, or the bright circumference around sun or moon, as when viewed through mist. "Aureole" stems ultimately from *aurum*, the Latin for gold, and is introduced by Benjamin into his *Baudelaire* essay by way of Baudelaire's prose-poem on the poet's loss of his halo or aureole. The loss of the aureole suggests the loss of the Sublime's high, breaking light, yet this is hardly the primary meaning of *aura* in Benjamin. His *aura* is properly an invisible breath or emanation; an air, as of nobility, characterizing person or thing; a breeze, but most of all a sensation or shock, the sort of illusion of a breeze that precedes the start of a nervous breakdown or disorder. There are, however, more individual aspects of Benjamin's *aura* that will take us further into a theory of the Sublime.

One deep source of Benjamin's *aura* is Freud's *Beyond the Pleasure Principle*, which Benjamin assimilated to what he called Valéry's notion that lyric poetry could take "as its basis an experience for which the shock experience has become the norm." This formulation of Benjamin's allowed him to associate Freud's concepts of defense with Valéry's poetic idea that lyric perceptions belong in the category of "surprise." From Valéry to Baudelaire was a natural step back in time, and allowed Benjamin to concentrate upon the "figure of shock, indeed of catastrophe" in Baudelaire, a trope that Benjamin named as the *aura*: "To perceive the aura of an object we look at means to invest it with the ability to look at us in return." There is something ceremonial about that investiture, and so the disintegration of the *aura* in the reversal of shock is the destruction of a ceremonial image. Benjamin's literary examples tend to be taken from Baudelaire, Valéry and Proust, but Yeats provides even richer exemplification of the same phenomena.

Gershom Scholem, Benjamin's close friend, defined the critic's sense of true actuality as involving always a quality of the ephemeral, and illustrated this definition by the image of the angel in Benjamin's work. In a letter to Scholem, Benjamin cited "a Talmudic legend [that] even the angels—new ones each moment in innumerable bands—are created so that, after they have sung their

hymn before God, they cease and dissolve into the naught."
Scholem's commentary upon this is remarkable. He speaks of

> . . . the formation and disappearance of angels before God, of
> whom it is said in a Kabbalistic book that they "pass away as
> the spark on the coals." To this, however, was added for Ben-
> jamin the further conception of Jewish tradition of the personal
> angel of each human being who represents the latter's secret
> self and whose name nevertheless remains hidden from him. In
> angelic shape, but in part also in the form of his secret name,
> the heavenly self of a human being (like everything else
> created) is woven into a curtain hanging before the throne of
> God. This angel, to be sure, can also enter into opposition to,
> and a relation of strong tension with, the earthly creature to
> whom he is attached. . . .

"True actuality" is the particular strength of the *aura*, for Benjamin. The distintegration of the *aura* is like the dissolution of the
angels once they have sung their hymn. The curiously Shelleyan
image of the spark on the coals passing away is another fading of
the *aura*, but we come closest to Benjamin's idea of the Sublime as
negative moment in the personal angel of hidden name, who represents the secret self, and who can oppose and baffle the individual to whom he is attached. I suggest that Benjamin's *aura* is related not only to this daemonic figure, and to the evanescent
angels, but also to the Jewish Gnostic and Kabbalist hypostasis
of the *zelem*, which is in turn related to the Gnostic and later
Neoplatonist idea of the astral body. Just as Emerson's image of
the reader's Sublime, the "lustre," goes back I think to the Cambridge Neoplatonist Cudworth's exposition of the astral body, so
Benjamin's *aura* has an ultimate ancestor in the Kabbalistic *zelem*.
Scholem says of the *zelem* or "image" (*Genesis* 1:26) that it

> . . . is the principle of individuality with which every single
> human being is endowed, the spiritual configuration or essence
> that is unique to him and to him alone. Two notions are com-
> bined in this concept, one relating to the idea of human indi-
> viduation and the other to man's ethereal garment or ethereal
> (subtle) body which serves as an intermediary between his

material body and his soul. . . . An ancient belief concerning such an ethereal body . . . was that the *zelem* was actually a man's true self. . . . Without the *zelem* the soul would burn the body up with its fierce radiance.

Like Benjamin's *aura*, the *zelem* is a final evidence of an authentic individuality, and its image of a luminous envelope suits Benjamin's curiously visionary materialism, his sense that the *aura* is a final defense of the soul against the shock or catastrophe of multiplicity, against masses of objects or multitudes of people in the streets. What Scholem's researches show us is that an agonistic element in esoteric origins is what attracted Benjamin to those origins. The personal angel, like the *zelem*, is both a mark of individuality and an antagonist. In Benjamin's theory of the Sublime, the *aura* is indeed both the shock of reversal and loss and what he calls it in his beautiful essay on Leskov, the beautiful halo of the storyteller. Emerson, in his essay *The Poet*, had invoked the Cambridge Platonist Cudworth's image of *aura* for what he regarded as the authentic mark of creativity: "The condition of true naming, on the poet's part, is his resigning himself to the divine *aura* which breathes through forms, and accompanying that." Yet, more often, Emerson attributes *aura* or "lustre" not so much to a condition of true naming as to the agon of true un-naming. To accept an anterior naming is to submit, but in the Sublime reversal one's own lustre derives from not using the rotted names, from throwing away the lights, the definitions, and from saying that what one sees in the dark is this or that, but not what another ever described before one.

3

I verge upon the conclusion that the Sublime *is* the truth that strong poetry has to be agonistic, whether its writers consciously do or do not desire to enter the contest. But I take it that poetic ambivalence in regard to the taboo of such agon is the threshold to the Sublime, as Angus Fletcher has demonstrated in his book

Allegory and in his more recent essay on Coleridge's "Positive Negation." Longinus had pointed the Sublime at "the eagerness of mutual rivalry and the emulous pursuit of the foremost place." Kant also, rather more subtly, had posited an agonistic Sublime, the poet's response to the Sublime in nature being a consciousness "sensible of the appropriate sublimity of the sphere of its own being, even above nature." Fletcher interprets Coleridge's Sublime as a problem in personification, once there has been a trespass of the taboo, that is, after an overcoming of influence-anxiety, an overcoming in which the poet momentarily is one with a phantom person or daemon:

> . . . To envision and realize the phantom person poetically the poet must empty his imagery of piety and sense, allowing in their place some measure of daemonic possession. The necessary poetic act will be to utter, to speak, nothingness. To achieve this defining negativity, the poem *Limbo* typically seeks to *posit* negation as the ultimate daemon. . . .

Fletcher's insight associates the daemonic agent with the agonistic spirit, an association that restores to us one of the vitalizing origins of Western poetry. E. R. Dodds, in *The Greeks and the Irrational*, traces the transition from Homer to the Classical Age as a movement from "Shame-Culture to Guilt-Culture," but this movement is clearly more evident from Homer *or* the Classical Age *to* the Romans. Pindar and Sophocles are far closer to the agonistic spirit than Virgil is, since "tradition" and "authority," as Hannah Arendt has shown, are Roman and not Greek ideas. Dodds indicates that a new type of daemon makes an appearance among the post-Homeric Greeks, a destiny or fortune "as much part of a man's natal endowment as beauty or talent." By a brilliant surmise, Dodds associates this new daemonic endowment with the element of guilt and anxiety that attended post-Homeric Greek instances of agon, and he then identifies the anxiety with the struggle of a son against a father. Dodds notes that "when Plato wants to illustrate what happens when rational controls are not functioning, his typical example is the Oedipus dream."

Though Dodds does not cite Plato's anxiety in regard to Homer, we can apply Dodds's analysis to Plato's agon with Homer, as outlined in Eric Havelock's *Preface to Plato*. The Sublime ambivalence of Plato's polemic against Homer has its daemonic and Oedipal components, and these helped to give Plato one of the great ancestral poems of the Western Sublime, the Myth of the Cave in *The Republic*. I will suggest now that the Myth of the Cave is another founding paradigm for the Sublime crisis-poem, with its three crossings or negative turnings, and so is another instance of Emerson's point in his wry remark upon Plato: "Great havoc makes he among our originalities."

Plato's own summary (*Republic* VII, 532) names his parable as a progress of thought or a dialectic, while another passage (VII, 516d) overtly identifies the Cave with the Hades of Homer. Plato parodistically descends into the Homeric Sublime to place therein his own dialectic. Men fettered all their lives watch a puppet-show, seeing by "the light from a fire burning higher up and at a distance behind them." A first turning or crossing, which I have called by the Protestant name of Election, begins the dialectic of freedom:

> . . . When one was freed from his fetters and compelled to stand up suddenly and turn his head around and walk and to lift up his eyes to the light, and in doing all this felt pain and, because of the dazzle and glitter of the light, was unable to discern the objects whose shadows he formerly saw, what do you suppose would be his answer if someone told him what he had seen before was all a cheat and an illusion, but that now, being nearer to reality and turned toward more real things, he saw more truly?

Plato says that this release takes place in the course of nature, but the liberating and guiding agency appears to be daemonic. It is evidently the philosophical ephebe's own daemon who is the

> . . . someone [who] should drag him thence by force up the ascent which is rough and steep, and not let him go before he had drawn him out into the light of the sun, do you not think

that . . . when he came out into the light, that his eyes would be filled with its beams so that he would not be able to see even one of the things that we call real?

Dazzled by the light of common day, the ephebe is at a turning or crossing of Solipsism, cut off momentarily from what Emily Dickinson called "neighbors and the sun." Painful step-by-step in consciousness, the philosopher-to-be at first discerns the shadows, then reflections in water, later the things themselves, until at last he turns to the light of the stars and the moon. From there the necessary turn is to the idea-of-ideas, the sun itself. Seeing the truth, the philosopher is moved by pity for his fellows in the cavern, and re-descends to them, suffering a third blinding, but this final turning or crossing, of Identification with others and finally with martyrdom and death, is a blinding by the darkness, and not by light, as with the first two Crossings:

> If such a one should go down again and take his old place would he not get his eyes full of darkness, thus suddenly coming out of the sunlight?

In so reading the parable of the cavern, I follow Heidegger, and his pupil Hannah Arendt, who in her book *Between Past and Future* traces the turnings and crossings against yet within tradition, as made by Kierkegaard, Marx and Nietzsche, back to Plato's "first great turning operation." Arendt reads the parable as Plato's quest for authority, an agonistic quest because the precursor from whom authority must be usurped is Father Homer. Here is Arendt's professedly Heideggerian interpretation:

> . . . the sky of ideas stretches above the cave of human existence, and therefore can become its standard. But the philosopher who leaves the cave for the pure sky of ideas does not originally do so in order to acquire those standards and learn the "art of measurement" but to contemplate the true essence of Being. . . . The ideas become measures only after the philosopher has . . . returned to the dark cave of human existence. . . .

If I translate this into aesthetic terms, it becomes the formula that when the Sublime ebbs, truth-as-measurement takes over, leading finally into the realm of death. For the Sublime Crossing represses truth-as-measurement, and is a direct attempt to confront what Heidegger calls *Unverborgenheit* ("unrevealedness"). But what is "measurement" between poem and poem? I move toward another fundamental formula for an *antithetical* criticism of poetry, which is that *allusion is concealed measurement, just as echo is repressed quotation*, and that what I have been calling the poetic Sublime is closer to echo than to allusion. To explain my formula and its corollary, I need to follow a winding path of discourse, which begins with the most troublesome of Freudian tropes for the critic of poetry, the persuasive trope of the dynamic unconscious.

You cannot *know* the Freudian unconscious, by Freudian definition. But you *can know* the Gnostic Alien God through *being known by him*, by Gnostic definition. You *can know* Emerson's Trustee, the aboriginal self or deep source. The Freudian unconscious is therefore not any hypostasis either of orthodoxy (Jehovah, the Neoplatonic One) or of heresy (Gnosis, Kabbalah). But the Freudian unconscious, while unknowable, always can be *interpreted*. This is because everything it brings about is *over-determined*. However, what Freud named the unconscious is already an interpretation, *his interpretation*, his will-to-power over the text-of-life. Because his will was so disinterestedly analytic and (societally considered) benign, it is perhaps unwise to dispute his interpretation in regard to the text-of-life. But there is no unconscious in the life-of-the-text. When I speak of repression, in a text, I do not mean the accumulation or aggregation of an unconscious. I mean that I can observe and frequently identify *patterns of forgetting* in a poem, and that these tend to be rather more important than the poem's allusions, even where those allusions are patterned. What makes a poem strongest is *how* it excludes what is almost present in it, or nearest to presence in it. Criticism (strong) begins by finding the Sublime moment which is the most intense

Negative crossing in the poem. By locating this Crossing of Solipsism, the critic discovers *what* it is that the poem *represses* in order to have persuaded us of the illusion of its own closure. That *what* is, in the first place, necessarily another poem. Poems are *to other poems* what people are *to themselves*. But poems are not *to themselves* what people are *to themselves*. When a person says: "I and the Abyss," he is saying: "I and my unconscious." But when a poem says: "I and the Abyss," it is saying: "I and the other strong poems that impinge upon me."

Why then invoke the Freudian term "repression" as a supposed aid to the study of poetry? I revert here to the formula of displacement regarding the triads of Proclus and of Peirce, unlikely duo, that I employed in a short book called *Kabbalah and Criticism*. The meaning of a poem hovers always between and betwixt three signs: that poem, any precursor poem, and the trope of the self that we can call any reader. The reader *qua* reader is an interplay of repressive forces. Another interplay goes on between the reader's confrontation of the two poems. I read *Resolution and Independence*, and then I read the *Prothalamion*, its precursor text. I encounter Wordsworth's anxiety as to the continuity of his own joy and vital force. I brood upon Spenser's sullen care and discontent at his lack of preferment. To read the two poems together is to see that they are connected quite apart from my own anxieties, and yet to see also that I would not be so obsessively concerned with their intertextual relation if I were not repressing related anxieties of my own. Wordsworth's strength is manifested not by the presence of Spenser's poem in his own text, but by the precise figurations of its absence. The strength of my reading, of either poem, when I attempt to communicate such a reading to auditors or other readers, depends upon at least a partial repression of my passion for the text, since a total return of that passion would prevent any reading whatsoever, in any true sense of "reading." It is just here that my own mode of criticism arouses the weakest kinds of misreading and misrepresentation, and so I want to address myself to the process of figuration that we call "reading."

To read actively is to make a fiction as well as to receive one, and the kind of active reading we call "criticism" or the attempt to decide meaning, or perhaps to see whether meaning *can* be decided, always has a very large fictive element in it. I continue to be surprised that so many literary scholars refuse to see that every stance in regard to texts, however professedly humble or literal or prosaic or "scientific" or "historical" or "linguistic," is always a poetic stance, always part of the rhetoric of rhetoric. "Reading" is a heuristic process, a path-breaking into inventiveness. All of the most "commonsensical" or determinedly naive of critics rely, however implicitly, upon paradigms or philosophical models that are themselves poetic, even if like the Platonic models they are anti-poetic in their intentions.

4

I offer the instance of what I would call the Sublime moment proper, the gap of negation or disjunctive generation of meaning that I have been naming the Crossing of Solipsism, an abyss of middleness in every strong "modern" (post-Miltonic) poem. This is the moment of turning-around that Plato equated with passing out of the Cave and being blinded by the trope-of-tropes, the sun, and so ultimately by the First Idea of the sun, as Stevens called it. Rhetorically, I have mapped this moment as the revisionary ratio of *daemonization*, the advent of a Counter-Sublime. Topologically it is a movement from the place-of-a-voice that speaks of cause-and-effect to the place-of-a-darker-voice that speaks of comparison, in the particular sense of harsh questions: more? the same as? or less? This darker voice measures and quantifies, and secures the force-of-measurement by a linguistic equivalent of the psychic process that Freud called "repression," a process that in language must be always *the repression of quotation*. Every critic and every poet comes up to this agonistic place in every reading and every writing of a strong or canonical poem, a poem that has triumphed by imposing itself upon tradition. To become memorable, a poem must overcome both its own memory and some particular elements in the reader's memory, insofar as both these memories collect the anterior traces *of other poems.*

"Overcoming," in the context of a voice that asks the questions that compare forces, is the trope of transcendence, of a rhetorical flight beyond prior fixations of consciousness. Overcoming is overthrowing or hyperbolizing, but not through exaggeration. Rather, this casting-beyond intensifies through comparison, through the measurement of voicings that are equal to, less than, and in aspiration more than, the challenging voices of anteriority. Again, we move to the consideration of poetic agon, and to the belated realization that the modern crisis-ode descends, however remotely, from Pindar's epinician or victory odes, so that Hart Crane spoke truly when he saw himself as the Pindar of the Machine Age, hymning however a great defeat rather than the American victory prophesied by Emerson.

The topos of comparison is a scene where the voice of the dead breaks through as an image of voice itself, an image of the power that is voicing in a poem. To speak may be to fall into tautology, but the repetition or redundancy of strong poetry is a very deep or Schopenhauerian tautology. Voicing goes back to the root *wekw,* which allies such words as "vowel," "vocation," and "epos" with the Muse Calliope. The only privilege of strong poetry is that it struggles to repress a voice *by voice,* as well as to sublimate a writing by writing. But this is not the originary privilege of a free and open word. For what does it mean to repress voicing by voicing? How can one vocation displace another, without itself being wounded into silence? To answer such questions is to attempt to say perhaps what cannot be said, or to enter upon the enterprise that Freud despairingly termed "speaking to the winds" in his late essay *Analysis Terminable and Interminable,* an essay upon perpetual crisis or crises which we can call "poetic."

Poetic crisis—the occasion of strong Post-Enlightenment poems— is always a crisis in which a quotation or quotations from another poem or poems are being repressed. The overcoming of crisis—in a poem—is never a true overcoming but is always an out-talking of a rival poem. This hyperbolical out- or over-talking achieves what Longinus called elevation or the Sublime (or what other, later theorists and poets have called, variously, a visionary gleam [Wordsworth], a lustre [Emerson], and an *aura* [Walter Benjamin]). Because that Sublime comes from a momentary out-talking or over-taking of anteriority or the burden of the *already said*, it is always marked as a negative moment, a crossing between figurations rather than a figuration in itself. Considered as rhetoric this moment or gap is a transitional flow between a metonymy of cause and effect and a hyperbole or transcendental over-throw, a cast of what the Romantics insisted upon calling the Imagination. As such there is no referential aspect whatsoever to this hyperbole; it is not a sign that refers to other signs, but represents instead the force by which poetic language seeks to restitute its own vastation—its voiding and avoidance of its own tendency *towards quotation,* towards a repetition that would have the status of a tautology. Considered psychoanalytically, this negative moment or crossing marks the repetition of a primal repression (Scene of Instruction) that has been evaded by a partial return of the repressed, and which is now re-abyssed or voided by a fresh enforcement of repression. Considered theologically or better yet, theosophically, this Crossing of Solipsism or voiding of the sense of others and otherness, and so of the possibility of any Eros save self-love, represents a renewal of the Gnostic "call" of the Alien God, the true estranged Divinity who has (had) been thrust aside by Jehovah the Demiurge, mere god of nature and the Creation, rather than spirit of creativity itself.

What are the consequences, for practical criticism, of so apparently outrageous an antithetical formula? At first, surely, they must seem wholly unacceptable, as we can see by considering an always crucial proof-text, the *Intimations* ode of Wordsworth. Our formula asserts that this most influential of crisis-lyrics *says* that it laments and confronts the *loss* of a visionary gleam, a preternatural light that surrounded the child and even the youth Wordsworth. But what the poem *means* is that the occasion for lamentation is not actually the *loss* of the gleam but instead is its own repressed and *belated* (*nachträglich*) realization that the presence of the gleam was caused—in the first place and always—*by the words of an anterior poetry, by quotation, by the recollection of texts not one's own.* And even *that* initial presence of the visionary gleam was caused by a *repressive de-contextualization* of nearly all of the anterior text or texts, a kind of all-but-primal repression that destroyed everything in the earlier text that *from the start did not seem to be one's own,* that did not seem to have been written by one's own self.

I am suggesting that the Sublime is always a quotation, a *measuring* (etymological meaning of "quoting") that becomes a quota, and so destroys the context of a text. This means that the Sublime asks: "What?" (*hwa, qua*) and not "How?" Such asking is a forgetting (failure in translation, repression) and so a re-presentation. Though this seems clearer of the Romantic, Modern Sublime (Wordsworth, Stevens) than of the older Sublime, nevertheless the Sublime always *was* this. Homer and the Bible were not Sublime until the critics and Talmudists learned how to quote from them.

All Sublimes are transcendent, down to Emerson's American Sublime, and all this transcendence transcends not the world but anterior texts. Perhaps we need to begin a study of the *psychology of quoting.* I have never known a person whose writing was quoted by anyone else who did not believe that he or she had been distorted or misrepresented by being quoted out of context. Yet all quotation is necessarily out of context, and not to a greater or lesser degree. The truth may be that there is no difference between the act of quoting with a favorable or with an unfavorable intention. All quotation may be an un-favoring process, in regard to the text that is being "read," "reviewed," "studied." But this is *not* because "unity" or "context" is being violated, but only that "unity" and even "context" are revealed as being illusions. We all of us are condemned to do what Emerson did cheerfully, and

Benjamin with an elegiac grace: to read any text only for the lustres or *auras*.

5

I want to return, here at this discourse's point-of-abandonment, to the Sublime extracts with which I began, to those six moments whose glory is in their own pride and willfulness, their own highly individual ways of beholding the disintegration of the *aura* in the experience of shock. Earlier, I compared the Sublime turning proper or Crossing of Solipsism to the second of Plato's turnings, the passing of his potential philosopher out of the mouth of the cave and into the momentarily blinding light of the idea of ideas, the inconceivable idea of the sun, not as the sun but as a sun might be. This turning is away from the other image-watchers in the cave, but dialectically is only a stage and not a finality. Plato will conclude his myth with a third turning, a Crossing of Identification in which the philosopher redescends into Hell, to attempt an enlightenment of those he has left behind. But I believe that the negative moments of our crisis-poetry are more disjunctive than the Platonic turnings. The love that dies in the Crossing of Solipsism is not revivified in the final Crossing of Identification, and the *aura* that is regained when the Sublime lyric attempts closure differs in kind as well as in degree from the great light that falls outwards and downwards in the Sublime moment proper.

The Sublime moment of modern lyric is not a sublimation, whether in Plato's or Nietzsche's or in Freud's sense. Because it is a kind of repression, its truest trope may be that of a monumental burial, of an empty pyramid, to cite an image played with by Hegel and by Derrida, and in a different tradition by Shelley and by Melville. A strong poet wants his pyramid; he does not wish the unmarked grave of Moses or of Oedipus. Wordsworth, Keats, Tennyson, Warren and Ashbery all derive authority from having marked out their own graves, from having buried much of their own power, but then from having refused, in their poems, to accept this burial as an occasion for lament. Rather, this burial stimulates a Longinian sense that Leopardi best recaptured in prose when he wrote that "always to accuse things of insufficiency and nothingness and to suffer the want and the void—this seems to me the best proof of the grandeur and nobility of human nature." Leopardi saw that the direction of meaning in the Sublime moment is diagonal, a slanting movement through desire and the void, a chiasmus as curious as the one hinted by Plato's Aristophanes in the *Symposium* when he says that what lovers really want of one another is always a "longing for a something else—a something to which they can neither of them put a name."

A recent essay, "The Sublime: In Alchemy, Aesthetics and Psychoanalysis," by Jan Cohn and Thomas H. Miles traces the curious crossing or diagonal of meaning in the word "Sublime" itself. In an engaging footnote they state the puzzle that I think I can subsume:

> One wonders why the meaning of elevation and loftiness carried in the word *sublime* should be developed from a root with the meaning of diagonal, rather than from a more dramatic vertical denotation. . . .

A Sublime rising, assuming that this is a true etymology, would be a rising up, *along a diagonal line*, from below to above. At the mid-point of that diagonal path is the Sublime turning proper, what I have called the Crossing of Solipsism, or the passage out of Plato's cave into the light of the Ideas. Why must the path be diagonal rather than perpendicular? The question may seem zany, or as some of my unamiable critics say, "psychokabbalistic," but it seeks to surmise something hidden in the linguistic history of the word, "Sublime."

I verge here upon a formulation that I take to be definitive of strong or Sublime poetry: it is the topos where the power of "the father" never can be overcome, because its labor endlessly remystifies the precursor. The topos of the strong poem is a mingled staging of three problematics: naming/un-naming; quantification;

negativity. The crisis of naming/un-naming is the Crossing of Election; the crisis of quantification is the Crossing of Solipsism; the final crisis, of negativity, is the Crossing of Identification. Three crossings: if the first un-names the father, it still does not forget that only he *gives* a new name. If the second out-measures the father, it still does not forget that only he provides the standard of measurement, and so it approaches him slant-wise, on the diagonal. If the third casts out and so projects the father, it still does not forget that only he among all images is neither origin nor desire, but rather is the inaugurating lie that makes language both possible and necessary.

No one "fathers" or "mothers" his or her own poems, because poems are not "created," but are interpreted into existence, and by necessity they are interpreted from other poems. Whenever I suggest that there is a defensive element in all interpretation, as in all troping, the suggestions encounter a considerable quantity of very suggestive resistance. All that I would grant to this resistance is its indubitable idealism, its moving *need* of the mythology of creative imagination, and of the related sub-mythology of an "objective" scholarly criticism. Both the mythology and the sub-mythology are modes of *lying for time*, while the actuality of the Sublime, of strong poetry, is a chiasmus, a diagonal *lying against time*. There isn't any moral difference between the two kinds of lying, but it is a dark irony that only a strong poem, a lie against time, can be so misread as to sustain the continuance of an institutionalized lie for time, the fourfold lie that any text whatsoever can possess or create unity, presence, meaning, form.

Is our choice then only to be between a nihilism and a collective Narcissism? The strong poem, as I have tried to show, has no choice; the quest for the Sublime demands, of poet and of reader, both transgressions: to celebrate the Abyss, and to worship, lovingly, one's own self as it is confronted by the Abyss, whether or not the Abyss returns our gaze as *aura*. But to so doubly transgress is possible only because of the indubitable *gain* that the anxiety of influence represents. Poetic transgression embraces the void only in opposition to *the place of the father*, and embraces the self only in substitution for the embrace of the father. Since the father, in a poem, ensues from a process of: initial identification, agonistic negation, self-substitution, we can say that the father *is* the poem, or is the aspect of the poem that is a fiction-of-duration. We have the irony that we do not father our own text, but that necessarily *our own text fathers us*. In Kabbalah, this is no irony but is the explicit ground of the text-of-self.

The gain-of-anxiety, for the strong poet *and* the strong reader, is the certain location of a place—even though the place be an absence, the place-of-a-voice—for this setting of a topos makes a poem possible. "We only know what we ourselves have made" is the great Vichian adage, and if we know both a place and a father, it is because we have made them both, and then turned from and against them in the ambivalence of synecdoche, in the vicissitudes of drive. We mark the spot by wishing to slay the father, there, at *that* crossing, and we then know the spot because it becomes the place where the voice of the dead father breaks through. The marking, the will-to-inscribe, is the *ethos* of writing that our most advanced philosophers of rhetoric trace, but the knowing is itself a voicing, a *pathos*, and leads us back to the theme of presence that, in a strong poem, persuades us ever afresh, even as the illusions of a tired metaphysics cannot.

10
Wallace Stevens:
A Poem of Our Gnosis

The imaginative literature of our country, particularly from Emerson on, is our Gnosis, that is, *the* American religion. I give a reading here of Wallace Stevens's *The Poems of Our Climate*, as an instance of this religion, as a text of the American Gnosis.

In an eloquent study of American poetry, published in 1965 (*Connoisseurs of Chaos*), Denis Donoghue made a fine and accurate distinction between Stevens and Eliot in terms of their rival relationship to a crucial precursor, Walter Pater, a writer whose work should be for all of us what Yeats said it was for him: a sacred book. Donoghue wrote that

> . . . much of Eliot's work can be considered as a translation of Walter Pater's exquisite moments into spiritual terms, so as to blur the distinction between the greatest sanctity and the greatest consciousness. Those who are incapable of such intense consciousness are beneath contempt and probably beneath the dignity of damnation. Much of Stevens' work, on the other hand, is an attempt to render to Pater the things that are Pater's.

As I turn to *The Poems of Our Climate*, I would add to Donoghue's maxim that this meditation also renders to Emerson the things that are Emerson's, and to Nietzsche the dark italics that are Nietzsche's. But perhaps this should go without saying, because

Pater, Emerson and Nietzsche are bewilderingly close in their deepest perceptions, and it was natural for Stevens, or for Yeats, or for Hart Crane, to fuse together the insights of these three philosophers of Romanticism in its belated phase, just prior to the advent of Freud.

I follow Donoghue then in citing Pater and his contemporaries as the meditative context for *The Poems of Our Climate*, and I take from Pater's early essay *Wincklemann* the following passage as epigraph to Stevens's poem:

> . . . painting and poetry . . . can accomplish their function in the choice and development of some special situation, which lifts or glorifies a character, in itself not poetical. To realize this situation, to define, in a chill and empty atmosphere, the focus where rays, in themselves pale and impotent, unite and begin to burn. . . .

That is the work of Stevens's poem: the definition, in a chill and empty atmosphere, of a focus where pale and impotent rays unite in the flame of a Gnosis. Begin then with the poet as flower-arranger, making his own knowing into the seeing of a chill and empty atmosphere:

> Clear water in a brilliant bowl,
> Pink and white carnations. The light
> In the room more like a snowy air,
> Reflecting snow. A newly-fallen snow
> At the end of winter when afternoons return.
> Pink and white carnations—one desires
> So much more than that. The day itself
> Is simplified: a bowl of white,
> Cold, a cold porcelain, low and round,
> With nothing more than the carnations there.

There is an overtone of fleshly regret in those "pink and white carnations," and the precise stationing in our climate, at the end of winter, before the thaw, suggests also that this still life does not decline life. But there is an enigma, a palpable and Paterian irony, in the curiously flat, toneless declaration:

Pink and white carnations—one desires
So much more than that.

I think the best way to understand this irony is to dramatize it,
imagine it as spoken by one of the Paterian exquisites either in
one of Oscar Wilde's plays or in one of his critical dialogues. Presumably any one of us desires so much more than pink and white
carnations, but a Wildean young man could say that and mean:
one desires so much *less* than that. Stevens writes: "simplified,"
but he means "reduced," and what he reduces is Keats's Grecian
urn, with "a bowl of white, / Cold, a cold porcelain, low and
round" replacing the "silent form . . . Cold Pastoral" of Keats's
vision. Stevens's mad lecturer, in *Extracts from Addresses to the
Academy of Fine Ideas*, had invoked and admonished Keats as the
Academy's Secretary for Porcelain:

> Let the Secretary for Porcelain observe
> That evil made magic, as in catastrophe,
> If neatly glazed, becomes the same as the fruit
> Of an emperor, the egg-plant of a prince.
> The good is evil's last invention. . . .

"Evil," as elsewhere in Stevens, means the necessary pain and
suffering attendant upon being a natural man or woman, so that
the "evilly compounded, vital I" of the next stanza must mean
something like "made up of necessary suffering, and so at last inventive of pleasure":

> Say even that this complete simplicity
> Stripped one of all one's torments, concealed
> The evilly compounded, vital I
> And made it fresh in a world of white,
> A world of clear water, brilliant-edged,
> Still one would want more, one would need more,
> More than a world of white and snowy scents.

I locate the Gnosis here in the subtle evasion of "brilliant-
edged." The brilliance, the shining forth, is neither in art nor in
nature, neither in the brilliant bowl with its clear water and carna-

tions, nor in the bitterness of the earth. No, precisely the brilliance emerges from the edge, the demarcation made less ghostly, between the illusory project of art, "a world of white, / A world of clear water," and the unnamed world of the real, the world that Stevens everywhere calls by the Emersonian name of "poverty," meaning imaginative need. At his poem's prime crossing, "brilliant-edged," Stevens cannot cross to a beyond, and so he compels his reader to meditate upon poverty, upon a lack of feeling and so upon a loss of power. I cite our father Emerson, inventor of our American Gnosis, upon this loss, from his central text, *Self-Reliance:*

> Life only avails, not the having lived. Power ceases in the instant of repose; it resides in the moment of transition from a past to a new state, in the shooting of a gulf, in the darting to an aim. . . .

I read honest spiritual failure in Stevens's second stanza, that is, his knowing that he has failed to know this Emersonian and Whitmanian crossing, this transcendental over-throw. He is instead with the skeptics of an American Gnosis, despite his own desires; momentarily he is closer to Melville than to Dickinson, to Hawthorne than to Thoreau. The "complete simplicity" of his reductiveness, even if it made the illusion of an ever-early candor, would abandon him still at the hard brilliance of the edge, and at the murmuring of an understatement that converts the American Sublime into a pathetic American Grotesque:

> Still one would want more, one would need more,
> More than a world of white and snowy scents.

I have cited Pater and Emerson, so far. It is Nietzsche, I think, who hovers strongly in the poem's third and final section:

> There would still remain the never-resting mind,
> So that one would want to escape, come back
> To what had been so long composed.
> The imperfect is our paradise.
> Note that, in this bitterness, delight,
> Since the imperfect is so hot in us,
> Lies in flawed words and stubborn sounds.

"What had been so long composed" is the Nietzschean fiction of the sensible world, the human poem of ordinary perception, the grand bitterness of earth, "imperfect" only because perpetually unfinished. Delight consists in flawed or wind-blown words and in sounds that stubbornly resist being made keener. Yes, but at least as strongly, the joy of poetry lies *against* time, rather than *about* time. Does that make it less of an untruth? Surely not, but the truth is mortal, would make us perish immediately, and so we need the lie of life, and the life of lying. I want to get us in a little closer to this poem's dialectic, which is to say, its Gnosis. We have a Gnostic triad: stanza I, Negation; stanza II, Evasion; stanza III, Extravagance. I read off therefore the phases of this difference, as befits a Stevensian rabbi.

I, Negation: Keats's urn estranges even as it befriends, and yet it remains pastoral. Stevens's bowl negates cold pastoral and so gives us only "Cold, a cold porcelain." The crucial negation indeed is that our placing our bowl into stance has left us with less than we had when we started, "with nothing more than the carnations *there*." We have moved some carnations, from here to there, but Keats could do more than that, or at least dramatized the *illusio* of having done more than that.

II, Evasion: And yet, we have made and known an edge more brilliant than before between our poem and the staleness of what passes as and for reality, and more brilliant than Keats's similar edge because more evasive of both poem and of mortality. We respect epistemology less than the Hazlittian Keats did, and if we know both less and less surely, we know better why we must evade knowing.

III, Extravagance: Our mind is "never-resting," rather than merely restless. It wanders beyond limits, *extra vagans*, and comes back to a reality it knows to be fictive. Indeed, the mind is never-resting because it knows its own status as fiction, and in knowing that, it knows delight, as untruth and as poetry, but more crucially it is released from the coldness of porcelain; it knows the heat of the unfinished and of the unfinishable. One of the "flawed words" would yet be that "first word" that Stevens would celebrate at the end, would *know* as *A Discovery of Self*:

One thinks when the houses of New England catch the first sun,
The first word would be of the susceptible being arrived,
The immaculate disclosure of the secret no more obscured.

Call that "secret" the American Gnosis, the knowledge that is

The accent of deviation in the living thing
That is its life preserved, the effort to be born
Surviving being born, the event of life.

11
Hart Crane's Gnosis

> O Thou steeled Cognizance whose leap commits
> The agile precincts of the lark's return. . . .

I remember reading these lines when I was ten years old, crouched over Crane's book in a Bronx library. They, and much else in the book, cathected me onto poetry, a conversion or investment fairly typical of many in my generation. I still have the volume of Crane that I persuaded my older sister to give me on my twelfth birthday, the first book I ever owned. Among my friends there are a few others who owned Crane before any other book. Growing up in the thirties, we were found by Crane's poetry, and though other poets followed (I went from Crane to Blake) the strength of first love still hovers whenever they, or I, read Crane.

The Marlovian rhetoric swept us in, but as with Marlowe himself the rhetoric was also a psychology and a knowing, rather than a knowledge, a knowing that precisely can be called a Gnosis, transcending the epistemology of tropes. What the Australian poet Alec Hope, echoing Tamburlaine, perceptively called "The Argument of Arms" is as much Crane's knowing and language as it was Marlowe's. "Know ye not the argument of arms?" Tamburlaine calls out to his protesting generals before he stabs his own son to death for cowardice. As Hope expounds it, "the argument of arms" is poetic warfare, the agonistic interplay of the Sublime mode:

There is no middle way and no compromise in such a world. Beauty is the rival of beauty as force of force, and only the supreme and perfect survives. Defeat, like victory, is total, absolute, final.

This is indeed Marlowe's knowing, and it would be pointless for a humanist critic to complain that such a vision is human-all-too-human. *Power* is the central poetic concept in Marlowe as it will be in Milton, and as it came to be in the American Milton, Emerson (a prose Milton, granted), and in Crane as a kind of American Marlowe. Hope rightly points to Hazlitt on *Coriolanus* as the proper theorist of the union of the Argument of Arms and the Argument of Poetry. Hazlitt also would not gain the approval of the natural supernaturalist kind of critical humanist:

> The principle of poetry is a very anti-leveling principle. It aims at effect, it exists by contrast. It admits of no medium. It is everything by excess. It rises above the ordinary standard of sufferings and crimes.

But Crane is a prophet of American Orphism, of the Emersonian and Whitmanian Native Strain in our national literature. His poetic of power is therefore best caught by the American theorist proper:

> . . . though Fate is immense, so is Power, which is the other fact in the dual world, immense. If Fate follows and limits Power, Power attends and antagonizes Fate. We must respect Fate as natural history. For who and what is this criticism that pries into the matter? Man is not order of nature, sack and sack, belly and members, link in a chain, nor any ignominious baggage; but a stupendous antagonism, a dragging together of the poles of the Universe. . . .

This might be Melville, meditating upon his own Ahab, but of course it is the uncanny Sage of Concord, satirized by Melville as Plotinus Plinlimmon and as Confidence Man; yet the satire was uneasy. Crane is not very easy to satirize either, and like Shelley, with whom his affinities were deep, Crane goes on burying his critical undertakers. Whitman and Dickinson, Frost and Stevens all had time enough, but Crane, perhaps more gifted than any of them, was finished at an age when they had begun weakly or not at all. A Gnosis of man as a stupendous antagonism, Orphic and Promethean, needs time to work itself through, but time, reviled by all Gnostics with a particular vehemence, had its literal triumph over Crane. As with Shelley and Keats, we have a truncated canon, and yet, as with them, what we have is overwhelming. And what it overwhelms, amidst much else, is any privileging of understanding as an epistemological event, prior to being the catastrophe creation of an aesthetic and spiritual value.

I am concerned here with Crane's "religion" *as a poet* (not as a man, since that seems an inchoate mixture of a Christian Science background, an immersion in Ouspensky, and an all but Catholic yearning). But by poetic "religion" I mean American Orphism, the Emersonian or national religion of our poetry, which Crane inherited, quite directly, from his prime precursor Whitman. True precursors are always composite and imaginary, the son's changeling-fantasy of the father that his own poetry reinvents, and there is usually a near-contemporary agon, as well as a struggle with the fathering force of the past. The older contemporary antagonist and shaper for Crane was certainly Eliot, whose anti-Romantic polemic provoked in Crane an answering fury of High Romanticism, absurdly undervalued by Crane's critical contemporaries, but returning to its mainstream status in the generation that receives the recent abundance of poetic maturation in Ashbery, Merrill, Ammons, Hollander and others.

The governing deities of American Orphism, as of the ancient sort, are Eros or Phanes, Dionysus or Bacchus, and Ananke, the Necessity who appears as the maternal ocean in Whitman and Crane most overtly, but clearly and obsessively enough in Stevens also. Not so clear, though just as obsessive, must be our judgment upon Melville's representations of an Orphic Ananke in the great shroud of the sea. Melville's "that man should be a thing for immortal souls to sieve through!" is the apt epigraph of a crucial chapter on Greek Shamanism in E. R. Dodds's great book *The*

Greeks and the Irrational. Dodds traced to Scythia the new Orphic religious pattern that credited man with an occult self of divine origin. This self was not the *psyche*, but the daemon; as Dodds says, "the function of the daemon is to be the carrier of man's potential divinity and actual guilt." Crane's daemon or occult self, like Whitman's, is the actual hero and victim of his own poetry. Crane as American Orpheus is an inevitable image, exploited already by writers as diverse as Yvor Winters in his elegy for Crane and Tennessee Williams in *Suddenly Last Summer.* The best of the Orphic hymns to Crane is the astonishing poem *Fish Food* of John Brooks Wheelwright, except that Crane wrote his own best Orphic elegy in "Atlantis," his close equivalent of Shelley's *Adonais.* But I narrow my subject here of Crane's "Orphism" down to its visionary epistemology or Gnosis. Crane's Eros, his Dionysus, above all his Whitmanian Ananke, remain to be explored, but in these remarks I concern myself only with Crane as "daemon," a potential divinity knowing simultaneously its achievement and its guilt.

The assumption of that daemon, or what the poets of Sensibility called "the incarnation of the Poetic Character," is the inner plot of many of the lyrics in *White Buildings.* The *kenosis* or ebbing-away of the daemon is the plot of the *Voyages* sequence, where the other Orphic deities reduce Crane to a "derelict and blinded guest" of his own vision, and where the "ocean rivers" churn up the Orphic heritage as a "splintered garland for the seer." Certainly the most ambitious of the daemonic incarnations is the sequence *For the Marriage of Faustus and Helen,* which is Crane at his most triumphantly Marlovian, but so much else is at play there that I turn to two lesser but perfect hymns of Orphic incarnation, *Repose of Rivers* and *Passage.*

Crane is a great master of transumptive allusion, of achieving poetic closure by a final trope that reverses or sometimes even transcends both his own lyric's dominant figurations and the poetic tradition's previous exploitations of these images. So, *Repose of Rivers* concludes:

> . . . There, beyond the dykes
>
> I heard wind flaking sapphire, like this summer,
> And willows could not hold more steady sound.

The poem's opening stanza gives a more complex version of that "steady sound" because the synaesthetic seeing/hearing of "that seething, steady leveling of the marshes" is both an irony and an oxymoron:

> The willows carried a slow sound,
> A sarabande the wind mowed on the mead.
> I could never remember
> That seething, steady leveling of the marshes
> Till age had brought me to the sea.

Crane is recalling his version of a Primal Scene of Instruction, a moment renewing itself discontinuously at scattered intervals, yet always for him a moment relating the inevitability of sexual orientation to the assumption of his poethood. The slow-and-steady dance of the wind on the marshes became a repressed memory until "age" as maturation brought the poet to the sea, central image of necessity in his poetry, and a wounding synecdoche here for an acceptance of one's particular fate as a poet. The repressed reveals itself as a grotesque sublimity, with the second stanza alluding to Melville's imagery in his story *The Encantadas:*

> Flags, weeds. And remembrance of steep alcoves
> Where cypresses shared the noon's
> Tyranny; they drew me into hades almost.
> And mammoth turtles climbing sulphur dreams
> Yielded, while sun-silt rippled them
> Asunder . . .

The seething, steady leveling of the mammoth turtles, their infernal love-death, is a kind of sarabande also. In climbing one another they climb dreams of self-immolation, where "yielded" means at once surrender to death and to one another. The terrible slowness of their love-making yields the frightening trope: "sun-silt rippled them / Asunder," where "asunder" is both the post-coition

parting and the individual turtle death. Crane and D. H. Lawrence
had in common as poets only their mutual devotion to Whitman,
and it is instructive to contrast this stanza of *Repose of Rivers*
with the Tortoise-series of Lawrence in *Birds, Beasts, and Flowers.*
Lawrence's tortoises are crucified *into* sex, like Lawrence himself.
Crane's Melvillean turtles are crucified *by* sex. But Crane tells a
different story about himself: crucified *into* poetry and *by* poetry.
The turtles are drawn into a sexual hades; Crane is *almost* drawn,
with the phrase "hades almost" playing against "steep alcoves."
Embowered by steep alcoves of cypresses, intensifying the dominant noon sun, Crane nearly yields to the sexual phantasmagoria
of "flags, weeds," and the sound play alcoves/almost intensifies
the narrowness of the escape from a primary sexuality, presumably
an incestuous heterosexuality. This is the highly oblique burden
of the extraordinary third stanza:

> How much I would have bartered! the black gorge
> And all the singular nestings in the hills
> Where beavers learn stitch and tooth.
> The pond I entered once and quickly fled—
> I remember now its singing willow rim.

What he would have bartered, indeed did barter, was nature for
poetry. Where the second stanza was a *kenosis*, an emptying-out,
of the Orphic self, this stanza is fresh influx, and what returns
from repression is poetic apperception: "I remember now its singing willow rim," a line that reverberates greatly against the first
and last lines of the entire poem. The surrendered Sublime here
is a progressive triad of entities: the Wordsworthian Abyss of birth
of "the black gorge"; "the singular nestings," instructive of work
and of aggression; most memorably the pond, rimmed by singing
willows, whose entrance actually marks the momentary daring of
the representation of Oedipal trespass, or perhaps for Crane one
should say "Orphic trespass."

If everything heretofore in *Repose of Rivers* has been bartered
for the antithetical gift of Orpheus, what remains is to represent

the actual passage into sexuality, and after that the poetic maturation that follows homosexual self-acceptance. Whether the vision
here is of an actual city, or of a New Orleans of the mind, as at
the end of the "River" section of *The Bridge*, the balance of pleasure and of pain is left ambiguous:

> And finally, in that memory all things nurse;
> After the city that I finally passed
> With scalding unguents spread and smoking darts
> The monsoon cut across the delta
> At gulf gates . . . There, beyond the dykes
>
> I heard wind flaking sapphire, like this summer,
> And willows could not hold more steady sound.

The third line of the stanza refers both to the pathos of the city
and to Crane's own sexual initiation. But since "all things nurse"
this memory, the emphasis must be upon breakthrough, upon the
contrast between monsoon and the long-obliterated memory of
sarabande-wind. "Like this summer," the fictive moment of the
lyric's composition, the monsoon of final sexual alignment gave
the gift of an achieved poethood, to hear wind synaesthetically,
flaking sapphire, breaking up yet also distributing the Shelleyan
azure of vision. In such a context, the final line massively gathers
an Orphic confidence.

Yet every close reader of Crane learns to listen to the wind for
evidences of *sparagmos*, of the Orphic breakup, as prevalent in
Crane's winds as in Shelley's, or in Whitman's. I turn to *Passage*,
White Buildings's particular poem of Orphic disincarnation, where
the rite of passage, the movement back to unfindable and fictive
origins, is celebrated more memorably in the opening quatrain
than anywhere else even in Crane, who is clearly the great modern poet of *thresholds*, in the sense definitively expounded in
Angus Fletcher's forthcoming book of that title.

> Where the cedar leaf divides the sky
> I heard the sea.
> In sapphire arenas of the hills
> I was promised an improved infancy.

The Fletcherian *threshold* is a daemonic crossing or textual "image of voice," to use Wordsworth's crucial term. Such a chiasmus tends to hover where tropes collide in an epistemological wilderness. Is there a more outrageously American, Emersonian concept and phrase than "an improved infancy"? Crane presumably was not aware that *Passage* centered itself so directly at the Wordsworthian heart of the crisis poem, in direct competition with *Tintern Abbey* and the *Intimations of Immortality* ode. But the American version as established in the *Seadrift* poems of Whitman was model enough. Crane, inland far though he finds himself, hears the sea. The soft inland murmur promised Wordsworth so improved an infancy that it became an actual intimation of a more-than-poetic immortality. But for Whitman the secret of the murmuring he envied had to be listened for at the water-line. Crane quests for the same emblem that rewarded *Repose of Rivers*, but here the wind does not flake sapphire in the arenas of these inland hills, where the agon with the daemon, Whitman's dusky demon and brother, is to take place.

In Whitman's great elegy of Orphic disincarnation, *As I Ebb'd with the Ocean of Life*, the daemon comes to the poet in the shape of a sardonic phantom, "the real Me," and confronts Whitman, who may hold his book, *Leaves of Grass*, in hand, since the phantom is able to point to it:

But that before all my arrogant poems the real Me stands yet un-
    touch'd, untold, altogether unreach'd,
Withdrawn far, mocking me with mock-congratulatory signs and bows,
With peals of distant ironical laughter at every word I have written,
Pointing in silence to these songs, and then to the sand beneath.
I perceive I have never really understood any thing, not a single object,
    and that no man ever can,
Nature here in sight of the sea taking advantage of me to dart upon
    me and sting me,
Because I have dared to open my mouth to sing at all.

In Crane's *Passage* the sulking poet, denied his promise, abandons memory in a ravine, and tries to identify himself with the wind; but it dies, and he is turned back and around to confront his mocking daemon:

> Touching an opening laurel, I found
> A thief beneath, my stolen book in hand.

It is deliberately ambiguous whether the real Me has stolen the book, or whether the book of Hart Crane itself is stolen property. Unlike the abashed Whitman, Crane is aggressive, and his phantom is lost in wonderment:

> "Why are you back here—smiling an iron coffin?"
> "To argue with the laurel," I replied:
> "Am justified in transience, fleeing
> Under the constant wonder of your eyes—."

But nature here, suddenly in sight of the sea, does take advantage of Crane to dart upon him and sting him, because he has dared to open his mouth to sing at all:

> He closed the book. And from the Ptolemies
> Sand troughed us in a glittering abyss.
> A serpent swam a vertex to the sun
> —On unpaced beaches learned its tongue and drummed.
> What fountains did I hear? what icy speeches?
> Memory, committed to the page, had broke.

The Ptolemies, alluded to here as though they were a galaxy rather than a dynasty, help establish the pyramid image for the serpent who touches its apex in the sun. The glittering abyss belongs both to time and the sun, and the serpent, drumming its tongue upon the beach where no Whitmanian bard paces, is weirdly prophetic of the imagery of Stevens's *The Auroras of Autumn*. The penultimate line glances obliquely at Coleridge's *Kubla Khan*, and the poem ends appropriately with the broken enchantment of memory, broken in the act of writing the poem. It is as though, point for point, *Passage* had undone *Repose of Rivers*.

The Bridge can be read as the same pattern of Orphic incarnation/disincarnation, with every Sublime or daemonic vision subsequently undone by an ebbing-out of poethood. That reading, though traditional, seems to me a weak misreading, inadequate to *The Bridge*'s strong misreadings of its precursors. Nietzsche and Pater, both of whom Crane had pondered, taught a subtler *askesis*, and *The Bridge* advances upon *White Buildings* (except for *Voyages*), by mounting a powerful scheme of transumption, of what Nietzsche called the poetic will's revenge against time and particularly against time's proclamation of belatedness: "It was." Crane shrewdly wrote, in 1918: "one may envy Nietzsche a little; think of being so elusive,—so mercurial, as to be first swallowed whole, then coughed up, and still remain a mystery!" But veteran readers of Crane learn to observe something like that when confronted by the majesty of *The Bridge* at its finest, as here in the final quatrains of the "Proem":

> Again the traffic lights that skim thy swift
> Unfractioned idiom, immaculate sigh of stars,
> Beading thy path—condense eternity:
> And we have seen night lifted in thine arms.
>
> Under thy shadow by the piers I waited;
> Only in darkness is thy shadow clear.
> The City's fiery parcels all undone,
> Already snow submerges an iron year . . .
>
> O Sleepless as the river under thee,
> Vaulting the sea, the prairies' dreaming sod,
> Unto us lowliest sometime sweep, descend
> And of the curveship lend a myth to God.

Crane in *White Buildings* is wholly Orphic, in that his concern is his relation, as poet, *to* his own vision, rather than *with* the content of poetic vision, to utilize a general distinction inaugurated by Northrop Frye, following after Ruskin. The peculiar power of *The Bridge*, at its strongest, is that Crane succeeds in becoming what Pater and Nietzsche urged the future poet to be: an ascetic of the spirit, which is an accurate definition of a purified Gnosis. Directly before these three final quatrains of "To Brooklyn Bridge," Crane had saluted the bridge first as Orphic emblem, both harp and altar, but then as the threshold of the full triad of the Orphic destiny: Dionysus or prophet's pledge, Ananke or prayer of pariah, and Eros, the lover's cry. It is after the range of relations to his own vision has been acknowledged and accepted that a stronger Crane achieves the Gnosis of those three last quatrains. There the poet remains present, but only as a knowing Abyss, contemplating the content of that knowing, which is a fullness or presence he can invoke but scarcely share. He sees "night lifted in thine arms"; he waits, for a shadow to clarify in darkness; he knows, yet what he knows is a vaulting, a sweep, a descent, above all a curveship, a realization of an angle of vision not yet his own.

This peculiarly effective stance has a precursor in Shelley's visionary skepticism, particularly in his final phase of *Adonais* and *The Triumph of Life*. Crane's achievement of this stance is the still-unexplored origin of *The Bridge*, but the textual evolution of "Atlantis," the first section of the visionary epic to be composed, is the probable area that should be considered. Lacking space here, I point instead to the achieved stance of *Voyages VI* as the earliest full instance of Crane's mature Orphism, after which I will conclude with a reading of "Atlantis" and a brief glance at Crane's testament, *The Broken Tower*.

The governing deities of the *Voyages* sequence are Eros and Ananke, or Emil Oppfer and the Caribbean as Whitmanian fierce old mother moaning for her castaways. But the Orphic Dionysus, rent apart by Titanic forces, dominates the sixth lyric, which like Stevens's *The Paltry Nude Starts upon a Spring Journey* partly derives from Pater's description of Botticelli's Venus in *The Renaissance*. Pater's sado-masochistic maternal love-goddess, with her eyes smiling "unsearchable repose," becomes Crane's overtly destructive muse, whose seer is no longer at home in his own vision:

> My eyes pressed black against the prow,
> —Thy derelict and blinded guest
>
> Waiting, afire, what name, unspoke,
> I cannot claim: let thy waves rear

> More savage than the death of kings,
> Some splintered garland for the seer.

The unspoken, unclaimed name is that of Orpheus, in his terrible final phase of "floating singer." Crane's highly deliberate echo of Shakespeare's Richard II at his most self-destructively masochistic is assimilated to the poetic equivalent, which is the splintering of the garland of laurel. Yet the final stanza returns to the central image of poetic incarnation in Crane, *Repose of Rivers* and its "hushed willows":

> The imaged Word, it is, that holds
> Hushed willows anchored in its glow.
> It is the unbetrayable reply
> Whose accent no farewell can know.

This is the achieved and curiously firm balance of a visionary skepticism, or the Orphic stance of *The Bridge*. It can be contrasted to Lawrence again, in the "Orphic farewell" of *Medlars and Sorb Apples* in *Birds, Beasts and Flowers*. For Lawrence, Orphic assurance is the solipsism of an "intoxication of perfect loneliness." Crane crosses that intoxication by transuming his own and tradition's trope of the hushed willows as signifying an end to solitary mourning, and a renewal of poetic divination. *Voyages* VI turns its "imaged Word" against Eliot's neo-orthodox Word, or Christ, and Whitman's Word out of the Sea, or death, death that is the Oedipal merging back into the mother. Crane ends upon "know" because knowledge, and not faith, is his religious mode, a Gnosis that is more fully developed in *The Bridge*.

The dozen octaves of the final version of "Atlantis" show Crane in his mastery of the traditional Sublime, and are wholly comparable to the final seventeen stanzas of Shelley's *Adonais*. Crane's absolute music, like Plato's, "is then the knowledge of that which relates to love in harmony and system," but Crane's love is rather more like Shelley's desperate and skeptical outleaping than it is like Diotima's vision. For six stanzas, Crane drives upward, in a hyperbolic arc whose burden is agonistic, struggling to break beyond every achieved Sublime in the language. This agon belongs to the Sublime, and perhaps in America it *is* the Sublime. But such an agon requires particular contestants, and "Atlantis" finds them in *The Waste Land* and, yet more repressedly, in Whitman's *Crossing Brooklyn Ferry*, the great addition to the second, 1856, *Leaves of Grass*, and Thoreau's favorite poem by Whitman.

Much of Crane's struggle with Eliot was revised out of the final "Atlantis," but only as overt textual traces; the deep inwardness of the battle is recoverable. Two modes of phantasmagoria clash:

> Through the bound cable strands, the arching path
> Upward, veering with light, the flight of strings,—
> Taut miles of shuttling moonlight syncopate
> The whispered rush, telepathy of wires.
> Up the index of night, granite and steel—
> Transparent meshes—fleckless the gleaming staves—
> Sibylline voices flicker, waveringly stream
> As though a god were issue of the strings. . . .

> A woman drew her long black hair out tight
> And fiddled whisper music on those strings
> And bats with baby faces in the violet light
> Whistled, and beat their wings
> And crawled head downward down a blackened wall
> And upside down in air were towers
> Tolling reminiscent bells, that kept the hours
> And voices singing out of empty cisterns and exhausted wells.

The latter hallucination might be called an amalgam of *Dracula* and the Gospels, as rendered in the high style of Tennyson's *Idylls of the King*, and obviously is in no sense a source or cause of Crane's transcendental opening octave. Nevertheless, no clearer contrast could be afforded, for Crane's lines answer Eliot's, in every meaning of "answer." "Music is then the knowledge of that which relates to love in harmony and system," and one knowledge answers another in these competing and marvelous musics of poetry, and of visionary history. Crane's bridge is to Atlantis, in fulfillment of the Platonic quest of Crane's Columbus. Eliot's bridge is to the Inferno, in fulfillment of the neo-Christian condemnation of Romantic, Transcendentalist, Gnostic quest. Crane's Sibylline voices stream upward; his night-illuminated bridge becomes a transparent musical score, until Orpheus is born out of the flight of strings. Eliot's Sibyl wishes to die; her counterpart plays a vampiric score upon her own hair, until instead of an Orphic birth upwards we have an impotent triumph of time.

This contrast, and others equally sharp, constitute the context of Crane's aspiration in "Atlantis." But this aspiration, which is for knowledge, in the particular sense of Gnosis, yields to Eliot, as it must, much of the world of things-as-they-are. The closing images of "The Tunnel," the section of *The Bridge* preceding "Atlantis," combine *The Waste Land's* accounts of loss with Whitman's darker visions of those losses in *Crossing Brooklyn Ferry:*

> And this thy harbor, O my City, I have driven under,
> Tossed from the coil of ticking towers. . . . Tomorrow,
> And to be. . . . Here by the River that is East—
> Here at the waters' edge the hands drop memory;
> Shadowless in that abyss they unaccounting lie.
> How far away the star has pooled the sea—
> Or shall the hands be drawn away, to die?

> Kiss of our agony Thou gatherest,
>   O Hand of Fire
>   gatherest—

Emerson's was a Gnosis without Gnosticism; Crane's religion, at its darkest, shades from Orphism into Gnosticism, in a negative transcendence even of the Whitman who proclaimed: "It is not upon you alone the dark patches fall, / The dark threw its patches upon me also." The negative transcendence of "Atlantis" surmounts the world, history and even precursors as knowing, in their rival ways, as Eliot and Whitman. Crane condenses the upward intensities of his first six octaves by a deliberate recall of his own Columbus triumphantly but delusively chanting: "I bring you back Cathay!" But Crane's Columbus invoked the Demiurge under Emily Dickinson's name for him, "Inquisitor! incognizable Word / Of Eden." This beautiful pathos of defeat, in "Ave Maria," was consonant with Whitman's *Prayer of Columbus*, where the battered, wrecked old mariner denied all knowledge: "I know not even my own word past or present." Crane's American burden, in the second half of "Atlantis," is to start again where Dickinson and Whitman ended, and where Eliot had sought to show no fresh start was possible. Knowledge in precisely the Gnostic sense—a knowing that knows the knower and is, *in itself*, the form of salvation—becomes Crane's formidable hymn addressed directly to itself, to poem and to bridge, until they become momentarily "—One Song, one Bridge of Fire!" But is this persuasively different from the "Hand of Fire" that gathers the kiss of our agony?

The dialectic of Gnosticism is a triad of negation, evasion and extravagance. Lurianic Kabbalah renders these as contraction, breaking-of-the-vessels and restitution. Fate, freedom, power is the Emersonian or American equivalent. All of these triads translate aesthetically into a dialectic of limitation, substitution and representation, as I have shown in several critical books starting with *A Map of Misreading*. Crane's negation or limitation, his contraction into Fate, is scarcely different from Eliot's, but then such rival negative theologies as Valentinian Gnosticism and Johannine Christianity are difficult to distinguish in their accounts of how to express divinity. Gnostic evasion, like Crane's notorious freedom and range in troping, is clearly more inventive than authorized Christian modes of substitution, just as Gnostic extravagance, again like Crane's hyperbolical Sublime, easily surpasses orthodox expressions of power.

Crane's elaborate evasiveness is crucial in the seventh stanza of "Atlantis," where the upward movement of the tropology has ended, and a westward lateral sweep of vision is substituted, with the bridge no longer confronted and addressed, but seen now as binding the continent:

We left the haven hanging in the night—
Sheened harbor lanterns backward fled the keel.
Pacific here at time's end, bearing corn,—
Eyes stammer through the pangs of dust and steel.

And still the circular, indubitable frieze
Of heaven's meditation, yoking wave
To kneeling wave, one song devoutly binds—
The vernal strophe chimes from deathless strings!

The third line implies not merely a circuit of the earth, but an achieved peace at the end of days, a millennial harvest. When the bridge returns in this stanza's last four lines, it has become heaven's own meditation, the known knowing the human knower. And such a knowing leads Crane on to the single most central stanza of his life and work:

O Thou steeled Cognizance whose leap commits
The agile precincts of the lark's return;
Within whose lariat sweep encinctured sing
In single chrysalis the many twain,—
Of stars Thou art the stitch and stallion glow
And like an organ, Thou, with sound of doom—
Sight, sound and flesh Thou leadest from time's realm
As love strikes clear direction for the helm.

Contrast the precise Shelleyan equivalent:

The One remains, the many change and pass;
Heaven's light forever shines, Earth's shadows fly;
Life, like a dome of many-colored glass,
Stains the white radiance of Eternity,
Until Death tramples it to fragments.—Die,
If thou wouldst be with that which thou dost seek!
Follow where all is fled!—Rome's azure sky,
Flowers, ruins, statues, music, words, are weak
The glory they transfuse with fitting truth to speak.

Superficially, the two stanzas are much at variance, with Crane's tone apparently triumphal, Shelley's apparently despairing. But the pragmatic or merely natural burden of both stanzas is quite suicidal. The bridge, as "steeled Cognizance," resolves the many into

One, but this music of unity is a "sound of doom" for all flesh and its senses living in time's realm. Love's "clear direction," as in Shelley's climactic stanza, is towards death. But Shelley is very much involved in his own relation, as poet, to his own vision. Crane's role, as known to the bridge's knower, forsakes that relation, and a terrifyingly free concentration on the content of poetic vision is the reward. "Of stars Thou art the stitch and stallion glow" Marlowe himself would have envied, but since both terms of the trope, bridge and stars, exclude the human, Crane is impelled onwards to extraordinary achievements in hyperbole. When the bridge is "iridescently upborne / Through the bright drench and fabric of our veins," then the human price of Gnosticism begins to mount also. Crane insists that all this is "to our joy," but that joy is as dialectical as Shelley's despair. And Crane, supremely intelligent, counts the cost, foreknowing all criticism:

> Migrations that must needs void memory,
> Inventions that cobblestone the heart,—
> Unspeakable Thou Bridge to Thee, O Love.
> Thy pardon for this history, whitest Flower,
> O Answerer of all,—Anemone,—
> Now while thy petals spend the suns about us, hold—
> (O Thou whose radiance doth inherit me)
> Atlantis,—hold thy floating singer late!

Would it make a difference if this read: "Cathay,—hold thy floating singer late!" so that the prayer of pariah would belong to Columbus and not to Orpheus? Yes, for the final stanza then would have the Orphic strings leap and converge to a question clearly different:

> —One Song, one Bridge of Fire! Is it Atlantis,
> Now pity steeps the grass and rainbows ring
> The serpent with the eagle in the leaves . . . ?

Crane's revision of the Orphic stance of *White Buildings*, of lyrics like *Repose of Rivers* and *Passage*, here allows him a difference that is a triumph. His serpent and eagle are likelier to be Shelley's than Nietzsche's, for they remain at strife *within* their border of covenant, the ring of rainbows. Atlantis is urged to hold its Orpheus late, as a kind of newly fused Platonic myth of reconcilement to a higher world of forms, a myth of which Gnosticism was a direct heir. "Is it Cathay?," repeating the noble delusion of Columbus, is not a question hinting defeat, but foreboding victory. Yet Orphic victories are dialectical, as Crane well knew. Knowledge indeed is the kernel, for Crane astutely shows awareness of what the greatest poets always know, which is that their figurations intend the will's revenge against time's "it was," but actually achieve the will's limits, in the bewilderments of the Abyss of troping and of tropes.

The coda to Crane's poetry, and his life, is *The Broken Tower*, where the transumption of the Orphic quest does allow a final triumph:

> And so it was I entered the broken world
> To trace the visionary company of love, its voice
> An instant in the wind (I know not whither hurled)
> But not for long to hold each desperate choice.

Crane mentions reading other books by Pater, but not the unfinished novel *Gaston de Latour*. Its first few chapters, at least, would have fascinated him, and perhaps he did look into the opening pages, where the young Gaston undergoes a ceremony bridging the spirit and nature:

> Gaston alone, with all his mystic preoccupations, by the privilege of youth, seemed to belong to both, and link the visionary company about him to the external scene.

The "privilege of youth" was still Crane's when he died, and *The Broken Tower* remains as one of those links. Such a link, finally, is not to be judged as what Freud called "a false connection" or as another irony to be ironically recognized, but rather as a noble synecdoche, self-mutilating perhaps as is a steeled Cognizance, but by its very turning against the self, endlessly reconstituting the American poetic self, the *pneuma* or spark of an American Gnosis.

12

Measuring the Canon:
John Ashbery's
Wet Casements and Tapestry

I begin with a critic's apologia for some autobiographical remarks, but they do come under the heading of what these days is called "reception." Anyway, the apologia may be redundant, since Oscar Wilde was always right, and here is his *persona* Gilbert speaking in the grand dialogue *The Critic as Artist*:

> That is what the highest criticism really is, the record of one's own soul. It is more fascinating than history, as it is concerned simply with oneself. It is more delightful than philosophy, as its subject is concrete not abstract, real and not vague. It is the only civilized form of autobiography, as it deals not with the events, but with the thoughts of one's life; not with life's physical accidents of deed or circumstance, but with the spiritual moods and imaginative passions of the mind. . . .

The only civilized form of autobiography—I know no more adequate characterization of the highest criticism. And so I start with autobiography. I heard Ashbery's poem *Wet Casements* read aloud by its poet at Yale, before I had seen the text. Only the pathos of the traditional phrase "immortal wound" seems to me adequate to my response, both immediate and continuing. For me, it had joined the canon, directly I had heard it, and it transcended the poet's customary, beautifully evasive, rather flat delivery. What persuaded me, cognitively and emotionally, was the poem's immediate authority in taking up and transuming the major American trope of "solitude," in the peculiar sense that Emerson invented, by way of misprision out of Montaigne. Montaigne, in his essay *Of Solitude*, warned that "this occupation with books is as laborious as any other, and as much an enemy to health." But American solitude seems to be associated always with bookish ideals, even if not directly with books, from Emerson and Thoreau to the present moment. Emerson, in his essay *The Transcendentalist*, prophesied that his disciples would choose solitude:

> They are lonely; the spirit of their writing and conversation is lonely; they repel influences; they shun general society; they incline to shut themselves in their chamber in the house. . . .

It seems a more accurate prophecy of Emily Dickinson than of Walt Whitman, but that is because Whitman's *persona*, his mask, was so profoundly deceptive. Though Whitman proclaims companionship, his poetry opens to glory only in solitude, whether that be in the phantasmagoria of *The Sleepers*, in the struggles with his waxing and waning poetic self in the *Sea Drift* pieces, or more intensely in the uniquely solitary elegy for Lincoln, *When Lilacs Last in the Dooryard Bloom'd*.

The poetry of our century has its major spokesmen for solitude in Wallace Stevens and Robert Frost, both of whom flourished best when most perfectly alone. Stevens particularly is closest to a sense of triumph when he proclaims his isolation:

> In solitude the trumpets of solitude
> Are not of another solitude resounding;
> A little string speaks for a crowd of voices.

The darker side of solitude, the estrangement from life brought about by so literary an ideal, is more a burden of contemporary American poetry. Prophecy here belongs to Hart Crane, who drowned himself in 1932, three months before what would have been his thirty-third birthday. His elegy for himself, the immensely poignant *The Broken Tower*, possibly takes from Walter Pater's unfinished prose romance, *Gaston de Latour*, a beautiful phrase, "the visionary company," and converts it into an image of loss, of hopeless quest:

> And so it was I entered the broken world
> To trace the visionary company of love. . . .

Such a tracing would have taken the poet beyond solitude, but Crane's life and work ended more in the spirit of his late poem *Purgatorio*, which pictures the poet in exile and apart, cut off from country and from friends.

The contemporary poet John Ashbery is the culmination of this very American solitude. His recent poem *Wet Casements* records the loss of a beloved name, or perhaps just the name of someone once loved, and then expresses the creative anger of a consciousness condemned to a solitude of lost information, or a world of books. "Anger" becomes Ashbery's substitute word or trope for what Montaigne and Emerson called "solitude":

> I shall use my anger to build a bridge like that
> Of Avignon, on which people may dance for the feeling
> Of dancing on a bridge. I shall at last see my complete face
> Reflected not in the water but in the worn stone floor of my bridge.

Is this not the most American of solitudes, where even the self's own reflection is to be observed, not in nature, but in the self's own solitary creation? The solitude that Montaigne both praised and warned against, but which Emerson wholly exalted, attains a climax in Ashbery's final lines:

> I shall keep to myself.
> I shall not repeat others' comments about me.

Indeed, no American feels free when she or he is not alone, and it may be the eloquent sorrow of America that it must continue, in its best poems, to equate freedom with solitude.

Freedom, or rather the stances or positions of freedom, might be called the determining element, above all others, in canon-formation, the complex process through which a few poets survive, and most vanish. I want, in this chapter, to perform three separate but related critical acts, all of them quests for stances of freedom. Taking as my texts two poems by Ashbery, *Wet Casements* from *Houseboat Days*, and *Tapestry* from *As We Know*, I want to offer interpretations that will aid others in reading more fully and recognizing as canonical two marvelous short meditations. More briefly, I then will go on to an analysis of contemporary canon-formation, and will conclude with a defense of my own antithetical mode of criticism, as against all merely rhetorical analyses. To conduct a defense of that kind, however briefly, necessarily will involve a proclamation of credo as to the use of criticism and the use of poetry, at this time.

Like many other readers of Ashbery I first encountered the text of *Tapestry* in its magazine appearance, and like some of those readers I again responded immediately, as I had on first hearing *Wet Casements*. I do not believe that a canonical response is a mystery, but I defer an account of that response until I have offered a rather close reading of the poem. Though I have observed already that *Tapestry*, unlike *Wet Casements*, yields to rhetorical criticism, whether of the New or current Deconstructionist variety, I will read *Tapestry* rather strictly on the High Romantic crisis-poem model of six revisionary ratios, that is to say, by a kind of criticism overtly canonical and antithetical, a poor thing doubtless but my own.

In the broadest sense of High Romantic tradition, *Tapestry* is a poem in the mode of Keats's *Grecian Urn*, since its *topos* is at once the state of being of an art-work, and the stance or relation of both artist and viewer to the work. In a very narrow sense, there is a fascinating analogue to *Tapestry* in Elizabeth Bishop's wonderful poem, *Brazil, January 1, 1502*, which we can be sure that Ashbery both knows and admires. Bishop's epigraph, which is also her central trope, is from Kenneth Clark's *Landscape into Art*: ". . . embroidered nature . . . tapestried landscape." It is worth recalling, as we read both Bishop's poem and Ashbery's, that "tapestry" in its Greek original sense was a word for a carpet, and that what the two poets exploit is the carpet-like density of tapestry, its heavy fabric woven across the warp by varicolored designs. Bishop contrasts the tapestry-like Brazilian nature that greets her eyes in January with the same nature that greeted the Portuguese four hundred fifty years before. "The Christians, hard as nails, tiny as nails, and glinting," as she grimly calls them, are seen as lost in the illusions of a tapestry-like nature, as they pursue "a brand-new pleasure":

> they ripped away into the hanging fabric,
> each out to catch an Indian for himself—
> those maddening little women who kept calling,
> calling to each other (or had the birds waked up?)
> and retreating, always retreating, behind it.

This negative Eros, and nature/art continuum/conflation, alike are alien to Ashbery's poem. What he shares however is a deeper level of troubled meaning in Bishop's text, which is an apprehension that the dilemmas of poem and of poet are precisely those of tapestry; as Bishop phrases it: "solid but airy; fresh as if just finished / and taken off the frame," which I would gloss as: a representation yet also a limitation, with a black hole of rhetoric, or *aporia*, wedged in between. Ashbery is bleaker even than Bishop, or their common precursor in the later Stevens, and his opening swerve is an irony for that *aporia*, that impossible-to-solve mental dilemma:

> It is difficult to separate the tapestry
> From the room or loom which takes precedence over it.
> For it must always be frontal and yet to one side.

Reductively I translate this (with reservations and reverence) as: "It is impossible to separate the poem, Ashbery's *Tapestry*, from either the anterior tradition or the process of writing, each of which has priority, and illusion of presence, over it, because the poem is compelled always to 'be frontal,' confronting the force of the literary past, 'and yet to one side,' evading that force." The tapestry, and Ashbery's poem, share an absence that exists in an uneasy dialectical alternation with the presence of the room of tradition, and the loom of composition.

The next stanza moves from the artistic dilemma to the reader's or viewer's reception of poem or tapestry, conveyed by a synecdoche as old as Plato's Allegory of the Cave in *The Republic*:

> It insists on this picture of "history"
> In the making, because there is no way out of the punishment
> It proposes: sight blinded by sunlight.
> The seeing taken in with what is seen
> In an explosion of sudden awareness of its formal splendor.

"Sight blinded by sunlight" is Plato's trope, but for Plato it was a phase in a dialectic; for Ashbery it is a turning-against-the-self, a wound beyond rhetoric. Ashbery's genius makes this his reader's wound also; a poetic insistence, a moral proposal that contains the mystery and the authority of the canonical process, which after all is one of *measurement*, particularly in the sense of quantification. Ashbery's trope proper here, his wounded synecdoche, is the "history" he places between quotation marks. Though an intense reader of Whitman and of Stevens, Ashbery asserts he knows little of Emerson directly; but his "history" is precisely Emerson's, probably as filtered through Whitman. "History," like the tapestry and poem, is a textual weave always confronting the force of anteriority and yet evading that force "to one side." Emerson, repudiating Germanic and British "history" in favor of American "biography" or "self-reliance," remarked in an 1840 Journal entry: "self-reliance is precisely that secret,—to make your supposed deficiency redundancy." But "history" in Ashbery's making is his poem's Platonic prospect of the punishment of sight by sunlight, a kind of Oedipal blinding. This is Emerson's trope reversed into its opposite. Contrast to Ashbery the majestic final sentence of Emerson's manifesto, *Nature*:

> The kingdom of man over nature, which cometh not with ob-
> servation,—a dominion such as now is beyond his dream of
> God,—he shall enter without more wonder than the blind man
> feels who is gradually restored to perfect sight.

This is Emerson's triumphant Orphic poet speaking, while Ashbery's *persona*, at least since his great book *The Double Dream of Spring*, is what I remember describing once as a failed Orphic, perhaps even deliberately failed. Such a failure is the intentionality of the two remarkable lines that end *Tapestry*:

> The seeing taken in with what is seen
> In an explosion of sudden awareness of its formal splendor.

Emerson said of American poetic seeing that it was, in essence, more-than-Platonic. Indeed, I would cite this Emersonian blending of the mind's power and of seeing as being more a Gnostic than a Neoplatonic formulation:

> As, in the sun, objects paint their images on the retina of the eye, so they, sharing the aspiration of the whole universe, tend to paint a far more delicate copy of their essence in his mind. . . .
> . . . This insight, which expresses itself by what is called Imagination, is a very high sort of seeing, which does not come by study, but by the intellect being where and what it sees; by sharing the path or circuit of things through forms and so making them translucid to others.

As I have remarked, in other contexts, this is the indisputable American Sublime, by which I intend no irony but rather a noble synecdoche. That synecdoche Ashbery turns from, against himself, in favor of the mutilating synecdoche that executes two turns, both deconstructive, away from the Emersonian cunning. One is to refuse the valorization of seeing over what is seen; the other is to substitute for translucence "an explosion of sudden awareness" of the formal splendor of the seen. Against the passage of things through forms, we are given the more static splendor of the form, the tapestry's actual design. But this is hardly that wearisome Modernism, Poundian and Eliotic in its origins, that pretends to de-idealize a Romantic agon. Instead, it leads to what Romantic convention would accustom us to expect, a *kenosis* of the poet's godhead, an ebbing-away and emptying out of poetic energies:

> The eyesight, seen as inner,
> Registers over the impact of itself
> Receiving phenomena, and in so doing

Draws an outline, or a blueprint,
Of what was just there: dead on the line.

This is a *kenosis* of sight, like Whitman's in the *Sea-Drift* poems, or like Stevens in his Whitmanian *Stars at Tallapoosa:*

> The lines are straight and swift between the stars.
> The night is not the cradle that they cry,
> The criers, undulating the deep-oceaned phrase.
> The lines are much too dark and much too sharp.
>
> *   *   *
>
> Let these be your delight, secretive hunter,
> Wading the sea-lines, moist and ever-mingling,
> Mounting the earth-lines, long and lax, lethargic.
> These lines are swift and fall without diverging.

For Whitman, to be "dead on the line" was the experience of being "seiz'd by the spirit that trails in the lines underfoot," of pondering his own identity with the windrows and the sea-drift. For Ashbery his eyesight, confronting the tapestry, performs the psychic defense of isolation, burning away context until the self-reflexiveness of seeing yields an outline of what was *just* there, in both senses of just, barely and temporally belated, *dead on the line*. In that immensely suggestive Ashberian trope, how are we to read that adverbial "dead"? Presumably not as meaning lifeless nor inanimate nor unresponsive nor out of existence, though these are the primary significations. Lacking excitement, weary, luster-less are possibilities, but more likely "dead on the line" means completely, precisely, abruptly on the line, the line of vision and tapestry, and the poetic line itself. But more probable even is the sports meaning of being out of play, as well as the technical mean-ing of being cut off from energy, from electric current. Let us translate "dead on the line" as being the burning-out-and-away of context, and most particularly of poetic context.

I recur here to one of my own critical notions, that of "crossing" or the disjunctive gathering of topological meanings between one kind of figuration and another. Outward reality, isolated to outline or blueprint, and rendered dead on the line, as tapestry or poem, is replaced by a tercet that substitutes a repressive "blanket" in a trope at once Keatsian and Stevensian:

> If it has the form of a blanket, that is because
> We are eager, all the same, to be wound in it:
> This must be the good of not experiencing it.

This revises a famous tercet of Stevens's *Final Soliloquy of the Interior Paramour*:

> Within a single thing, a single shawl
> Wrapped tightly round us, since we are poor, a warmth,
> A light, a power; the miraculous influence.

Both poets without design remind us of the Emersonian trope of "poverty" for imaginative need, but the High Romantic: "A light, a power; the miraculous influence" plays against the toneless: "This must be the good of not experiencing it," hyperbole against litotes. In the Sublime crossing to a greater inwardness, Stevens's pathos is strong, invoking the language of desire, possession and power, but Ashbery's language is again what we might call the real absence, the achieved dearth of the tapestry's substitution for experience. As Keats turns to another scene upon the Urn, so Ashbery moves his gaze to some other life, also depicted on the now blanket-like tapestry:

> But in some other life, which the blanket depicts anyway,
> The citizens hold sweet commerce with one another
> And pinch the fruit unpestered, as they will.

The humor charmingly conceals Ashbery's sublimating metaphor, which is his outside removal from this free world inside, or depicted anyway on the blanket-tapestry. The "as they will" at the tercet's close prepares for two Stevensian "intricate evasions of as" that govern the startling final stanza:

> As words go crying after themselves, leaving the dream
> Upended in a puddle somewhere
> As though "dead" were just another adjective.

This "dead" presumably is not identical with "dead on the line," since there "dead" is adverbial. I read this second "dead" as a trope upon the earlier trope "dead on the line," that is to say, as a transumption of Ashbery himself and of his Whitmanian-Stevensian tradition. "Words go crying after themselves" because words are leaves are people (readers, poets), and so "the dream / Upended in a puddle somewhere" is the Shelleyan dream of words or dead thoughts quickening a new birth, as though indeed "dead" were one more adjective among many.

I want to distinguish now, for later development, between strong poems that are implicitly canonical, like *Tapestry*, and those whose designs upon the canon are explicit, like *Wet Casements*. The implicitly canonical *Tapestry* yields to merely rhetorical criticism, while *Wet Casements* requires a more antithetical mode of interpretation. Nevertheless, I have ventured an antithetical reading of *Tapestry*, pretty well relying upon my apotropaic litany of revisionary ratios, and now I will extend contrariness by a reading of *Wet Casements* neither formal nor antithetical, but free-style, eclectic, perhaps wholly personal.

Ashbery shies away from epigraphs, yet *Wet Casements* turns to Kafka's *Wedding Preparations in the Country* in order to get started. The epigraph though is more about not getting started:

> When Eduard Raban, coming along the passage, walked into the open doorway, he saw that it was raining. It was not raining much.

Three paragraphs on from this opening, Raban stares at a lady who perhaps has looked at him:

> . . . She did so indifferently, and she was perhaps, in any case, only looking at the falling rain in front of him or at the small nameplates of firms that were fixed to the door over his head. Raban thought she looked amazed. "Well," he thought, "if I could tell her the whole story, she would cease to be astonished. One works so feverishly at the office that afterwards one is too tired even to enjoy one's holidays properly. But even all that work does not give one a claim to be treated lovingly by every-

one; on the contrary, one is alone, a total stranger and only an object of curiosity. And so long as you say 'one' instead of 'I' there's nothing in it and one can easily tell the story; but as soon as you admit to yourself that it is you yourself, you feel as though transfixed and are horrified."

That dark reflection is the *ethos*, the universe of limitation, of the poem *Wet Casements*, whose opening irony swerves from Kafka's yet only to more self-alienation:

> The conception is interesting: to see, as though reflected
> In streaming windowpanes, the look of others through
> Their own eyes.

"Interesting" is one of Ashbery's driest ironies, and is a trope for something like "desperate," while the "look of others through / Their own eyes" is an evasion, wholly characteristic of Ashbery's self-expression through his own reflexive seeing. Yet the conception *is* interesting, particularly since it is both concept and engendering. How much can one catch of the look of others or of the self, through their eyes or one's own, when the look is reflected in wet casements, in streaming windowpanes? The question is desperate enough, and the slightly archaic "casements" of the title means not just any windows opening outwards, but the casements of Keats's odes, open to the vision of romance. Keats concluded his *Ode to Psyche* with the vision of "A bright torch, and a casement ope at night, / To let the warm love in!" In *Ode to a Nightingale*, there is the still grander trope of the bird's song: "that oft-times hath / Charmed magic casements, opening on the foam / Of perilous seas in fairy lands forlorn." *Wet Casements* is a strange, late, meditative version of the Keatsian ode, obviously not in mere form, but in rhetorical stance. Perhaps we might describe it as Keats assimilated to the Age of Kafka, and still it remains Keats. Lest I seem more extreme even than usual, I turn to the merely useful point that must be made in starting to read Ashbery's poem. It could not be entitled *Wet Windows*, because these have to be windows that open outwards, just as Kafka's Raban walked into the open doorway to see that it was raining. There must be still, even in Kafka and in Ashbery, what there always was in Keats, the hope, however forlorn, of open vision, and of a passage to other selves. Yet *Wet Casements* is a beautifully forlorn poem, a hymn to lost Eros, not an *Ode to Psyche* triumphantly opening to Eros even as a poem attempts closure. The conception is indeed interesting, to see the self-seen look of others reflected in a window closed against the rain, but that could and should be opened outwards in a season of calm weather. "A digest," Ashbery writes, meaning a daemonic division or distribution of self-images, ending with the overlay of his own "ghostly transparent face." We are back in one of Ashbery's familiar modes, from at least *Three Poems* on, a division of self and soul of a Whitmanian rather than Yeatsian kind, where "you" is Ashbery's soul or re-imagined character, in the process of becoming, and "I" is Ashbery's writing self or reduced personality. But the "you" is also the erotic possibility of otherness, now lost, or of a muse-figure never quite found. This is the "you" described in the long passage that is a single sentence and that takes up exactly half of the poem's length:

You in falbalas

Of some distant but not too distant era, the cosmetics,
The shoes perfectly pointed, drifting (how long you
Have been drifting; how long I have too for that matter)
Like a bottle-imp toward a surface which can never be approached,
Never pierced through into the timeless energy of a present
Which would have its own opinions on these matters,
Are an epistemological snapshot of the processes
That first mentioned your name at some crowded cocktail
Party long ago, and someone (not the person addressed)
Overheard it and carried that name around in his wallet
For years as the wallet crumbled and bills slid in
And out of it.

Call it a Whitmanian "drifting," an episode in Ashbery's continuous, endless Song of Himself. "Drifting" is the crucial word in the passage, akin to Whitman's "sea-drift" elegiac intensities. What precisely can "drifting" mean here? "You"—soul of Ashbery,

lost erotic partner, the other or muse component in lyric poetry—
are attired in the ruffles, frills, cosmetics, ornamental shoes of a
studied nostalgia, one of those eras Stevens said the imagination
was always at an end of, a vanished elegance. Like an Arabian
Nights bottle-imp you are drifting perpetually towards a fictively
paradoxical surface, always absent. If it were present, if you could
approach it ever, then you would be pierced through, you would
have pierced through, into a true present, indeed into the ontological timelessness of an energy of consciousness that would pass
judgment upon all drifting, have its own opinion, presumably negative, of drifting. Again, why "drifting"? The best clue is that the
drifter is "an epistemological snapshot of the processes" of time itself, which has a wallet at its back, a crumbling wallet, with bills
and alms for oblivion sliding in and out of it. The unreachable
surface of a present would have timeless energy, but "drifting"
means to yield with a wise passivity to temporal entropy, and so
to be reduced to "an epistemological snapshot" of time's revenges.

Yet that is only part of a dialectic; the other part is naming,
having been named, remembering, having been remembered. Your
overheard name, carried round for years in time's wallet, may be
only another alm for oblivion, and yet its survival inspires in you
the poet's creative rage for immortality, or what Vico called "divination": "I want that information very much today, / Can't have
it, and this makes me angry." The striking word is "information,"
reminding Ashbery's readers of the crucial use of that word in W*et
Casements*'s meditative rival, *Soonest Mended* in *The Double
Dream of Spring*:

> Only by that time we were in another chapter and confused
> About how to receive this latest piece of information.
> W*as* it information? Weren't we rather acting this out
> For someone else's benefit, thoughts in a mind
> With room enough and to spare for our little problems. . . .

"Information" in both poems means a more reliable knowledge
communicated by and from otherness, than is allowed by one's

status as an epistemological snapshot of a drifter through temporal processes. But the casements do not open out to otherness and to love, and where information is lacking, only the proper use of the rage to order words remains:

> I shall use my anger to build a bridge like that
> Of Avignon, on which people may dance for the feeling
> Of dancing on a bridge.

The round-song of the bridge of Avignon charmingly goes on repeating that the bridge is there, and that people dance upon it. As a trope for the poem *Wet Casements*, this tells us both the limitation and the restituting strength of Ashbery's ambitions. But the song of the self, as in Whitman, movingly and suddenly ascends to a triumph:

> I shall at last see my complete face
> Reflected not in the water but in the worn stone floor of my bridge.

The dancers are Ashbery's readers, who as Stevens once said of *his* elite, will do for the poet what he cannot do for himself: receive his poetry. Elegantly, Ashbery reverses his initial trope, where the reflection in streaming windowpanes did not allow seeing the complete face either of others or of the self. The worn stone floor of the bridge of words has replaced the wet casements, a substitution that prompts the strongest of all Ashberian poetic closures:

> I shall keep to myself.
> I shall not repeat others' comments about me.

If the sentiment is unlike Whitman's, its sermon-like directness still would have commended it to Whitman, or to Thoreau, or even to the Founder, Emerson. For this is the Emersonian Sublime, a belated declaration of self-reliance, or a repression of every fathering force, even the American ones. I note Ashbery's uncharacteristic but very welcome bluntness, and turn to consider how and why I would assign a canonical strength both to this poem and to *Tapestry*. Yet this means I must turn first to the vexed problematic of the canonical process itself.

There is no innocence, and only a small degree of chance, in the canonical process. As a Western procedure, it has combined three main elements: the Jewish tradition of forming Scripture, with its Christian misprision and subsequent refinements, is ideologically the most important. The Alexandrian Hellenistic tradition of literary scholarship is the most instrumental for us, since it inaugurated the canonization of what we would now call secular texts. But the Greek poets themselves, at least from Hesiod on, invented poetic self-canonization, or self-election. I am going to suggest the antithetical formula that a contemporary American poem, to have any hope of permanence, necessarily builds the canonical ambition, process and agon directly into its own text, as Hesiod, Pindar, Milton, Pope, Wordsworth and Whitman did also, as indeed all the poetic survivors have done.

Homer and his unknown precursors were primarily storytellers, and to tell a story is very different from the act of measuring the canon. That act is a genealogy, and perhaps necessarily a cataloging. We sometimes call Whitman the American Homer, but it might be more accurate to call him the American Hesiod. Nietzsche followed Burckhardt in seeing the agonistic spirit as being central to Greek culture, and here is Nietzsche upon *Homer's Contest:*

> Every talent must unfold itself in fighting. . . . Whereas modern man fears nothing in an artist more than the emotion of any personal fight, the Greek knows the artist *only as engaged in a personal fight*. Precisely where modern man senses the weakness of a work of art, the Hellene seeks the source of its greatest strength. . . . What a problem opens up before us when we inquire into the relationship of the contest to the conception of the work of art!

This agonistic spirit, as expounded by Nietzsche, finds expression in the genealogies and catalogues of Hesiod, who in sorting out and so canonizing the gods, becomes the first Greek theologian. But though epic and drama were conducted as contests, it was in the Greek lyric that the agon became truly internalized, to

the extent that the canonical process itself became the structure—
rather than the gesture—of the poet's stance. Here is the final
stanza of Pindar's *First Olympian Ode* (as rendered by Richmond
Lattimore):

> For me
> the Muse in her might is forging yet the strongest arrow.
> One man is excellent one way, one in another; the highest
> fulfills itself in kings. Oh, look no further.
> Let it be yours to walk this time on the height.
> Let it be mine to stand beside you
> in victory, for my skill at the forefront of the Hellenes.

Hieron of Syracuse and his fellow contestants in the race for
horse and rider are clearly not so much in Pindar's mind as are Si-
monides and Bacchylides. Milton, opening *Lycidas* with that awesome and shattering "Yet once more," sweeps past Virgil and
Spenser and inaugurates a new internalization of the agon, not
to be matched until Wordsworth's *Intimations* ode confidently
chants: "Another race has been and other palms are won." This
is the tradition of the explicitly canonical, subverted by Keats in
his implicitly canonical odes. Yet how am I employing the traditional term "canonical" here? Metaphorically, I must admit, that is
to say by what I would call "a strong misreading," and here I must
present a highly compressed account of a theory of canonization.

A strong poem, which alone can become canonical for more
than a single generation, can be defined as a text that must engender strong misreadings, both as other poems and as literary criticism. Texts that have single, reductive, simplistic meanings are
themselves already necessarily weak misreadings of anterior texts.
When a strong misreading has demonstrated its fecundity by pro-
ducing other strong misreadings across several generations, then
we can and must accept its canonical status.

Yet by "strong misreading" I mean "strong troping," and the
strength of trope can be recognized by skilled readers in a way that
anticipates the temporal progression of generations. A strong trope
renders all merely trivial readings of it irrelevant. Confronted by

Ashbery's "dead on the line" or his "I want that information very much today, / Can't have it, and this makes me angry," the weak reader is defeated by the energy of the Sublime. "Dead," "line," "information" and "angry" are available only to the agonistic striver in the reader, not to the reductionist who inhabits always the same reader. Longinus on the Sublime and Shelley defending poetry both make the crucial point that strong, canonical, Sublime poetry exists in order to compel the reader to abandon easier literary pleasures for more difficult satisfactions, or as Freud would have said it, for works where the incitement premium is higher.

There is a true law of canonization, and it works contrary to Gresham's law of currency. We may phrase it: *in a strong reader's struggle to master a poet's trope, strong poetry will impose itself, because that imposition, that usurpation of mental space, is the proof of trope, the testing of power by power.* The nature of that trope in the poetry of the last three hundred years is increasingly transumptive, and with a brief examination of transumption I will offer also an assertion of how criticism can meet the challenge of the canonical process, and then conclude with a coda on the use of poetry.

Transumption is diachronic rhetoric, figuration operating across a time-frame, which is of course a conceptual temporality, or trope of time, not time itself, whatever we take that to be. Theorists from Samuel Johnson to Angus Fletcher and John Hollander have noted that Miltonic simile is uniquely transumptive in nature, that it crowds the imagination by joining Milton to an ancient and complete truth, and by making every poet's figuration that comes between that proper truth and Milton's text into a trope of belated error, however beautiful or valuable. By joining himself to an ever-early candor, Milton thus assured not only his own place in the canon, but taught his poetic successors how to make themselves canonical by way of their transumptive imagery. This remains the canonical use of strong poetry: it goes on electing its successors, and these Scenes of Instruction become identical with the continuity of poetic tradition.

The use of criticism can only be like this use of poetry. Criticism too must display a power at once interpretive and revisionary, and thus, as Hollander says, in some sense make the echo even louder than the original voice. In a time when nearly every other activity of the mind has suffered a de-mystification or a de-idealization, the writing and reading of poetry has retained a curious prestige of idealism. Curious because the nature of poetry, during the last two hundred years or so, may have changed in ways we scarcely begin to apprehend.

Poetry from Homer through Alexander Pope (who died in 1744) had a subject matter in the characters and actions of men and women clearly distinct from the poet who observed them, and who described and sometimes judged them. But from 1744 or so to the present day the best poetry internalized its subject matter, particularly in the mode of Wordsworth after 1798. Wordsworth had no true subject except his own subjective nature, and very nearly all significant poetry since Wordsworth, even by American poets, has repeated Wordsworth's inward turning.

This no longer seems to be a question of any individual poet's choice, but evidently is a necessity, perhaps a blight, of the broad movement that we see now to be called Romanticism *or* Modernism, since increasingly the latter would appear to have been only an extension of the former. What can be the use of a poetry that has no true subject except the poet's own selfhood? The traditional use of poetry in the Western world has been instruction through delight, where teaching has meant the common truths or common deceptions of a societal tradition, and where esthetic pleasure has meant a fulfillment of expectations founded upon past joys of the same design. But an individual psyche has its own accidents, which it needs to call truths, and its own necessity for self-recognition, which requires the pleasures of originality, even if those pleasures depend upon a kind of lying-against-time, and against the achievements of the past. The use of such a poetry demands to be seen in a de-idealized way, if it is to be seen more truly.

The philosopher of modern poetry is the Neapolitan rhetorician Giambattista Vico, who died in 1744, the same year as the poet Pope. In his *New Science* (1725), Vico strikingly de-idealized the origin and purpose of poetry. Vico believed that the life of our primitive ancestors was itself what he termed "a severe poem." These giants, through the force of a cruel imagination, defended themselves against nature, the gods, and one another by metaphoric language, with which they "divinated," that is, at once they sought to become immortal gods and also to ward off potential and future dangers from their own lives. For them, the function of poetry was not to liberate, but to define, limit, and so defend the self against everything that might destroy it. This Vichian or de-idealizing view of poetry is the truth about all poetry, in my judgment, but particularly modern poetry. The use of poetry, for the reader as for the poet, is at a profound level an instruction in defense. Poetry teaches a reader the necessity of interpretation, and interpretation is, to cite the other great philosopher of modern poetry, Nietzsche, the exercise of the will-to-power over a text.

The strong American poets—Emerson, Whitman, Dickinson, Frost, Stevens, Hart Crane—and the strongest of our contemporaries—Robert Penn Warren, Elizabeth Bishop, A. R. Ammons, James Merrill, W. S. Merwin, John Hollander, James Wright and John Ashbery—can give their American readers the best of pragmatic aids in the self-reliance of a psychic self-defense. In the struggle of the reader both with and against a strong poem, more than an interpretation of a poem becomes the prize. What instruction is more valuable than that which shows us how to distinguish real from illusory dangers to the self's survival, and how to ward off the real menaces?

13

John Hollander's
Spectral Emanations:
The Menorah
as the White Light of Trope

Interpretation, like philosophy, begins in wonder, but otherwise
unlike philosophy it pursues that course which Angus Fletcher has
called "lateral fall," or wandering. The wonderful difficulty of
John Hollander's *Spectral Emanations* has already proved a stum-
bling-block to some reviewers who have been concerned to treat
the volume *Spectral Emanations: New and Selected Poems,* in
which it appears, as the work of the very witty Neoclassical lyricist
and verse-essayist he was twenty years ago, but has remained only
occasionally, and as the work of his left hand, as it were, since
1965. His new long poem comes to us at the head of an important
group of new poems, including among others the somewhat Bor-
gesian *Collected Novels,* a poetic replacement for an oeuvre scattered along a road not taken; *Nocturne* and *The Lady of the Cas-
tle,* two different modes of fearful confrontation with a female
daemon; and *On the Calendar.* This last is a sequence of short,
prophetic scenarios falling on the thirty-one days of an imaginary
month, each foreseeing a different way of death for the speaker,
avoiding pointedly that form of execution on a gallows which
would too literally have manifested the poem's *Galgenhumor.* This
new group and, indeed, the whole volume of selections from all

the poet's prior work save for *Reflections on Espionage*, as well as some helpful and rather poignant notes and glosses, provides a useful context for the title poem. The whole volume, however, I have reviewed elsewhere, and should like in these pages to attend to the difficulties and the splendid achievement of Hollander's *Poem in Seven Branches in Lieu of a Lamp*, as it is subtitled.

Spectral Emanations is manifestly a sequence of seven poems, each one named by one of the seven spectral colors, and each followed by a prose section of varying length and character. The whole is prefaced by a prologue called "The Way to the Throne Room," a parable of what looks like a kind of bardic ordeal in which are manifested the dangers that lie even in that trope of questing in which the poet, searching for a late sublimity linking form and subject, is always engaged. The narrator answers correctly seven questions apparently about the preparation and lighting of an oil lamp, the answers consisting in the identification of a number of angelic figures: "*Who trimmed the wick? Gananiel,* I confessed, *the lopper of branches, the one who limits that the many may flourish. Surely he did it.*" "*Who struck a light? Bhel,* I reconstructed, *the starred one, that we may see, that we may write our poor books, white fire on black fire.*" The name "Gananiel" would suggest, from the Hebrew root, a gardening angel, and that of "Bhel" is the Indo-European base (often prefaced by an asterisk because it is a reconstructed and not attested form, glossed by Calvert Watkins as "To shine, flash, burn; shining white and various bright colors; fire"). "Bhel" is treated with mythological playfulness in an episode in Hollander's recent poem *Blue Wine*. This serio-comic suite of explanations—mock-rabbinic *midrashim*, or interpretations—of what blue wine might be appears in his book *Blue Wine and Other Poems* (1979). It was apparently occasioned by Hollander's having seen his friend Saul Steinberg's parodic wine-labels, pasted on bottles filled with a blue fluid, in the artist's apartment one day. The episode in question, a Homeric fantasy, intrudes upon its Tennysonian voyaging a local myth of the dispersal of *Bhel* by *Kel* (the Indo-European base for "cover, conceal") into various kinds of light, all named in words descending from *bhel. Steinberg's first language was Rumanian, which may account for the "vin albastru" ("blue wine") in the final, explanatory episode. I suspect that the whole poem may have resulted from Hollander's own uneasiness, whether conscious or not, about the "Blue" section of *Spectral Emanations*, the completion of all of which enabled him to write more freely of azure matters.

Having answered the questions, the quester moves through a series of seven antechambers, each of which constitutes a trap for some part of the company of all the lost adventurers, his peers, who are not to reach the throne room, or what we might read as the seat of vision in the *merkabah* or throne-chariot of Ezekiel. Unlike the two younger brothers in Hollander's mixed verse and prose romance for children, *The Quest of the Gole*, who fail to complete a Sublime quest by succeeding so well at a lower one, these candidates lapse in variously intense ways:

On the way to the fourth chamber, strange pictures hung: a glass of green fur, an open apple, a house of loss; and portraits of the Baron of Grass, the Count of Nought. Those who approached to read the titles had to go all the way back.
On the way to the fifth chamber, all was smooth and slate, as if beauty were a disease of surface, an encroachment of depth. Many fell asleep, and had to be removed.

It will be seen that the progression from the surrealistic sportiveness of the fourth anteroom ("un verre de vair vert"? Having to "go all the way back" sounds suspiciously like the children's game of "Giant Steps") to the Tennysonian swoon of the fifth is like a shift of phase in a romance of mythological island-hopping.

It is enough to say here that the narrator himself fails in the last antechamber, responding inappropriately to the glimmering of marble slabs there: "They / dazzled mine eyes, and it was not at my own tears that I / cried out O *water! Water!* Thus I was never to enter." It is clear that the text of *Spectral Emanations*, a self-proclaimed replacement for an irrecoverable Jewish lamp, is to attempt sublimity only in an awareness of how its own route of ascent must by nature stop short of it. The solar spectrum itself, an image whose magic has been long since eradicated, could not, as I shall shortly show, provide a form for organized imagining, and it is by means of a re-entry into a height of abstraction and visual arc previously identified with sublimity—a re-entry through an almost fanciful intermediate trope—that a sequence of colors becomes a major myth.

In Hawthorne's *The Marble Faun*, Hilda and Kenyon have been walking through Rome towards her dove-surrounded tower room. (Hollander's *The Muse in the Monkey Tower*, which he had earlier intended for the prologue, indirectly proclaims Hilda to be the muse of his long poem, then barely started.) They have been discussing color, whiteness, religion, art and purity, and finally come to speak of the golden lamp or menorah of the Second Temple in Jerusalem, brought to Rome by Titus, on whose triumphal arch it may still be seen. Hilda says that it remained in Rome until the time of Constantine, when it fell off the Milvian bridge during the battle with Maxentius; it still lies at the bottom of the Tiber. "Such a candlestick," she says, "cannot be lost forever." She suggests that its recovery might be "an admirable idea for a mystic story or parable, or seven-branched allegory, full of poetry, art, philosophy, and religion. . . . As each branch is lighted, it shall have a differently colored lustre from the other six; and when all seven are kindled, their radiance shall combine into the white light of truth."

This much of Hawthorne's chapter entitled "Hilda and a Friend" Hollander quotes as epigraph; what he suppresses may give us a glimpse into his point of departure: "The theme is better suited for verse than prose; and when I go home to America, I will suggest it to one of our poets. Or, seven poets might write the poem together, each lighting a separate branch of the Sacred Candlestick." Hollander's way, through Hilda's conceit, to the polychromatic Sublime is parallel to another circular route of re-entry: like Hilda, his muse goes home to America and almost to Judaism at once. The

Judaic material in his earlier work was primarily essayistic or elegiac (in the reincantation of the *Lamentations of Jeremiah* in the
"Ninth of Ab" section of *Visions from the Ramble* in 1965). Only
in some of the poems in *Tales Told of the Fathers* (1975)—I
would include *The Ziz* and *Cohen on the Telephone*, as well as
the title poem, among these—did he approach the almost self-
defeating task of diasporic Jewish myth-making. Hawthorne's flickering Protestant heroine's misprision of the menorah became a
more solid trope than any unmediated vision of replacement or,
to use the poem's term, *restitution*. In a letter to Richard Poirier,
Hollander has suggested that, in thinking of Hilda as the poem's
muse, he had forgotten how much Hawthorne's louche Semitic
Miriam, her dark companion, had replaced her. Perhaps this is as
much as to say that *Spectral Emanations* succeeds in being American by being Judaistic, and vice versa.

In his own epigraph, which continues after Hilda's observation,
the poet proclaims his intention and scheme in a way not wholly
oblique: "The text which follows intends to hoist up another lamp
from other waters than those of the Tiber. Lost bronze is silent,
let alone lost gold; even the newest oil has no echo. I have here
kindled the lights of sound, starting with the red cry of battle,
followed by the false orange gold, true yellow goldenness, the
green of all our joy, blue of our imaginings, the indigo between
and the final violet that is next to black, for that is how our scale
runs. . . ." It is instructive to juxtapose this table of the spectral
scheme with the one given at the beginning of the prose following
"Departed Indigo":

> There are six songs, no seven, that need to be sung in the
> darkness:
>
> The Battle on the Plains, where heroes stood and fell; the
> Finding of the Treasure where it was hard to get to; the Found-
> ing of the Fields, where all expanded in peace; the Visit to the
> Sky, which was no wearying journey; the Farewell to the Guide,
> when the next stage was reached; the Darkening of It All, when
> it had become too late.

After the formulaic opening (it echoes a device of the Biblical proverb), these versions of the "subjects" of the sequence of colors connect the visionary pattern of the many-colored lamp with the pattern of a journey into a center and out of it again, and with the theme of an American Sublime, like a heroism or a patriotism, which is palpably unavailable and for whose loss some restitution must be made. This is made explicit in the next passage from the "Indigo" prose:

> At first our heroes stood for us, then among us, when we stood for ourselves; now they do not even represent our sorrows. The Paul Bunyan balloon was deflated and put away when Thanksgiving had passed. Miss America farted into the microphone as if thereby to bear true witness to beauty, but that was only last season's attraction. No hero sums us up, no clown can contain us, and the Book of the People of the Book is in tatters.

I shall not shrink from pointing out here the almost schematic map of anxiety about figuration: sublimity has failed (even the commercial parades are over), the antithetical mockery of satire and anti-heroism has little force as pious fables, and there must be transumption of fable and of centrality if there is to be any at all.

The seven sections of *Spectral Emanations* depend for their form and scale on the seven-branched quality of the menorah itself, evoking not so much the traditional calendrical and mystical significances of the number seven as an importance totally ad hoc to the myth of the poem. There are exactly 504 lines in the whole poem, or $7! \div 10$, divided into sections 72 lines long. The lines are syllabic, starting with six ("Red") and proceeding by augmentation to eight ("Orange"), ten ("Yellow"), twelve ("Green"), then down again by twos to six ("Violet"). These lines are grouped differently in each poem, from the epical twelves of the stanzas of "Red" to the sparkling tercets of "Violet." In a note we are told that Philo of Alexandria had associated a different planet with each branch of the temple menorah. Hollander follows his Hellenistic precursor in his use of planetary allusions in each section, save that, as he says in a note, "Saturn and Mars have had to exchange their places"—"bloodied Saturn" appearing in "Red," and a statue of Mars in "Yellow." (He grimly comments later that the confusion of these "is always more than a matter of mechanics of vision.") Thus we have the displacement of Saturn by Mars at the left-hand, westernmost and, here, red first branch of the menorah; the whole array goes as follows: Mars (R), Jupiter (O), Saturn (Y), Sun (G), Mercury (B), Venus (I), Moon (V).

"Red" is certainly Mars's poem. The first of the sequence, it is a representation of redness as primitive, both creatively (the Adamic earth) and destructively (the blood of warfare, or the crude heroic). The poem was composed, we are told, during the 1973 Arab-Israeli war, and concerns the death of a soldier in a desert battle. The soldier is known only as J; he is both the soldier and the prophet Jonah (like him, J is "exceedingly glad" of a gourd-shaped shadow which affords him some shade). The poet connects the destroyed soldier and the reluctant prophet of destruction by reference to the fact that the Book of Jonah is read on the afternoon, in Jewish liturgy, of the Day of Atonement (on which the 1973 war broke out). The poem is spectacular and violent, but before the protagonist's destruction by "the fiery worm" of a rocket, a vision links the battle of "Red" to all the fables of desert warfare everywhere in Western history. The "unwilling prophet of / His past" sees "screaming / Seals ripped open" and echoes of Mycenae ("Bronze / Spears smash grayware pitchers"). Gideon's battles in the Bible ("Torches splash fear near tents"), classical, medieval and romantic warfare all emerge:

> . . . as can by
> Opened can the film of
> The ages runs in coils
> Across his mind's sky.

This celebration of the "wide realm of the red" is followed by perhaps the most beautiful of the prose "commentaries," and certainly the most pure prose-poem of them all, a meditation on the primitiveness of red starting out with the hieroglyph of its name in

Semitic: an ox, a door, some water (the aleph, daleth, mem of the word "adom" were originally pictograms for these). It ends with a vision of an epic bard (one of the seven poets suggested by Hilda perhaps):

> The red singer sits looking back toward the violet becoming black. His songs are capable of the opened and the spilled; only for them the wind sings in his hair. He stands outside the door; his shadow falls across it. Blown dust makes a false threshold.

"Orange" follows, a rather brassy poem which moves from an evocation of morning awakening, rising orange-colored sun, and breakfast, "the rising hemisphere of / Huge Florida orange," to metallic gold, the brutish version of value or worth which follows upon the primitive grandeur of battle. Its mythological figures are Midas, whose golden touch here turns even an erotic partner into a lump of gold; and Jupiter, coming to Danaë in a shower of gold coins, imbruting himself thereby. Here, the only heroic diction in "Orange" is flung up in criticism:

> . . . Not with the juice of sunlight
> Streaming with magnificence does
> The crude chrysomorph enter her,
> But like light interred in the hard
> Shining that dazzles poor eyes with
> Mere models of the immortal.

Gold as the travesty of fruitful goldenness, Jupiter as the usurper of the milder harvester, Saturn, is the subject of "Orange." A glimpse of a way back to the Saturnian gold appears in a mention of a reality principle, "the living dullard / Of daylight"; he reappears in the prose commentary as the poem's clown, Roy G Biv, the traditional mnemonic acronym of the color-names whom Hollander associates with lead because of a Hebrew pun on the word *Biv* ("sewer pipe"). Biv mocks the systems of tropes by which gold is made noble, or by which colors can be mixed; he is what we might call an Idiot Answerer who smashes the myths of gold in order to move us on to the realm of what Milton calls the "vegetable gold" of Paradise, the region of Yellow:

Dirty gold sublimed from the black earth up
In bright air: these are the awaited stalks,
The ripeness possible to imagine
Even among mezzotints of winter,
And to remember having imagined
Oddly amid the late spring's lackadaisies
And all of the earlier primulas.

With this opening, the powerful poem of "Yellow" asserts its own aspirations to sublimity, even as its opening words have become transformed by the time the colon in the second line has been reached. "Yellow," save possibly only for "Violet," is the strongest verse section of the whole poem, a romantic crisis-ode of great beauty. The floral yellow of the opening stanza modulates through a moment of self-representation:

. . . the attentive images of
Jonquils peering out at themselves along
the wide bank

to the yellow of candle-flames burning in sunlight, among golden grain, "the bright fruit / Of what we after all have"—fruit, flame, eye and flower. This modulation follows the first of the three poetic crossings (Election, Solipsism, Identification) which I have elsewhere mapped as the structure of the poem of crisis. The Crossing of Election from irony to synecdoche covers the gulf of doubt: "Am I truly a poet?" Here, the reflections of the jonquils, the last trope on one side of the crossing, are followed by the turn away toward a new source of figuration:

. . . Which would be no fulfillment
In any event, of early pallor:
It would remain an interpretation
Of the flimsy text, half remembered,
Dimming evermore and diminishing.

The second eighteen-line stanza performs the two tasks of celebrating the myth of yellow, now totally free of even a tincture of its prior neighbor, orange, and of confirming the poetic voice of the propounder of true fictions. Its climax starts with an echo of a Jewish prayer made at annual festivals, said in thanks for having been sustained and preserved and enabled to experience the present moment, and proceeds through to a gentle but still energetic revision of the hard, ironic images of entrepreneurial awakening in "Orange":

> To have been kept, to have reached this season,
> Is to have eternized, for a moment,
> The time when promise and fulfillment feed
> Upon each other, when the living gold
> Of sunlight struck from the amazing corn
> Seems one with its cold, unending token,
> The warm time when both seem reflections from
> The bright eyes of the Queen of the Peaceful
> Day being welcomed with these twin burnings,
> These prophetic seeds of the Ripener,
> Brightness rising and getting on with things.

Yellow has redeemed even orange, the goldenness of American corn (maize) has reversed the traditional trope and declared metallic gold only to be an image of itself; the presiding figure who in fact emanates both of these is Hollander's version of the Sabbath Queen, celebrated in the liturgical imagery of normative rabbinic Judaism, but associated Kabbalistically, as he may have learned from Scholem, with the Eros of symbolic marriage.

In any event, the second Crossing of Solipsism, as I have called it—the realization in figure of the will's question, "Am I able to love"—occurs with the startling opening of the next stanza. The opening word, "Or," is both the name of gold in romance languages and the poet's figurative gold of word-hoard; Hollander must be consciously or unconsciously echoing the rhetorically complex "or" by which Milton moves from simile to simile, classical comparison to comparison, a move which, if it implies that the reader is to take his pick, is lying. "Or" is followed by a strange metrical effect, a compression into the pure syllabic lines of the jingle of minor romantic song, such as Thomas Moore's:

> . . . In the air there is a soft *gleaming*
> As of fair light in certain *hair*, and wind

Through the pale curtains *streaming* like moonlight
In the dark *air.* . . .

(Italics mine, to mark the rhymes of the hidden verse.) But this
mode of evocation is rejected in a turn, with the italics here the
poet's own, toward keener sounds of evocation: "*This has been all
of silver,*" he says, and then proceeds to describe the birth of the
true erotic and poetic counterpart, as "the man of earth inhales a
girl of air," bringing with her a "return of everlastingness" and
leaving even the creator-lover's emptied arms "with light beyond
seeming," the sublimed trope of worth beyond counting.

The final crossing, that of Identification, occurs in the middle
of the final stanza at a point of transumptive vision,

When the world's yellow is of burning sands
Leading down to the penultimate blue
Of, say, the Ionian sea,

and where the blue of the clearest of water ("penultimate" both
in relation to violet in the larger scheme, and in relation to the
trope of death) reveals the final meaning of the blessedness of yellow to the swimmers, whose golden bodies are "in their purest /
And most revealing element at last." The adventures of "Orange"
were a travesty of pathos, as well as of worth; the arioso of "Yellow" has redeemed them both.

The prose of "Yellow," like that of the "Indigo" section, is the
most explicit commentary on a transition from one color region to
another. It starts with what is surely a rhymed quatrain printed as
italicized prose and ascribed to a mythical French Jewish poet, but
proceeds through two anecdotes to gloss the creative and imaginative progress from the orange-gold to the yellow-golden. The first
describes an imaginary painting that might have been done by the
American Romantic Thomas Cole, as one of his visionary *Course
of Empire* series. (Hollander had written an interpretive essay
about it some years earlier.) It is seen from the point of view of a
spectator, perhaps a traveler from some other antique land, as in
Cole's huge scenes of *Fulfillment* (with its crowds of worshippers,

in form somewhere between John Martin and Cecil B. De Mille) and *Destruction*. "Their famous chryselephantine Saturn," he says, has loomed up behind them as they watch triumphal parades. "But it would only be after that lowering crimson, rhymed in the red fires of the Conquerors come that same evening," he continues, that they should discover the statue, about to fall into ruins, "to have been one of Mars, sword curved in the same flat crescent as scythe, gatherer of red rather than of yellow." The whole first sequence from red to yellow, including the Saturn-Jupiter-Mars displacement, is here summed up.

The second anecdote is a parable of transumptive figuration, of copying as *copia*, of incorporation and originality: "Hilda laid on the gold leaf. The copy she was making of 'The Miracle of the Field' flourished and sprouted under her shining care. . . ." Hawthorne had himself implied that Hilda's copies were more authentic works of art than the original paintings of others (and in this, Hilda may be also the muse of that remarkable prose romance, *The Recognitions* of William Gaddis); the painting Hollander has invented for her is of a myth of imaginative transformation, a field of golden grain, probably, and evolving from the fields in such of his relatively recent poems as *Rotation of Crops* and *Being Alone in the Field*. The anecdote concludes with an assurance that "This was true plenty."

"Green" is a vision of summer and love. At the midpoint of the sequence, its expansive, long lines and its high rhetoric have a relaxed quality that starts with the opening chant of a summer evening, whose darkening will bring green to black, with the poem's own hope of "some hushed / Nocturnal verdant." The delimitation of green from the blue that borders it is not handled in the quizzical parodies of argument that the author's earlier poems employ, but rather by an embodiment in a *locus amoenus*, a paradisal landscape:

> In the high day, clear at the viridian noon,
> Blue water, enisled in the broad grass singing hot
> Choruses of summer, lies still; and far away

Half-gesturing lakes surrounded by dense, quiet
Spruces recall the silence that we are told lies
As a green hedge around blue wisdom. At the edge
Of things here and now, soft-looking cedars, waving
Away at azure, keep the sky at a distance. . . .

There may be an echo here of a Talmudic saying to the effect that silence is a hedge around wisdom. The movement of the poem's green going brings it past a stanza of love being made on a lawn, and another of a poetic wanderer, a Whitmanian "nomad among the verdures" who partakes of the intensity of this central, high greenness. Hollander quotes from Goethe's *Theory of Color*, one of his precursor texts for a mythology of hue: "*Man will nicht weiter, und man kann nicht weiter*" ("one neither desires, nor is capable of," anything beyond green), and in a final stanza he specifically rejects a series of prior readings of the meaning of green ("no flag of what state one is in" is clearly a turn, albeit somewhat uneasy, against Whitman's unfurling of the trope of grass: "I guess it is the flag of my disposition").

Hollander's hymn to green is followed by a prose section which is less like incantation than any of the others. The procession through the first, or "warm," half of the spectrum from heroic through ironic to meditative lyric has been paralleled by a counter-progression in the prose pieces, from lyric (in "Red") to the narrative romance of the twelve-page "Leaves from a Roman Journal" (in "Green"). This quirky and poignant story of a caper—the rescuing of the historical menorah from the Tiber's bed and the transporting of it secretly to Jerusalem—shares some tonal and parabolic elements with *Reflections on Espionage*; its unnamed narrator, one of a group of seven conspirators (their names are those of the colors in various languages, and the narrator must be the missing indigo), sometimes sounds like a prosy Cupcake, Hollander's pastoral poet-spy. "Leaves from a Roman Journal" has all the trappings of a romance novella, including a mock table of contents of the story of what is happening, should it be written up; however, this section is darkened by the true grimness of a pre-

ceding personal confession, allusive of the narrative prayer (a re-
minder of the history of providence) in the Passover service, whose
refrain is *Dayenu*—"it would have been sufficient." There is also
a good deal of anxiety expressed by the conspirators about unearth-
ing and destroying various false simulacra of the Lamp (as it is
called throughout). I shall only observe here that the playful and
the literal version of "The Recovery of the Sacred Candlestick," as
Hilda called it, constitute an exorcism of the various spectres of
reductiveness, of failed figuration, which might turn the poem's
own poetic quest awry. The quest is protected in the poem by its
dreamy occurrence in the region of summer night, amidst

> The patience of the deep that black has when green ends
> The still unquenchable absorption of its gaze.
> It will not be, can never be a mere return.

"Blue" I must confess to liking the least of the seven. It may be
here only that scheme has blocked high eloquence, and it is not
irrelevant that this was the first of the seven verse sections to be
written. The language of the four strophes, two of four quatrains
and two of five, is most palpably Stevensian, as are some of the
versions of the trope of blue itself. Its fables and their ordering
cleave perhaps too closely to the line of *Notes Toward a Supreme
Fiction*, and its mythopoeia of tinctures of *l'azur*—two moons,
"two modes of night," sea-blue and sky-blue—may be, despite an
elegant and exuberantly pleasurable rhetoric, less fully realized
than we might hope for a region following upon green. Mercury's
assigned appearance in the poem is a kind of sad prankster substitute for Venus as an evening star:

> Mercury leered out of the bold cobalt
> He was returning to, remembering
> Azure anterior to this night's share.

But he returns, far more effectively, as the liquid metal bearing
his name in the prose following "Blue," an Ashberyan instruction
manual for building a contraption for creating a poetic self. It is
a mysterious machine whose structure seems more important than

what it does (which remains undisclosed until the end). Akin to Elizabeth Bishop's monument, to the machine in Kafka's penal colony and, perhaps ultimately, to the allegory of the decay of the body in *Ecclesiastes* with its breaking of golden skull and loosing of silver spinal cord, the manual warns against too open an acceptance of its own tropes:

> Do not make the mistake of sentimentalizing the mechanical parts: for the flywheel, archaic and precise with its gleaming spokes, is a horror of solemnity, going berserk at the insinuations of jiggle—the twin moons of the governor are a cramp on exuberance—the pistons slide joylessly in their cold oil—the shining brass gauges were unwisely calibrated in a time of hope.

Activity, whether athletic, artistic, sexual or moral, will suffer by being represented in reduced—here, mechanical—terms. It emerges only at the end of the commentary that the machine is a system for the deconstruction—and here I employ the word in a sense far less figurative than that of Derrida and de Man—of all "those to be dealt with," the "despots," finally identified in the last paragraph: "If you get it to work properly, it will put an end to them, your predecessors." The element of destructiveness in blue, which had not arisen in the verse, is revealed in the baroque wit of the prose to be a crucial element of imaginative creativity, even as the Kabbalah reminds us of how vessels must be broken that light may re-emanate.

"Departed Indigo" pauses for a moment, on the way toward the ultimate darkenings of violet, to propound a lovely fiction of beneficent night. It starts out from what would, in the poet's earlier work, have been a more philosophical exercise, perhaps a pseudo-Wittgensteinian questioning of the meaning for nature of the contraction of the conventional spectral colors from seven to six, as they are taught in schools today. But this poem turns to fable instead, and supposes an Astraea-like lady (although no virgin) departing the fallen world at a recent time, but inhabiting the color of the night sky in among the stars:

> . . . the rich, hopeful darkness seems
> Deepened by her presence, under
> Which we live and, hushed, still breathe the
> Night air's perfume of discernment.

Along with "Red," the hymn to indigo is more immediately accessible out of context than some of the others. Its prose I have already touched upon; aside from recapitulating the system of songs of the entire work, it moves to a close with a charming and domestic version of the rising of nighttime's blue from our own midst, with perhaps a reminiscence of the rising of the kite at the beautiful ending of Beckett's *Murphy*:

> And so at the end of the day, the sky deepening as we walked back from the Prater, or home from the zoo, or along the river away from the fun-fair, the youngest child's balloon, the dark one, escaped from a fist tired at last, vanishing into its own element of the color between day and night.

The central visual trope of Jewish tradition is not the Shield of David or six-pointed star, since that is a very late emblem, unmentioned in the Bible and the Talmud, and absent even from the literature of Hellenistic Jewry. It is the menorah, the lampstand of seven branches, that necessarily challenges any Jewish writer as the inevitable trope for the long history of the Jews. In Exodus, the Priestly author tells us that God commanded Moses to make a golden lampstand of seven branches, and then to set this menorah in the Tabernacle. The artisan Bezaleel supervised, and perhaps even made the menorah. In Solomon's temple there were a plethora of menorahs, presumably all carried off to Babylon by Nebuchadnezzar. The last chapter of the prophet Jeremiah mentions the removal of the menorahs, but when Ezra the Scribe recounts the restoration of the Temple vessels by Cyrus the Great, surprisingly he says nothing about the return of the sacred lampstand. Jewish legends account for this omission by suggesting that Nebuchadnezzar had been fobbed off with Solomonic copies, so that the true Mosaic menorah of Bezaleel had been kept in hiding, perhaps in Jerusalem, all through the Babylonian Exile.

Zerubbavel began the Second Temple in the year 516 B.C.E. The prophet Zechariah, the Book of David and most urgently, the Wisdom of Ben Sirach or Ecclesiasticus all refer to the presence of the menorah in the Second Temple, which may have been still the original lampstand. When Antioches Epiphanes looted the Temple in 170 B.C.E., in the Age of the Maccabees, Josephus ambiguously says that the Syrian tyrant carried off "lampstands," and again legend suggests that these also, however golden, were mere replicas of the Mosaic original. When in 164 B.C.E., Judas Maccabaeus retook Jerusalem, he set up his famous Hanukkah replica, made of the iron spearheads of his victorious troops. Why the true lampstand was not brought out of hiding just then no legend tells us. The Maccabean war-lampstand was replaced ultimately by the famous menorah of gold set in the Temple of Herod the Great. Whether we can surmise any connection between this lampstand and the original is left open by tradition.

But tradition is less reticent about the probable lack of identity between Herod's menorah and the one that Titus caried in triumph to Rome. Legend is best summed up here by L. Yarden in his definitive study of the Menorah, *The Tree of Light:*

> . . . it is not at all certain that the chief specimen of the menorah, that is, the lampstand that stood in the central hall of the sanctuary, did really fall into Roman hands. Josephus . . . nowhere expressly states that this was the case. On the contrary, in his account in *The Jewish War* . . . he merely relates that after the fall of the Temple one of the priests—a certain Jeshua, Thebuthi's son—handed over to Titus, upon assurance of self-conduct, "two lampstands similar to those [sic] deposited in the sanctuary. . . ."

Presumably it was one of these two replicas that is displayed upon the Arch of Titus, and subsequently fell off the Milvian bridge into the Tiber when Constantine triumphed, according to Christian legend. Hollander's fictive Jewish questers have therefore every reason to be anxious about replicas, and so necessarily does the poet writing his belated poem. But what kind of poem, or trope-of-tropes so to speak, was the sacred menorah itself? Fed by the pure oil of pounded (not pressed) olives, the menorah was held to be an analogue of God's own light, the burning bush in which Yahweh first appeared to Moses. Before I can venture an interpretation of this trope whether in the Temple or in Hollander's poem, I must cite the history of its interpretation. Behind the image of the menorah as Tree of Life is the more primal mythological image of the Tree of Life, which goes back at least to Gilgamesh, more than 4,000 years ago, and which in Jewish legend appears as the Tree of Life and Death in Adam's Paradise. Aaron's rod, which we can call the sceptre of Moses, is by tradition a branch of this tree, and so eventually is the cross of Christ, according to Paul in Romans 15:12.

The Mandaean Gnostics, who rejected both Moses and Jesus and elevated John the Baptist in their place, worshiped a Tree of Light directly opposed to the fertility goddess and her Tree of Life. In Gnostic interpretation, the fiery light substitutes for female sexuality, and the more extreme Mandaean stylization probably gives us a valid clue as to the stylization of the burning bush into the sacred lampstand, since so much Jewish symbolism comes out of the direct struggle against the female gods of Canaan. Yarden interestingly theorizes that the menorah evolved by the combination of the burning bush and the almond tree, sacred to the Mesopotamian Great Mother. This would help account for the remarkable passage in Numbers 17:8, where "Moses went into the tent of testimony; and behold, the rod of Aaron . . . had sprouted, and put forth buds, and produced blossoms, and it bore ripe almonds." Anyone who has seen a Jerusalem spring remembers that the almond tree bursts forth first into white and pink blossoms, just as it is the last tree to shed its leaves. The Old Semitic name for the almond tree is *Amygdala*, another name for Cybele or the Great Mother. The first Biblical name for the almond tree is *Luz*, still its name in Arabic; and in the Aramaic, the vernacular of the Jews after spoken Hebrew had lapsed, *Luz* also means the indestructible bone in the spinal column, which the

Pharisees believed would serve as the center about which the body would resurrect, the basis for a powerful conceit in Thomas Lovell Beddoes's *Death's Jest-Book*. This normative Jewish transumption of the almond tree attained its ultimate form in the menorah as an emblem of the people's survival.

With only a few remarks upon the traditional interpretations, normative and esoteric, of the menorah I will come to Hollander's poetic interpretation of the seven-branched lampstand in his "Violet." The first and greatest interpreter of the menorah was the prophet Zechariah, who in the fifth of his visions read the seven lamps of the menorah as representing the seven eyes of God, meaning the sun and the known planets. Besides this vision of menorah-as-cosmos, Zechariah prophesied in the menorah a prolepsis of Israel's freedom, the Messianic redemption. Both Josephus and Philo of Alexandria elaborate upon Zechariah's cosmological vision. In the normative, Talmudical tradition Zechariah's prophecy is codified into an identity between menorah and Torah, as we might expect. In the Kabbalistic tradition, the seven lamps were identified with the seven lower *sefirot* or spectral emanations, to use Hollander's rather Blakean trope. There is menorah symbolism, possibly based on material from the *Zohar*, in the opening scene of Goethe's *Faust*, as Yarden has shown. But though Hollander draws upon Goethe's color speculations, he indicates Hawthorne's *The Marble Faun*, rather than *Faust*, as his Romantic starting-point for menorah-questing. The general scheme of Hollander's sequence I have traced elsewhere; I turn now to consider only its conclusion in the poem "Violet" and in its prose coda.

"Violet," as color or trope, verges upon finality, upon the end of color or trope in blackness. Hollander begins his lyric with what will be his obsessive figuration throughout, which is his experiential expectation that derives from participating in group singing. As we begin singing a song we already know, then we necessarily know in advance what it will sound like to sing the song's last words. Just so the Yiddish fiddler, whether of Chagall's painting or Chekhov's poignant story *Rothchild's Fiddle*, coldly hums

the finality of our individual lives. Troping upon closure, the poet
looks out of his house of song to envision no resurrection:

> . . . no cock
> Crowing in the morn at
> Break of ultimate day. . . .

But if there is no hope of resurrection, of *Luz* as Tree of Life
and so as menorah constituting the spinal nucleus of a Messianic
age, how then shall this poet form the last room in his Stevensian
ennui of apartments, and place something in an otherwise bare
chamber of codas, other than an empty death? Beyond belatedness, the poetic grain spoiled and still ungathered, the poet is
forced to substitute for the lampstand the hopeless emblem of the
descendants of the Marranos. Hollander in a note cites the Jewish
historian Cecil Roth, who wrote of villagers in northern Portugal
"still lighting candles in pitchers on Friday nights, a mere half-
century ago, without knowing why they did so save that it was an
old family custom." The American emblem of the scholar-poet's
creative solitude, the Emersonian-Stevensian single candle of the
imagination, is darkly assimilated into this post-Marrano heritage,
as if to suggest again the double wounding into forgetfulness of
American Jewish consciousness per se. Late wanderers and won-
derers, errant both questingly and mistakenly, we hear the illumination purposelessly: "It will light up no path." To which however
this poet's antithetical spirit ruggedly replies, in a trope again both
American and Judaic: "Neither will it go out." Here in the region
of poetic endings, America as *Abendland*, "the easternmost / Edge
of the sunset world," the violet end of the color spectrum, two
precursor poems merge their concluding visions to frame Hollander's elegiac dying fall. We overhear faintly the end of Elizabeth Bishop's triadic *Roosters* in "what text will / The dallying
night leave?" and of Keats's ode *To Autumn* in "no wailful choir
of / Natural small songs." Yet there is a text, and a choir, *both*
enshrined in the menorah itself as trope: Tree of Light, burning
bush, seven tongues of fire or lower *sefirot*, spectral emanations

re-enacting the Lurianic and Romantic dialectic of contraction, smashing of the vessels, and reconstitution. What is recompounded, to use Hollander's own word, is what the rabbis called the *makom*, the place of the divine voice, the topos of an image of voice, in secular poetic terms.

It is American, Emersonian and Stevensian again, that Hollander's recompounding ensues in "a final / White," hardly Stevens's ever-early candor, but closer to the "here being visible is being white" of *The Auroras of Autumn*. Appropriately it is neither Stevens nor Keats who is invoked in the closing strophes of "Violet" but the Orphic, vatic and apocalyptic Shelley of the *Ode to the West Wind* and the final stanzas of *Adonais*:

> . . . but let be

> Heard their own undersong
> Filling this vast chamber
> Of continuing air

> With the flickering of
> Cantillation, quickened
> Soon in the ringing dew.

That last triad is American and Judaic, but the Shelleyan Sublime is neither, which may be why the prose following "Violet" becomes at once so personal and so Hebraic, paradoxically Hollander's most powerful poetic writing to date, though it is prose poetry and not in verse. Against the darkness, the poet drinks the violet wine of his own imaginings, after following the Passover ritual of symbolizing the ten plagues against Egypt, land of darkness, by flinging ten drops of wine, here into the night. If the ten Kabbalistic *sefirot* are suggested at first by those ten lost drops, later reflection sets the three higher *sefirot* "beyond color always," and so beyond the trope of the menorah. A child's memory of colored bowls in a pharmacist's window moves him also beyond his own troping, "not as if a radiance had been selectively stained," which is the work of his poem, but to the Judaic reawakening of the major American trope of the transcendental: "as if the color-

less had been awakened from its long exile in mere transparency."
That transvalued transparence would end "the diaspora of water"
and also the reign of the book for the people of the book. But a
diminuendo follows, with a low point reached in the fear "that the
first text was itself a rescension of whispers." Yet the four prose
strophes following, down to the beginning of the fourfold coda of
blessings, rise gradually from the blank anxiety. Morning could
bring a quest into other regions perhaps beyond dying, but this
quester holds back:

> But would stay to hum his hymn of the hedges, where truth
> is one letter away from death, and will ever so be emended.

Hollander puns here, audaciously, upon the myth of the golem,
a legend that the golem, like Adam, has *emeth* (truth) inscribed
upon the forehead, and that the golem, like Adam, eventually
asked that the initial "e" be erased so that *meth* (death) might
come to him. Emended, M-ended, emeth-ed and meth-ed make a
grim fourfold pun, the force of which is softened by the ensuing
fourfold blessing, a kind of rabbinic hedge defending the text.

In the first three blessings the divine "he" is omitted, for it
would hardly be normatively Judaic to celebrate God for the gift
of poetic language. But the passage from the visible to the audible,
to the three higher images of voice, "the three tones beyond," ac-
complishes something of a release. In those three tones beyond,
via a rich ambiguity of syntax, it will be *for us* to grow. When
however is the "when" of "when we have been stamped out and
burned not to lie in the ashes of our dust"? Figures of life beyond
life, yes, but the hidden trope is both Shelleyan and Lurianic, the
embers and sparks that are not stamped out, and indeed never are
to be burned out.

Canonization is the most disputable of processes when a contemporary critic attempts it in regard to contemporary work. "Violet" and its prose have the intricate authority of quiet persuasion,
of making yet another turn, as Goethe and Hawthorne did, upon
the trope of the menorah. As it was not *their* trope, it causes
Goethe and Hawthorne no anxiety. As Hollander evidences in his

poem's central prose, the story following the poem "Green," a Jewish poet employing menorah symbolism *gets* double anxieties of representation. Inauthenticity hovers in a mist about the menorah, replicas of which appear to have been fobbed off upon conqueror after conqueror. Somewhere, perhaps in some Dead Sea cave, the original Mosaic menorah doubtless abides, itself representing Bezaleel's anxiety of representation. Perhaps Hollander's somber power is to have found an inevitable trope for the anxious and continual quest for representation that every belated poet aspiring after strength necessarily must make.

I would say something more here about the form of *Spectral Emanations* as a contemporary long poem. Like James Merrill's tripartite angelic drama, its structure seems uniquely at one with its hope for its own unity. John Hollander's previous long poems had depended for their structure on forthright, creative Marvellian parody (*Upon Apthorp House*, an occasional poem that "got out of hand," as the author remarks in a note, and turned a meditation on a historic building at Harvard into a plangent study of his own nostalgias, poetic and scholarly) and on the loosely calendrical pattern of the separate parts of *Visions from the Ramble*. In the latter poem, a midsummer memory of past summers fires an explosion of pyrotechnical verbal patterning: the "Fireworks" section is a Pindaric ode with fully matched accentual strophes highlighted with sparks of internal rhyme and modulated echo, and it celebrates poetry itself. Starting with an elementary reversal of the opening *ariston men hudor* ("water is best") of Pindar's first Olympian ode, Hollander moves to a deliberate verbal misprision of *feux d'artifice* (literally, "fireworks"):

> Fire is worst, and fires of artifice thirst after more than
> Water does and consume
> More of the world. . . .

"Fireworks" displays a rich array of emblems of creation, and connects the preceding section called "Waiting," a memory of childhood July Fourth celebrations, with the central thematic celebration of the created occasion of which all of *Visions from the*

Ramble seems the cry, July ninth, the "American moment" of the Emersonian poet:

> Midway between the fourth of July and the fourteenth,
> Suspended somewhere in summer between the ceremonies
> Remembered from childhood and the historical conflagration
> Imagined in sad, learned youth. . . .

Visions from the Ramble plays, in its separate sections, on various genres: "West End Blues" is an elaborated imitation of a Catullan complaint, as much a farewell to the Columbia College which educated the poet (in the poem, its statue of Alma Mater looks "longingly downtown" towards careers in commercial publishing and journalism) as *Upon Apthorp House* was to the Harvard which continued to do so. The final "From the Ramble" transmutes the first-person meditations of previous sections, like "Sunday Evenings," with its twilit intimations of suicidal mortality, and "Humming," a midsummer digression on the sounds of cicadas. The machinery of this skilled transmemberment is Spenserian. In the tenth canto of Book VI of *The Faerie Queene*, Calidore encounters a vision on Mount Acidale of Spenser himself with his muse and the three Graces, surrounded by a ring of naked girls; in Hollander's poem, the girls and the muse merge with the Graces and with three pools in Central Park in New York City, and the Acidale episode becomes an encounter, fictionally "remembered," between the poet as a boy of ten and himself at about thirty-five, his age while writing the poem. Even the stanzaic form of this long episode refers obliquely to *The Faerie Queene*; the accented hexameter lines used throughout the poem are linked by assonance instead of rhyme, in the pattern of Spenser's stanzas, with a short final line substituted for the alexandrine. I quote from the poem's final stanzas:

> . . . This night, this newly darkened sky,
>   This scarred park rolling out behind us,
>
> Even this city itself, are ours, wholly unshared
> Because unremembered except by both of us, who have made
> Light come into darkness, graces dance on a bare
> Hilltop, a cycle of months spin around on a frail

Wheel of language and touch. O see this light! As a blaze
Of cloud above the western towers gleams for an instant
Up there! Firing the sky, higher than it should be able
To reach, a single firework launched from the unseen river
Rises and dies, as we kiss and listen.

The poet is here addressing the muse with whom he lay in River-
side Park at the whole poem's opening, but it is probably Spenser
he meant to hold hands with, a momentary precursor with whom
his problems of imaginative location would of course remain un-
shared.

If *Visions from the Ramble* does not ultimately succeed as a
long poem, it is for the familiar reason—the one for which *The
Bridge* is wrongly accused of failing—that the whole is no more
than the sum and, at times, the difference, of its parts. It is an
urban vision from *within* a visionary pasture itself, a garden built
to resemble a wild (Frederick Law Olmsted's "Ramble" in Central Park) in a city from which one looks, as the poet reminds us,
out towards skyscrapers (rather than up, or ahead, or behind, towards them, all of which would constitute more available glimpses
of the counter-Sublime and its consequences and which would
suggest other modes of pastoral or history). But unlike Crane's
great poem, Hollander's has no central trope which would inform
even the schemes of organization; Crane's bridge is ultimately a
transumption of all prior tropes of connection, and it asserts its
own transcendence in the only domain in which transcendence—
for a poet whose theology cannot be other than a pattern of utterance and death—remains to be found: in the tiny but vast gap between letter and figure. Hollander's poem has no central trope, but
even more important, it *is not such a trope itself*, and its relation
to prior modes of construction such as Pound's or, particularly,
Crane's, is merely formal. Scheme, in a sense, is part of the poem's
undoing.

It is all the more remarkable to encounter, in *Spectral Emanations*, the way in which the elements of rhetorical scheme, such as
format, verse form, scale, sequence of arrangement and so forth,
contribute to deeper configuration. Between the calculations of

Visions from the Ramble and the discoveries of meanings inherent
in his preordained schemes in the present text, Hollander had to
pursue a winding path through poems which, he now says, he
"could not understand," *The Night Mirror* being the first of these
perhaps, and certainly *The Head of the Bed*, about which I have
written elsewhere, and its dark minor counterpart, *The Shades*,
whose relation to the visionary *Farbenlehre* of the new work is
apparent.

There is an emblematic dimension to Hollander's trope of the
discretely compartmented solar spectrum, the fluid continuum of
color which is broken apart into *the colors* only by the human act
of naming (as the poet himself, in *Adam's Task*, playfully associates the original, unfallen naming of the animals in Paradise with
the First Poem—a revision of the Renaissance *topos* which associates *écriture* with Creation itself). That spectrum is naturally revealed in the Bow of the Covenant, whose demythologizing by
Newton into a mere common and prominent instance of prismatic
refraction was hailed by poets like Thomson in the eighteenth century, and bewailed by Keats in *Lamia*. The restoration of a trope
broken by the history of thought is never a simple matter: Thomas
Pynchon, for example, presented an image of the only possibility
for a serious (*Gravity's*) reconstruction of the apparently bent Bow
of the Covenant as a distorted circular arc, a parabolic one, the
missile trajectory of parable or fable, rather than the circular arc
of the literal. Hollander saw the emblematic nature of the rainbow
in the structure of the spectrum itself; characteristically for him,
he mythologized the epistemological problem of deciding where
one color left off and the next took over. This concern is at its most
explicit at the end of "Blue":

> Dawn comes when we distinguish blue from—white?
> No, green—and in agreement, eyeing the
> Dying dark, our morning wariness nods . . .

where the attention is heightened by the assonances and the word
play which avoids "weariness" in the last two lines. The problem

is repeated with more mythological assurance in "Departed In-digo": "Was she Madame de Violet / Or good Frau Blau? We were not told"—the two regions of the Jamesian seductress of night and the cheerful blue of midday are paralleled by the role of golden (orange) Venus, placed between the yellow flames of Vulcan and the "abashed reddening of / Her netted warrior." But the problem of boundaries, and the question of the *meaning of the transition* from one region of color to another, are general throughout the poem, and release its mythographic plot. (The question of where one condition or state stops and its bordering one starts is not only for philosophers. It has been central to the history of romance as well. A quest across the color spectrum—unlike one through clearly bounded regions, like the squares of a chessboard in *Through the Looking Glass,* or the circles of Hell—must be concerned with not only the meaning of where one is, but also when one is in fact there.)

In earlier poems like *At the New Year,* Hollander had brooded over the ghostly demarcations which mark the phases of our nat-ural and human cycles and, in an actual emblem poem from *Types of Shape,* had meditated upon the significance of the *Magen David,* the shield-of-David-as-hexagram, "of no great antiquity," as he cor-rectly observes in a subtitle, as a "liturgical symbol." *Graven Image* (in the volume *Spectral Emanations*) acknowledges, by its title, the aniconic strain in Judaism; for the belated diasporic poet, the forbidden images are not those of stone idols, but rather *eidola,* mythological images of poetry. "Craving the rich dark icons ever denied us," the poet goes on to explore, by the very act of produc-ing the typographical form, the significances lurking in the six-pointed star, commencing with the "momentary finial" of the up-per triangle:

A
bit
of an
image a
hint only

and ending with an ultimate commitment to a dark, pre-Judaic reading of the sign as the interpenetration of male and female genital forms:

> Let there be only
>   this final sign
>   this triangle
>   of the dark
>   about thy
>   opening
>   loves
>   own
>   V

The poem ends on its own omega, the capital letter whose form is synecdochic for that of half the image itself. On the way "down" the poem, the reading touches on the antithetical Nazi and Zionist uses of the emblem ("unshielding be it in blue or yellow"), but resolves to substitute its own misprision of the sign, the poem itself. The star, the poet says, "with the broad menorahs feathered wings was all / the symbol we were permitted"; it remained for his major poem of a decade later to reinterpret the menorah on a far grander scale, associating it with a tree (as it is in an incised carving on the Hellenistic synagogue in Sardis) and, specifically, in "Violet," with a substitute for the locus of the Divine Voice:

> —A tree of light. A bush
> Unconsumed by its fire.
> Branches of flames given
>
> Sevenfold tongue that there
> Might be recompounded
> Out of the smashed vessels
>
> Of oil, of blood and stain,
> Wine of grass and juice of
> Violet, a final
>
> White. . . .

This grand trope, at once a fresh Breaking of the Vessels and a superb *Tikkun* or restitution, is the inevitable apogee of Hollander's poem, which I do not hesitate to proclaim as one of the central achievements of his generation, matching the long poems of Merrill, Ashbery and Ammons.

14

Free and Broken Tablets:
The Cultural Prospects
of American Jewry

Though I have brooded for some years on American-Jewish self-identity, and on the cultural prospects of American Jewry, I feel very uneasy at addressing such matters directly. More than the usual disclaimers seem necessary. I am not a specialist in Jewish studies of any kind. Though I will draw much of my material from the more theoretical moments of reflection and summary by eminent Jewish historians, I myself am only an amateur student of Jewish history. Yet again, I will be speculating on the relation between Jewish survival and the Jewish religion, and *in* that relation, which may be an identity, a mystery transcending analysis may abide. I begin to sound like an echo of Wallace Stevens's self-mockery at the beginning of *An Ordinary Evening in New Haven*, when he says of the question that is a giant itself, "Of this, / A few words, an and yet, and yet, and yet." I write some of these pages having come down from New Haven, to pass an ordinary evening flying in on an El Al jet to Israel, and I add therefore a personal note to my very tentative beginnings. Between the setting down in New Haven of my notes, thoughts, quotations from authorities, and my continuing to write in the plane, my abstract gloom has been modified slightly by the evident vitality and diversity of my (mostly Jewish) fellow-passengers. But my subject is cultural prophecy—how vital and diverse, and more crucially, how

Jewish will such passengers be in thirty years? I return to my "an and yet, and yet, and yet," to a few more qualifications, and then I will begin.

Among my missing credentials, sociology is the largest lacuna, since any prophecy about American Jewry is necessarily also one about American society. But I am going to talk about a relation of people to text, a relation that is in a difficult sense a textual relationship, and there my competence begins. I am a student of texts, and of what some recent literary theorists call "textuality." My own work has tended more and more to concern itself with influences *between* texts, with "intertextuality" and with what I call "poetic misprision" or creative misunderstanding that takes place between texts. The cultural future of American Jewry, the very existence of American Jewry as such, hardly can be considered to be a literary or textual problem in any traditional sense. But I teach a great many students at Yale every year, and a great many of them are Jewish. It is very problematic to generalize from the experience of a single teacher, but I have discussed these matters with other teachers, both at Yale and at other universities, and so my observations are not entirely personal. There is a profound falling-away from what I would call "text-centeredness" or even "text-obsessiveness" among the current generation of American undergraduates, Gentile and Jewish alike. I can detect still some difference between Gentile and Jewish students in this regard, but it is not a substantial difference, and it seems to be diminishing. What the consequences might be, for American Jewry in particular, of such a falling-away from text-centeredness, is my concern in what follows.

What have our major historians concluded about the mystery of Jewish survival? Heinrich Graetz thought that Jewry had survived in the Diaspora because it was "a people for which the present meant nothing while the future meant everything." Yet Graetz also said that Jewish literature "makes up the kernel of Jewish history." To Graetz, Jewish history is one in which significant books are *deeds* with consequential ramifications.

Simon Dubnow's sociological alternative to this was to see Diaspora Jewry as a history of social organizations. If Dubnow proves to be wholly right, then I would say the future of American Jewry *as a Jewry* is very slim. Certainly the visible difference between reorganized American Jewry and the other 97 percent or so of Americans continues to wane.

Yehezkel Kaufmann, in his *Diaspora and Alien Lands*, wrote that the Jewish religion alone was the force that lets Jewries survive. "The Jewish religion" is by no means a single phenomenon, but however it is described or defined, my deep impression is that it is declining among undergraduates. When they are my age, in thirty years, there would be a significantly smaller and less influential American Jewry than now, if Kaufmann is wholly correct.

Kaufmann was a formidable historian, and I want to explore his contention a little further. He reminded us that "the change of language, which the Jewish people underwent, is particularly important in this connection—language is a people's primary expression of ethnicity." Kaufmann went on to observe that Jewry is unique in that it survives this linguistic assimilation, and he is right, since Aramaic, Ladino, Yiddish but also Greek, Arabic, German, French and English all have been major Jewish languages. In a curious leap of rhetoric, Kaufmann attributed this triumph over linguistic loss and substitution to Judaism *as a religious idea:* "The one and only primary cause for Israel's individuality in the Diaspora was its religion alone."

I hope that Kaufmann was not right, and I am going to dispute him, at least in part, by trying to re-cast his terms, which I think are too idealistic, in that they do admit of further reduction. For a "religious idea," in his formulation, I will substitute the idea of text-centeredness, and as I said before, even of text-obsessiveness. But before I make the substitution, I want to consider some thoughts of Simon Rawidowicz, one of the great theoreticians of interpretation in modern Jewish studies.

Rawidowicz speculated profoundly upon the Jewish obsession with *lastness:* ". . . how often are we full of doubt as to whether the future will give rise to further teachers, scholars and even plain ordinary Jews. Often it seems as if the overwhelming majority of our people go about driven by the panic of being the last."

Rawidowicz wishes to make the apparent Jewish weakness of this stance into a Jewish strength, but I find this stance to be truly dialectical anyway in American terms. There *could* be a certain kind of lastness about the next generation of American Jews, by which I mean current undergraduates. To explain this dark possibility, I return to Kaufmann, and I substitute for what he truly calls a religious idea a more reductive figuration, a textual idea. That is to say, it was an obsession with study, a condition of text-centeredness, that held the great Diaspora Jewries together. This is the common element in Babylon-Persia, Alexandria, Arabia-Spain, Provence, Renaissance Italy, East Europe and Germany-Austria. For this last Jewish culture I have in mind not so much Freud, Kafka and Walter Benjamin, who were in unbearably subtle ways more Jewish than Germanic, but Gershom Scholem, who seems to me the greatest living cultural figure in all of Jewry today. Scholem came to Zion, that is, to a cultural triumph of Jewishness, not through normative religion nor through ethnicity but through textuality, through a creative obsession with a tradition of very recalcitrant Jewish texts. I will return to Scholem at length later, because his essays on Jews and Judaism in crisis have convinced me that he is a better guide to the possibilities of a Jewish cultural survival in America than anyone else available to us.

I will state now the gloomier element in my argument, the one that I desperately don't want to believe. If American Jewry, of the supposedly most educated classes, assimilates totally and all but vanishes in thirty years, that is, except for the normative religious remnant, it will be because the text—all text—is dying in America, vanishing not into nature but into what Emerson grimly termed Necessity. A Jewry can survive without a Jewish language (and I will say something about this later in regard to Alexandrian Jewry and Philo), but not *without language,* not without an intense, obsessive concern that far transcends what ordinarily we call literacy.

In a Jewish tradition, let me consider the two alternatives. The more likely is that in thirty years America itself will cease to be a text, in the sense that Whitman said that "these States" were in themselves the greatest poem, or that Emerson wished to see each American as an incarnate book transcending nature. American Jewry, except for the normatively religious, will blend away into the quasi-intelligentsia, as in the fading lack of a textual difference between Yale's more than 1,000 Jewish undergraduates and its more than 3,000 Gentile undergraduates. Though an elite, of sorts, neither "group" could fairly be termed a textual elite any longer. Yet no special education under Jewish religious auspices can affect the students I teach, because they are not open to it, not even in their pre-college years. For many reasons—social, technological, perhaps belatedness itself—it just is becoming harder and harder to read deeply in America.

There is a more hopeful alternative, and I will return to it later, when I discuss some of Scholem's insights. Can a text of America survive in a new Jewish-American synthesis? I see no signs of this around me, and the new Castalia of Herman Hesse's *Glasperlenspiel* is not likely to come up in America. Yet if there *is* something undying in the Jewish concern with text, perhaps we might see a saving elitist remnant that in some odd Messianic sense will make "Jews" of all—Gentile or Jewish—who study intensively.

Yet this leads me to a further question: which of the previous great Diaspora Jewries does American Jewry resemble, in its cultural modes and aims? I am going to venture the odd judgment that the true analogue is the Hellenistic Jewry of the six great centuries of Alexandria, from the third century B.C.E. through the third century C.E. I have neither the competence nor the time here to go through the ten or so major Diaspora Jewries, and analyze both the analogies and the anomalies between them and American Jewry. But I will say something about several of them before I come to the definitive and frightening account of German cultural Jewry that Scholem has given us.

S. D. Goitein observed that a century after the death of Mohammed, the majority of the Jews lived under Islam. He added the more interesting observation that three centuries after the rise of Islam, Jewry flourished intellectually. Goitein, a careful but not a very speculative scholar, proceeded to ask the question which is central to my subject here: "How, then, should we explain this seeming contrast: a high degree of assimilation to the new Arabic-Muslim environment on the one hand, and rejuvenation and vigorous self-assertion on the other?"

It is no help at all that Goitein was too cautious a scholar to answer his own question. His excuse was that the historical data were lacking. All that I can take out of his paradox is the realization that *for a while* Arabic and Jewish obsessive delight in textual studies ran together, if not wholly in one current. Had there been a vigorous, large and flourishing American Jewry in the Age of Emerson, then perhaps the analogue would be useful, but American Jewry is culturally belated in America, another point to which I will return.

The great period of Jewish culture in Provence and southern France, generally from 1100 to 1400, is a somewhat more interesting analogue, for here the Jews were very active simultaneously in rabbinics, Kabbalah, philosophy, poetry, essays and in grammar. But, according to Twersky and other scholars, this was an instance of a thoroughly Torah-centered community that turned to cultivate the extra-Talmudic disciplines. And closer scrutiny tends to reveal that the Provencal Jewish scholars, except for Gersonides, were largely cultural middlemen, popularizers of greater figures like Maimonides and Alfasi. Caught between the Church and the Manichees, mysteriously affected both by the Cathars and by the rise of Troubadour verse, the Jewish cultural factors of Provence seem now a melancholy prophecy of the Spanish catastrophe, rather than a useful analogue to either a current or a projected American Jewry.

One might think of that Renaissance Italian Jewry that Cecil Roth studied, except that it was hardly a Diaspora culture until Pope Paul IV made it one, through his ghettoizing Bull of 1555. I turn instead to what was certainly a Jewry in exile, German-speaking Jewry, where the analogues to American Jewry would be a nightmare if it were not that the anomalies truly are greater, as I will try to show. And here at last I turn to Gershom Scholem.

If there is now a moral prophet in Jewry whom I can recognize, it must be Scholem, though he strongly denies the role, and insists that we are to regard him only as a historical scholar. It is significant that Scholem truly says of himself as a young man: "What interested me then was to find a way to the Jewish primary sources. I was not content with reading *about* things." But when he says truly also that "there is nothing Jewish that is alien to me," then he places himself in the prophetic current as well. Indeed, another remark of Scholem seems to me the best and most hopeful epigraph that I could have used for this talk: "We are unable to explain to ourselves what sparks function and sustain whatever remained alive in all these processes. It is altogether a riddle how Judaism and the Jewish people have held out. A large part of the Jewish people has almost always fallen away. So it is important to find out what has sustained us."

In his great essay *Jews and Germans*, Scholem sees the German Jews as victims of a century of their own emotional confusion. After quoting Charles Péguy's profound remark on the Jews: "Being elsewhere, the great vice of this race, the great secret virtue, the great vocation of this people," Scholem comments: "This 'being elsewhere' combined with the desperate wish to 'be at home' in a manner at once intense, fruitful and destructive. It is the clue to the relationship of the Jews to the Germans." Péguy and Scholem do not bother to cite the two German Romantic definitions that are at war here, probably because they assume we all know the definitions. One is the idealistic apothegm of Novalis, which is that the study of philosophy teaches us to be at home everywhere. The other is Nietzsche's uncanny definition of art as the desire to be different, the desire to be elsewhere. The German Jewish intellectuals foundered upon this conflict of definitions, both of which were used against them by the Germans.

Scholem never has made the mistake of analogizing German and American Jewry, and if we employ Scholem's dialectical recognitions, I think we will realize how he arrived at this wisdom. It is important to see that the Messianic idea in America (whether in its early version of Winthrop and the Puritans, or the later one of Emerson and the Transcendentalists) has waned even as the Messianic idea has waned among secularized American Jews. This is one of the many elements that connect what is problematic about American Jewry as much to the problematics of America as to those of the Diaspora. The German Jews assimilated to a Germany that had leaped straight out of a barbaric, mythological and romance conception of itself to a rather shaky Post-Enlightenment idealizing self-vision. But America is a theological and philosophical conception of itself, a concept with much Puritanism but little ethnic mythology at the root, which is to say, oddly, with less politics at the root. For a long time, Jewish assimilation in America was frequently a process of somehow becoming more Jewish by assimilating to Puritan Hebraism and its Election theology. Perhaps I am only saying that Calvinism is very different from Lutheranism, and is a touch more congenial to the spirit of Judaism. Perhaps I am saying something as pretentious, even, as this: that if America can be "saved," then American Jewry can be saved. What would make such a statement particularly pretentious is the sadness of another question: What has American Jewry engendered that American higher culture has absorbed? The probable answer is that American humor has been changed by Jewish humor into certain modes of self-mockery. But except for *Miss Lonelyhearts* by the anti-Semitic Nathanael West (or Nathan Weinstein) and a handful of scattered poems, such as John Hollander's *Spectral Emanations*, and stories, such as Cynthia Ozick's *Usurpation*, I do not find much contribution to high literature. There is of course the comic achievement of Saul Bellow. But when Bellow wants to represent an authentic spirituality, he has Mr. Sammler read Meister Eckhart or the narrator of *Humboldt's Gift* read Rudolf Steiner, which is rather a falling-away even within Gentile spirituality. In a darker mood, one could say that America for its size and resources is at this time culturally less than astonishingly productive—so therefore is American Jewry. But in a more positive mood one can say: it is still too soon. The American Renaissance was not more than one hundred years ago, and the significant mass of Jewry has not been in America for more than a hundred years. Are my complaints about a waning of text-centeredness in American Jewry only another version of that Continental and now chiefly Gallic contention that the Anglo-American pragmatic and empirical tradition keeps us from the dialectical, from the metaphysical, from the heroics of system and the grandiosity of the synthesizer?

My answer would be that I am concerned here, however ruefully, only with moral prophecy; will there be even as aggressive, alert and self-identified an American Jewry as there is now, thirty years hence? I am going to go a long way back to find a truer analogue, back to Alexandria, a hopeful analogue only in part, after which I will conclude with some final glances at some of our true prophets—at Jeremiah, Ezekiel and Second Isaiah, at Jehuda Halevi and Gershom Scholem.

It is difficult for any of us to be cheerful about an Alexandrian analogue, because normative Judaic tradition discarded Philo and his culture, possibly because, by a historical irony, Philo did so much to help engender Christian theology. But Philo was, as the great Jerusalem scholar Hans Lewy said, not only the first theologian but the first systematizer of Biblical theology. No one, except I suppose for Professor Wolfson of Harvard, ever has regarded Philo as a profound or original thinker. He culminated a long tradition of Alexandrian Jewish allegorists and he had curious flaws as a culminator. His Jewish learning was astonishingly small—indeed, he may not have known *any* Hebrew or at best only a very little. But—like all Hellenistic Jews—he was text-centered; like them, he believed that the Greek translation of the Scriptures by the Seventy was just as inspired as Moses had been. I quote Lewy's summary of Philo's religious context because it may be applicable to the coming religious chaos of much of American Jewry: "We must remember that in Philo's environment there did not exist anything like an authorized, canonized tradition of religious learning. Judaism has never been freer from dogmatical restrictions than it was in his time. Everyone who believed in the revelation of the Torah and followed its precepts was allowed to cherish his own views on the 'spirit' of the revealed letter and its religious content."

We can add to Lewy that if Oral Law affected Philo, we can be sure it was mostly the Oral Law of Plato and not of Palestine. Philo was so at ease in considering Greek as *the* Jewish language that he frequently wrote as follows: "the name in the Hebrew language is such-and-such, but in *our language* it is such-and-such." Philo so usurped Greek that he cheerfully attributes to the heroes of the Hebrew Bible a knowledge of Greek etymology. Thus, Abraham and God both know that one thing is identical to another because the two words have identical Greek roots! But this, I think, was an instance of that Alexandrian Gnostic modernity that rose as a defense against the malaise of belatedness. Elias Bickerman and his school have insisted that Torah survived only by the translation of its literature into the world language, Greek. And while the indebtedness of Akiba and the Pharisees to Platonic and Pythagorean thought is emotionally difficult for us to accept, it remains true that the Pharisees' notion that everyone in Israel was to achieve holiness through study of Torah was *not* a Biblical idea. Isaiah and Ezekiel did not believe that the Jewish nation would save itself through study, which is Plato's idea of salvation. Plato thought that education could so transform the individual and an entire people that the nation itself could fulfill the will of the divine. The Pharisees, as Saul Liebermann has argued persuasively against Bickerman, show *some* Hellenization, since he admits that the "Torah learning" idea is Platonic, but Liebermann also demonstrates that our Oral Law is not the Platonic Unwritten Law. The point, I think, is that Greek as the world language would have annihilated Jewry if even Akiba had not subtly come to terms with its influence, by a beautiful misprision of Plato. In Plato, the Unwritten Law often served to negate the Written Law, but the

Pharisees urged that the Oral Law be used to build a fence, a protective hedge, around the written Torah.

English is today the world language rather as Greek was in Hellenistic times, and in a curious sense English is becoming *the* Jewish language in that surely more Jews can use it whether as a first or second language than can use any other language, be it Hebrew or French, Yiddish or Spanish, or whatever. This in itself puts American Jewry in the linguistic situation of Hellenistic Jewry. But that consideration returns me to my rhetorical substitution of "text-centeredness" for Kaufmann's "religious idea." Is there a justification for my substitution that carries more authority than Alexandria or America, that can take us back to the first and most culturally productive of all our Diasporas?

The first Diaspora Jewry is of course Babylonian; Jeremiah was an older contemporary of Ezekiel and when Ezekiel's prophecy ended (after 571), the second Isaiah must already have been alive. To say that "a religious idea" sustained even this first Diaspora is to oversimplify. Gerhard von Rad notes that when the upper classes of both the Northern and then the Southern kingdoms had been deported to Babylon, many of the Jews reached a negative conclusion about Yahweh. We can cite Jeremiah 44:15 ff., where the Jews who have fled to Egypt tell Jeremiah that all had been well *in the time of their fathers,* when incense was burned in Jerusalem to the Queen of Heaven. Von Rad says, "In considering the question of the common element in these three prophets—Jeremiah, Ezekiel, Second Isaiah—we must remember that they belong to a time when men had become even more detached than before from the ties of religion."

We can say, that compared to Amos and First Isaiah, the three great prophets of the First Diaspora were modernists and acute subjective individualists. Jeremiah and Ezekial indeed are autobiographers, self-dependent men, addressing Jews who were critical and skeptical. The great confrontation of these later prophets was with the problematic status of Jewish text-centeredness, with the survival of the prophetic word. Belatedness thus is born as a Jewish literary, spiritual and political problem long before Alexandria.

I cite Scholem here for a last time, because of his deep Kabbalistic wisdom in confronting the pathos of Jewish belatedness:

> We know that even the deepest estrangement can again and again issue in a turning to Judaism—spontaneous and transforming those affected that way—whether we qualify it as a return or in some other way. . . .

As Scholem implies, to get from the "broken tablets" to "the freedom of the tablets" of the Law, there has to be a concern with "tablets," with text-centeredness and text-obsessiveness. Jewish literature has been written in an incredible diversity of languages, but only where "text-centeredness" existed among Jews *in that language.* Though nothing in later Jewish literature matches the Jahvist or Jeremiah or the two Isaiahs, if I could vote for a single post-Biblical Jewish work it would have to be the sublime dialogue, the *Kuzari* of Jehudah Halevi, which I cannot read in the original Arabic. Halevi was of course a linguistic genius; critics far more competent to judge poetry written in Hebrew than I am, tend to see Halevi as by far the crown of post-Biblical Hebrew poetry. But whether he chose Hebrew, Arabic or Castilian, Halevi represented a text-centered Jewry just as Philo did, or as Gersonides did or, however odd it sounds, just as Benjamin and Kafka did, even though they hardly wanted overtly to represent anything about Jewry whatsoever. An anti-Semitic Jewish writer like Nathanael West still hovers in the aura of a Jewish text-centeredness.

Jehudah Halevi ends the *Kuzari* by writing: "Jerusalem can only be rebuilt when Israel *yearns* for it to such an extent that we sympathize even with its stones and its dust." What informs that great prophecy is the idea of "yearning," an idea that was preserved only by the Jewish love for a text like the 102nd Psalm, which Halevi deliberately echoes here. An American Jewry that has lost its love for a text like the 102nd Psalm might recover, in time, such a love, if it were capable first of loving some text, any text. But if that love vanishes, and probably it will, then the other love will never come.

15
Coda:
The American Difference
in Poetry and Criticism

Wallace Stevens, in a letter written half a year before his death, remarked that Walt Whitman's "good things, the superbly beautiful and moving things, are those that he wrote naturally, with an extemporaneous and irrepressible vehemence of emotions." True and revelatory of Stevens's best work, rather than of Whitman's, the remark illustrates a central vehemence of American poetic traditions. The best poets of that climate are hermetic precisely when they profess to be vatic democrats, and they are curiously extemporaneous when they attempt to be most elitist. Whitman and Stevens, despite Stevens's protest, deeply resemble one another in this regard, and have large affinities with a company of major American poets that includes Emily Dickinson, Hart Crane and such extraordinary contemporary figures as John Ashbery, James Merrill and A. R. Ammons. A deep uncertainty concerning the American reader combines with ambitious designs upon that reader, and the result is a poetic stance more self-contradictory than that of most modern British poets of comparable achievement, from Thomas Hardy on to Geoffrey Hill, with D. H. Lawrence being the largest exception, as his Whitmanesque affinities clearly show.

Ralph Waldo Emerson may be regarded either as the primary source or as the initial representative of this American poetic difference. His audacity is still little appreciated in Great Britain, where many critics oddly think him somewhat tame and bland. His dialectics are subtle, but his actual stance is antinomian and even violent in relation to the pieties of all anterior creeds. A religious thinker who could say of the crucifixion that it was a Great Defeat whereas we, as Americans, demand Victory, a success to the senses as well as to the soul, Emerson is a writer who, like his admirer Nietzsche, would dare to say anything. Urging his American bards to be at once Gnostic and democratic, the prophetic Emerson encouraged, and goes on fostering, a split in American high culture that will evidently never end. The alternative convention in American literary aesthetics, which began with the anti-Emersonian protests of Hawthorne, Melville and Poe, and continued through the school of T. S. Eliot, finds its honorable last representative today in the distinguished poetry that Robert Penn Warren has been writing for the last decade. But Warren is a sunset hawk at the end of a counter-tradition. Emersonianism, with all its tangles of vision, style and stance, remains the dominant American poetic mode.

Three instances—from Whitman, Stevens and Ashbery—may be cited in illustration of the peculiarities of American poetic stance. Stevens kept insisting that he did not read Whitman, but when in a Yale lecture of 1947 he wished to give a demonstration of what he could admire as poetic strength, he chose to quote a brief lyric that Whitman wrote very late, *A Clear Midnight*:

This is thy hour O Soul, thy free flight into the wordless,
Away from books, away from art, the day erased, the lesson done.
Thee fully forth emerging, silent, gazing, pondering the themes thou
    lovest best,
Night, sleep, death and the stars.

The stance here is the Emersonian Dionysiac, returning to the commonal, away even from the differences and iterations of language. But the great and only apparent improviser, Whitman, "an American Bard at last," is totally individualized in what is after all his unitary and esoteric theme, the oceanic mother who compounds in herself, as she will for Stevens and for Hart Crane, "Night, sleep, death and the stars." The American poetic soul emerges as the Coleridgean moon of imagination, "silent, gazing, pondering," but with the destructive American Emersonian difference, an antithetical flight or repression away from art and nature alike, towards the solipsistic grandeur that is a new Gnosis.

Whitman's greatness may be in the ease or grace of this hermetic flight or repression, whereas Stevens had to attain it through rather too overt an esotericism or gaudy elitism, as here in the fable of the Arab-as-moon from *Notes toward a Supreme Fiction*:

> We say: at night an Arabian in my room,
> With his damned hoobla-hoobla, hoobla-how,
> Inscribes a primitive astronomy
>
> Across the unscrawled fores the future casts
> And throws his stars around the floor. By day
> The wood-dove used to chant his hoobla-hoo.
>
> And still the grossest iridescence of ocean
> Howls hoo and rises and howls hoo and falls.
> Life's nonsense pierces us with a strange relation.

Life's nonsense reduces us to relying upon the distinction between hoobla-how and hoobla-hoo, which is an instance of that Stevensian negative exuberance which has driven the eminent American critic (of the Poundian persuasion) Hugh Kenner to the sad conclusion that all Stevens represents is the ultimate culmination of the poetics of Edward Lear. Yet the distinction belongs firmly to Emersonian doctrine: the hoobla-hoo is the song of the bird of Aphrodite, the wood-dove, but the hoobla-how reductively refers to sexual limitation, due to age and a lifetime's repressiveness.

As the Coleridgean moon shines upon the aged Stevens, it compels him to confront what Whitman was too evasive to confront: the self-awareness of the erotic limits of poetic imagination. The future is death and death only, the word out of the sea uttered so persuasively by the Whitmanian terrible mother, yet Stevens masks his sexual anxieties by an elitist extravagance of trope. The moony Arab can afford to throw "his stars around the floor," but Stevens has lost so much that he can afford no more discarding gestures. Perhaps Stevens was addicted to loss; it might be urged that his disciple Ashbery scarcely knows how to proceed except by acknowledging loss. That may be the inevitable price of a tradition whose founders—Emerson and Whitman—so perpetually demanded victory.

It is the iridescent ocean, final and maternal form of "night, sleep, death and the stars," which is the largest figuration of Stevens's poetic (and sexual) dilemma. His esoteric diction barely disguises the human despair of a self-described "harmonious skeptic." Whitman could identify himself with the pondering moon, and more often with the sun, once even asserting, like Freud's mad Dr. Schreber, that he could send forth sunrise from himself.

The deliberate vagueness of the Stevensian moonlight produces the "unscrawled fores," or poems-not-to-be-written, but if these suggest poetic impotence, they testify also to a power of redundancy, to an imagination like the Arab's that can afford to throw its stars around the floor. By day one used to hear the wood-dove, but now one hears always the ocean mocking us with its erotic light. Pierced by the strange story of our inadequate relation to life, we end in its nonsense, which is that desire goes on even as the erotic fails. The poet could be speaking these realizations to a universal reader, but he has chosen an elite, capable of relating to so esoteric a mode. Stevens said once that the poet must direct himself not to a drab, but to a woman with the hair of a pythoness, which is a wonderful sentiment, but doubtless he implied also that such a muse would partake of Medusa.

Of the many contemporary heirs of Whitman and of Stevens, John Ashbery seems likeliest to achieve something near to their eminence. Yet their uncertainty as to their audience is far surpassed in the shifting stances that Ashbery assumes. His mode can vary from the apparently opaque, so disjunctive as to seem beyond interpretation, to a kind of limpid clairvoyance that again brings the Emersonian contraries together. Contemplating Parmigianino's picture in his major long poem, *Self-Portrait in a Convex Mirror*, Ashbery achieves a vision in which art, rather than nature, becomes the imprisoner of the soul:

> The soul has to stay where it is,
> Even though restless, hearing raindrops at the pane,
> The sighing of autumn leaves thrashed by the wind,
> Longing to be free, outside, but it must stay
> Posing in this place. It must move as little as possible.
> This is what the portrait says.
> But there is in that gaze a combination
> Of tenderness, amusement and regret, so powerful
> In its restraint that one cannot look for long.
> The secret is too plain. The pity of it smarts,
> Makes hot tears spurt: that the soul is not a soul,
> Has no secret, is small, and it fits
> Its hollow perfectly: its room, our moment of attention.

Whitman's Soul, knowing its true hour in wordlessness, is apparently reduced here and now to a moment only of attention. And yet even this tearful realization, supposedly abandoning the soul to a convex mirror, remains a privileged moment, of an Emersonian rather than Paterian kind. Precisely where he seems most wistful and knowingly bewildered by loss, Ashbery remains most dialectical, like his American ancestors.

The simple diction and vulnerable stance barely conceal the presence of the American Transcendental Self, an ontological self that increases even as the empirical self abandons every spiritual assertion. Hence the "amusement" that takes up its stance between "tenderness" and "regret," Whitmanian affections, and hence also the larger hint of a power held in reserve, "so powerful in its restraint that one cannot look for long." An American Orphic, wandering in the Emersonian legacy, can afford to surrender the soul in much the same temper as the ancient Gnostics did. The soul can be given up to the Demiurge, whether of art or nature, because a spark or *pneuma* is more vital than the *psyche*, and fits no hollow whatsoever. Where Whitman and Stevens are at once hermetic and off-hand, so is Ashbery, but his throwaway gestures pay the price of an ever-increasing American sense of belatedness.

Emerson's New England law of compensation, that "nothing is got for nothing," is my bridge from the dilemmas of American poetic tradition to the impasses of a native American kind of literary criticism. From Emerson himself through to Kenneth Burke, the American tradition of criticism is highly dialectical, differing in this from the British empirical tradition that has prevailed from Dr. Johnson to Empson. But this American criticism precisely resembles Whitmanian poetry, rather than the Continental dialectics that have surged from Hegel through Heidegger on to the contemporary Deconstruction of Jacques Derrida and Paul de Man. Hegelian negation, even in its latest critical varieties, is intellectually optimistic because it is always based upon a destructive concept of the given. Given facts (and given texts) may appear to common sense as a positive index of truth, but are taken as being in reality the negation of truth, which must destroy apparent facts, and must deconstruct texts. British or Humean literary critics maintain the ultimate authority of the fact or text. Emerson, and Kenneth Burke after him, espouse the Negative, but not at all in a Hegelian mode. Emerson, both more cheerful and less optimistic than Hegel, insisted that a fact was an epiphany of God, but this insistence identified God with Emerson in his most expansive and transcending moments. Burke remarks that everything we might say about God has its precise analogue in things that we can say about language, a remark which defines American poetry as the new possibility of a Negative that perpetually might restore a Transcendental Self.

The American critic here and now, in my judgment, needs to keep faith both with American poetry and the American Negative, which means one must not yield either to the school of Deconstruction or to the perpetual British school of Common Sense. Our best poets, from Whitman through Stevens to Ashbery, make impossible and self-contradictory demands upon both their readers and themselves. I myself urge an antithetical criticism in the American grain, affirming the self over language, while granting a priority to figurative language over meaning. The result is a mixed discourse, vatic perhaps, and at once esoteric and democratic, but that is the burden of American tradition. Stevens says it best for that burden but also for a possible freedom:

> There would still remain the never-resting mind,
> So that one would want to escape, come back
> To what had been so long composed.
> The imperfect is our paradise.
> Note that, in this bitterness, delight,
> Since the imperfect is so hot in us,
> Lies in flawed words and stubborn sounds.